BOOK 5 – FIXED INCOME, DERIVATIVES, AND ALTERNATIVE INVESTMENTS

LEVEL 1 BOOK 5: FIXED INCOME, DERIVATIVES, AND ALTERNATIVE
INVESTMENTS

©2009 Kaplan, Inc. All rights reserved.

Published in 2009 by Kaplan Schweser.

Printed in the United States of America.

ISBN: 1-4277-9492-8

PPN: 4550-0109

If this book does not have the hologram with the Kaplan Schweser logo on the back cover, it was
distributed without permission of Kaplan Schweser, a Division of Kaplan, Inc., and is in direct violation
of global copyright laws. Your assistance in pursuing potential violators of this law is greatly appreciated.

Required CFA Institute® disclaimer: "CFA® and Chartered Financial Analyst® are trademarks owned
by CFA Institute. CFA Institute (formerly the Association for Investment Management and Research)
does not endorse, promote, review, or warrant the accuracy of the products or services offered by Kaplan
Schweser."

Certain materials contained within this text are the copyrighted property of CFA Institute. The following
is the copyright disclosure for these materials: "Copyright, 2010, CFA Institute. Reproduced and
republished from 2010 Learning Outcome Statements, Level 1, 2, and 3 questions from CFA® Program
Materials, CFA Institute Standards of Professional Conduct, and CFA Institute's Global Investment
Performance Standards with permission from CFA Institute. All Rights Reserved."

These materials may not be copied without written permission from the author. The unauthorized
duplication of these notes is a violation of global copyright laws and the CFA Institute Code of Ethics.
Your assistance in pursuing potential violators of this law is greatly appreciated.

Disclaimer: The SchweserNotes should be used in conjunction with the original readings as set forth by
CFA Institute in their 2010 CFA Level 1 Study Guide. The information contained in these Notes covers
topics contained in the readings referenced by CFA Institute and is believed to be accurate. However,
their accuracy cannot be guaranteed nor is any warranty conveyed as to your ultimate exam success. The
authors of the referenced readings have not endorsed or sponsored these Notes.

©2009 Kaplan, Inc.

READINGS AND LEARNING OUTCOME STATEMENTS

READINGS

The following material is a review of the Fixed Income, Derivatives, and Alternative Investments principles designed to address the learning outcome statements set forth by CFA Institute.

STUDY SESSION 15

Reading Assignments

Equity and Fixed Income, CFA Program Curriculum, Volume 5 (CFA Institute, 2010)

STUDY SESSION 16

Reading Assignments

Equity and Fixed Income, CFA Program Curriculum, Volume 5 (CFA Institute, 2010)

STUDY SESSION 17

Reading Assignments

Derivatives and Alternative Investments, CFA Program Curriculum, Volume 6 (CFA Institute; 2010)

STUDY SESSION 18

Reading Assignments

Derivatives and Alternative Investments, CFA Program Curriculum, Volume 6 (CFA Institute, 2010)

LEARNING OUTCOME STATEMENTS (LOS)

The CFA Institute Learning Outcome Statements are listed below. These are repeated in each topic review; however, the order may have been changed in order to get a better fit with the flow of the review.

STUDY SESSION 15

The topical coverage corresponds with the following CFA Institute assigned reading:

60. Features of Debt Securities

The candidate should be able to:

a. explain the purposes of a bond's indenture and describe affirmative and negative covenants. (page 11)

b. describe the basic features of a bond, the various coupon rate structures, and the structure of floating-rate securities. (page 11)

c. define accrued interest, full price, and clean price. (page 13)

d. explain the provisions for redemption and retirement of bonds. (page 14)

e. identify the common options embedded in a bond issue, explain the importance of embedded options, and state whether such options benefit the issuer or the bondholder. (page 16)

f. describe methods used by institutional investors in the bond market to finance the purchase of a security (i.e., margin buying and repurchase agreements). (page 17)

The topical coverage corresponds with the following CFA Institute assigned reading:

61. Risks Associated with Investing in Bonds

The candidate should be able to:

a. explain the risks associated with investing in bonds. (page 24)

b. identify the relations among a bond's coupon rate, the yield required by the market, and the bond's price relative to par value (i.e., discount, premium, or equal to par). (page 26)

c. explain how features of a bond (e.g., maturity, coupon, and embedded options) and the level of a bond's yield affect the bond's interest rate risk. (page 27)

d. identify the relationship among the price of a callable bond, the price of an option-free bond, and the price of the embedded call option. (page 28)

e. explain the interest rate risk of a floating-rate security and why such a security's price may differ from par value. (page 28)

f. compute and interpret the duration and dollar duration of a bond. (page 29)

g. describe yield-curve risk and explain why duration does not account for yield-curve risk for a portfolio of bonds. (page 31)

h. explain the disadvantages of a callable or prepayable security to an investor. (page 33)

i. identify the factors that affect the reinvestment risk of a security and explain why prepayable amortizing securities expose investors to greater reinvestment risk than nonamortizing securities. (page 33)

j. describe the various forms of credit risk and describe the meaning and role of credit ratings. (page 34)

k. explain liquidity risk and why it might be important to investors even if they expect to hold a security to the maturity date. (page 35)

©2009 Kaplan, Inc.

l. describe the exchange rate risk an investor faces when a bond makes payments in a foreign currency. (page 36)

m. explain inflation risk. (page 36)

n. explain how yield volatility affects the price of a bond with an embedded option and how changes in volatility affect the value of a callable bond and a putable bond. (page 36)

o. describe the various forms of event risk. (page 37)

The topical coverage corresponds with the following CFA Institute assigned reading:

62. **Overview of Bond Sectors and Instruments**
The candidate should be able to:

a. describe the features, credit risk characteristics, and distribution methods for government securities. (page 45)

b. describe the types of securities issued by the U.S. Department of the Treasury (e.g. bills, notes, bonds, and inflation protection securities), and differentiate between on-the-run and off-the-run Treasury securities. (page 46)

c. describe how stripped Treasury securities are created and distinguish between coupon strips and principal strips. (page 48)

d. describe the types and characteristics of securities issued by U.S. federal agencies. (page 48)

e. describe the types and characteristics of mortgage-backed securities and explain the cash flow, prepayments, and prepayment risk for each type. (page 49)

f. state the motivation for creating a collateralized mortgage obligation. (page 51)

g. describe the types of securities issued by municipalities in the United States and distinguish between tax-backed debt and revenue bonds. (page 52)

h. describe the characteristics and motivation for the various types of debt issued by corporations (including corporate bonds, medium-term notes, structured notes, commercial paper, negotiable CDs, and bankers acceptances). (page 53)

i. define an asset-backed security, describe the role of a special purpose vehicle in an asset-backed security's transaction, state the motivation for a corporation to issue an asset-backed security, and describe the types of external credit enhancements for asset-backed securities. (page 58)

j. describe collateralized debt obligations. (page 59)

k. describe the mechanisms available for placing bonds in the primary market and differentiate the primary and secondary markets in bonds. (page 59)

The topical coverage corresponds with the following CFA Institute assigned reading:

63. **Understanding Yield Spreads**
The candidate should be able to:

a. identify the interest rate policy tools available to a central bank (e.g., the U.S. Federal Reserve). (page 67)

b. describe a yield curve and the various shapes of the yield curve. (page 68)

c. explain the basic theories of the term structure of interest rates and describe the implications of each theory for the shape of the yield curve. (page 69)

d. define a spot rate. (page 71)

e. compute, compare, and contrast the various yield spread measures. (page 72)

f. describe a credit spread and discuss the suggested relation between credit spreads and the well-being of the economy. (page 73)

g. identify how embedded options affect yield spreads. (page 73)

h. explain how the liquidity or issue-size of a bond affects its yield spread relative to risk-free securities and relative to other securities. (page 74)

i. compute the after-tax yield of a taxable security and the tax-equivalent yield of a tax-exempt security. (page 74)
j. define LIBOR and explain its importance to funded investors who borrow short term. (page 75)

STUDY SESSION 16

The topical coverage corresponds with the following CFA Institute assigned reading:

64. Introduction to the Valuation of Debt Securities
The candidate should be able to:
a. explain the steps in the bond valuation process. (page 84)
b. identify the types of bonds for which estimating the expected cash flows is difficult and explain the problems encountered when estimating the cash flows for these bonds. (page 84)
c. compute the value of a bond and the change in value that is attributable to a change in the discount rate. (page 85)
d. explain how the price of a bond changes as the bond approaches its maturity date and compute the change in value that is attributable to the passage of time. (page 88)
e. compute the value of a zero-coupon bond. (page 89)
f. explain the arbitrage-free valuation approach and the market process that forces the price of a bond toward its arbitrage-free value and explain how a dealer can generate an arbitrage profit if a bond is mispriced. (page 90)

The topical coverage corresponds with the following CFA Institute assigned reading:

65. Yield Measures, Spot Rates, and Forward Rates
The candidate should be able to:
a. explain the sources of return from investing in a bond. (page 98)
b. compute and interpret the traditional yield measures for fixed-rate bonds and explain their limitations and assumptions. (page 98)
c. explain the importance of reinvestment income in generating the yield computed at the time of purchase, calculate the amount of income required to generate that yield, and discuss the factors that affect reinvestment risk. (page 105)
d. compute and interpret the bond equivalent yield of an annual-pay bond and the annual-pay yield of a semiannual-pay bond. (page 107)
e. describe the methodology for computing the theoretical Treasury spot rate curve and compute the value of a bond using spot rates. (page 108)
f. differentiate between the nominal spread, the zero-volatility spread, and the option-adjusted spread. (page 112)
g. describe how the option-adjusted spread accounts for the option cost in a bond with an embedded option. (page 114)
h. explain a forward rate and compute spot rates from forward rates, forward rates from spot rates, and the value of a bond using forward rates. (page 114)

©2009 Kaplan, Inc.

The topical coverage corresponds with the following CFA Institute assigned reading:
66. Introduction to the Measurement of Interest Rate Risk
The candidate should be able to:

a. distinguish between the full valuation approach (the scenario analysis approach) and the duration/convexity approach for measuring interest rate risk and explain the advantage of using the full valuation approach. (page 132)

b. demonstrate the price volatility characteristics for option-free, callable, prepayable, and putable bonds when interest rates change. (page 134)

c. describe positive convexity, negative convexity, and their relation to bond price and yield. (page 134)

d. compute and interpret the effective duration of a bond, given information about how the bond's price will increase and decrease for given changes in interest rates, and compute the approximate percentage price change for a bond, given the bond's effective duration and a specified change in yield. (page 137)

e. distinguish among the alternative definitions of duration and explain why effective duration is the most appropriate measure of interest rate risk for bonds with embedded options. (page 140)

f. compute the duration of a portfolio, given the duration of the bonds comprising the portfolio, and explain the limitations of portfolio duration. (page 141)

g. describe the convexity measure of a bond and estimate a bond's percentage price change, given the bond's duration and convexity and a specified change in interest rates. (page 142)

h. differentiate between modified convexity and effective convexity. (page 144)

i. compute the price value of a basis point (PVBP), and explain its relationship to duration. (page 145)

STUDY SESSION 17

The topical coverage corresponds with the following CFA Institute assigned reading:
67. Derivative Markets and Instruments
The candidate should be able to:

a. define a derivative and differentiate between exchange-traded and over-the-counter derivatives. (page 159)

b. define a forward commitment and a contingent claim. (page 159)

c. differentiate the basic characteristics of forward contracts, futures contracts, options (calls and puts), and swaps. (page 160)

d. discuss the purposes and criticisms of derivative markets. (page 160)

e. explain arbitrage and the role it plays in determining prices and promoting market efficiency. (page 161)

The topical coverage corresponds with the following CFA Institute assigned reading:
68. Forward Markets and Contracts
The candidate should be able to:

a. explain delivery/settlement and default risk for both long and short positions in a forward contract. (page 165)

b. describe the procedures for settling a forward contract at expiration and discuss how termination alternatives prior to expiration can affect credit risk. (page 166)

c. differentiate between a dealer and an end user of a forward contract. (page 167)

d. describe the characteristics of equity forward contracts and forward contracts on zero-coupon and coupon bonds. (page 168)

    e.   describe the characteristics of the Eurodollar time deposit market and define LIBOR and Euribor. (page 170)

    f.   describe the characteristics and calculate the gain/loss of forward rate agreements (FRAs). (page 171)

    g.   calculate and interpret the payoff of an FRA, and explain each of the component terms. (page 171)

    h.   describe the characteristics of currency forward contracts. (page 173)

The topical coverage corresponds with the following CFA Institute assigned reading:

69. Futures Markets and Contracts

The candidate should be able to:

    a.   describe the characteristics of futures contracts. (page 180)

    b.   distinguish between futures contracts and forward contracts. (page 180)

    c.   differentiate between margin in the securities markets and margin in the futures markets, and explain the role of initial margin, maintenance margin, variation margin, and settlement in futures trading. (page 181)

    d.   describe price limits and the process of marking to market and compute and interpret the margin balance, given the previous day's balance and the change in the futures price. (page 183)

    e.   describe how a futures contract can be terminated at or prior to expiration. (page 184)

    f.   describe the characteristics of the following types of futures contracts: Eurodollar, Treasury bond, stock index, and currency. (page 185)

The topical coverage corresponds with the following CFA Institute assigned reading:

70. Option Markets and Contracts

The candidate should be able to:

    a.   define European option, American option, and the concept of moneyness of an option. (page 193)

    b.   differentiate between exchange-traded options and over-the-counter options. (page 194)

    c.   identify the types of options in terms of the underlying instruments. (page 195)

    d.   compare and contrast interest rate options with forward rate agreements (FRAs). (page 196)

    e.   define interest rate caps, floors, and collars. (page 197)

    f.   compute and interpret option payoffs, and explain how interest rate option payoffs differ from the payoffs of other types of options. (page 198)

    g.   define intrinsic value and time value and explain their relationship. (page 199)

    h.   determine the minimum and maximum values of European options and American options. (page 202)

    i.   calculate and interpret the lowest prices of European and American calls and puts based on the rules for minimum values and lower bounds. (page 202)

    j.   explain how option prices are affected by the exercise price and the time to expiration. (page 207)

    k.   explain put-call parity for European options, and relate put-call parity to arbitrage and the construction of synthetic options. (page 208)

    l.   contrast American options with European options in terms of the lower bounds on option prices and the possibility of early exercise. (page 210)

    m.   explain how cash flows on the underlying asset affect put-call parity and the lower bounds of option prices. (page 211)

©2009 Kaplan, Inc.

n. indicate the directional effect of an interest rate change or volatility change on an option's price. (page 211)

The topical coverage corresponds with the following CFA Institute assigned reading:

71. **Swap Markets and Contracts**
    The candidate should be able to:
    a. describe the characteristics of swap contracts and explain how swaps are terminated. (page 220)
    b. define, calculate, and interpret the payment of currency swaps, plain vanilla interest rate swaps, and equity swaps. (page 221)

The topical coverage corresponds with the following CFA Institute assigned reading:

72. **Risk Management Applications of Option Strategies**
    The candidate should be able to:
    a. determine the value at expiration, profit, maximum profit, maximum loss, breakeven underlying price at expiration, and general shape of the graph of the strategies of buying and selling calls and puts, and indicate the market outlook of investors using these strategies. (page 233)
    b. determine the value at expiration, profit, maximum profit, maximum loss, breakeven underlying price at expiration, and general shape of the graph of a covered call strategy and a protective put strategy, and explain the risk management application of each strategy. (page 237)

STUDY SESSION 18

The topical coverage corresponds with the following CFA Institute assigned reading:

73. **Alternative Investments**
    The candidate should be able to:
    a. differentiate between an open-end and a closed-end fund, and explain how net asset value of a fund is calculated and the nature of fees charged by investment companies. (page 243)
    b. distinguish among style, sector, index, global, and stable value strategies in equity investment and among exchange traded funds (ETFs), traditional mutual funds, and closed-end funds. (page 246)
    c. explain the advantages and risks of ETFs. (page 247)
    d. describe the forms of real estate investment and explain their characteristics as an investable asset class. (page 248)
    e. describe the various approaches to the valuation of real estate. (page 249)
    f. calculate the net operating income (NOI) from a real estate investment, the value of a property using the sales comparison and income approaches, and the after-tax cash flows, net present value, and yield of a real estate investment. (page 250)
    g. explain the stages in venture capital investing, venture capital investment characteristics and challenges to venture capital valuation and performance measurement. (page 253)
    h. calculate the net present value (NPV) of a venture capital project, given the project's possible payoff and conditional failure probabilities. (page 254)
    i. define hedge fund in terms of objectives, legal structure, and fee structure, and describe the various classifications of hedge funds. (page 255)
    j. explain the benefits and drawbacks to fund of funds investing. (page 256)

k. discuss the leverage and unique risks of hedge funds. (page 256)
l. discuss the performance of hedge funds, the biases present in hedge fund performance measurement, and explain the effect of survivorship bias on the reported return and risk measures for a hedge fund database. (page 257)
m. explain how the legal environment affects the valuation of closely held companies. (page 259)
n. describe alternative valuation methods for closely held companies and distinguish among the bases for the discounts and premiums for these companies. (page 259)
o. discuss distressed securities investing and compare venture capital investing with distressed securities investing. (page 260)
p. discuss the role of commodities as a vehicle for investing in production and consumption. (page 260)
q. explain the motivation for investing in commodities, commodities derivatives, and commodity-linked securities. (page 260)
r. discuss the sources of return on a collateralized commodity futures position. (page 261)

The topical coverage corresponds with the following CFA Institute assigned reading:
74. **Investing in Commodities**
The candidate should be able to:
a. explain the relationship between spot prices and expected future prices in terms of contango and backwardation. (page 277)
b. describe the sources of return and risk for a commodity investment and the effect on a portfolio of adding an allocation to commodities. (page 278)
c. explain why a commodity index strategy is generally considered an active investment. (page 279)

©2009 Kaplan, Inc.

The following is a review of the Analysis of Fixed Income Investments principles designed to address the learning outcome statements set forth by CFA Institute®. This topic is also covered in:

FEATURES OF DEBT SECURITIES

Study Session 15

EXAM FOCUS

Fixed income securities, historically, were promises to pay a stream of semiannual payments for a given number of years and then repay the loan amount at the maturity date. The contract between the borrower and the lender (the indenture) can really be designed to have any payment stream or pattern that the parties agree to. Types of contracts that are used frequently have specific names, and there is no shortage of those (for you to learn) here.

You should pay special attention to how the periodic payments are determined (fixed, floating, and variants of these) and to how/when the principal is repaid (calls, puts, sinking funds, amortization, and prepayments). These features all affect the value of the securities and will come up again when you learn how to value these securities and compare their risks, both at Level 1 and Level 2.

LOS 60.a: Explain the purposes of a bond's indenture and describe affirmative and negative covenants.

The contract that specifies all the rights and obligations of the issuer and the owners of a fixed income security is called the **bond indenture.** The indenture defines the obligations of and restrictions on the borrower and forms the basis for all future transactions between the bondholder and the issuer. These contract provisions are known as *covenants* and include both *negative covenants* (prohibitions on the borrower) and *affirmative covenants* (actions that the borrower promises to perform) sections.

Negative covenants include restrictions on asset sales (the company can't sell assets that have been pledged as collateral), negative pledge of collateral (the company can't claim that the same assets back several debt issues simultaneously), and restrictions on additional borrowings (the company can't borrow additional money unless certain financial conditions are met).

Affirmative covenants include the maintenance of certain financial ratios and the timely payment of principal and interest. For example, the borrower might promise to maintain the company's current ratio at a value of two or higher. If this value of the current ratio is not maintained, then the bonds could be considered to be in (technical) default.

LOS 60.b: Describe the basic features of a bond, the various coupon rate structures, and the structure of floating-rate securities.

A "straight" (option-free) bond is the simplest case. Consider a Treasury bond that has a 6% **coupon** and **matures** five years from today in the amount of $1,000. This bond is a promise by the **issuer** (the U.S. Treasury) to pay 6% of the $1,000 **par value** (i.e., $60) each year for five years and to repay the $1,000 five years from today.

With Treasury bonds and almost all U.S. corporate bonds, the annual interest is paid in two semiannual installments. Therefore, this bond will make nine coupon payments (one every six months) of $30 and a final payment of $1,030 (the par value plus the final coupon payment) at the end of five years. This stream of payments is fixed when the bonds are issued and does not change over the life of the bond.

Note that each semiannual coupon is one-half the coupon rate (which is always expressed as an annual rate) times the par value, which is sometimes called the *face value* or *maturity value*. An 8% Treasury note with a face value of $100,000 will make a coupon payment of $4,000 every six months and a final payment of $104,000 at maturity.

A U.S. Treasury bond is denominated (of course) in U.S. dollars. Bonds can be issued in other currencies as well. The **currency denomination** of a bond issued by the Mexican government will likely be Mexican pesos. Bonds can be issued that promise to make payments in any currency.

Coupon Rate Structures: Zero-Coupon Bonds, Step-Up Notes, Deferred Coupon Bonds

Zero-coupon bonds are bonds that do not pay periodic interest. They pay the par value at maturity and the interest results from the fact that zero-coupon bonds are initially sold at a price below par value (i.e., they are sold at a significant *discount to par value*). Sometimes we will call debt securities with no explicit interest payments *pure discount securities*.

Step-up notes have coupon rates that increase over time at a specified rate. The increase may take place one or more times during the life of the issue.

Deferred-coupon bonds carry coupons, but the initial coupon payments are deferred for some period. The coupon payments accrue, at a compound rate, over the deferral period and are paid as a lump sum at the end of that period. After the initial deferment period has passed, these bonds pay regular coupon interest for the rest of the life of the issue (to maturity).

Floating-Rate Securities

Floating-rate securities are bonds for which the coupon interest payments over the life of the security vary based on a specified interest rate or index. For example, if market interest rates are moving up, the coupons on straight floaters will rise as well. In essence, these bonds have coupons that are reset periodically (normally every 3, 6, or 12 months) based on prevailing market interest rates.

The most common procedure for setting the coupon rates on floating-rate securities is one which starts with a *reference rate* (such as the rate on certain U.S. Treasury securities

©2009 Kaplan, Inc.

or the London Interbank Offered Rate [LIBOR]) and then adds or subtracts a stated *margin* to or from that reference rate. The quoted margin may also vary over time according to a schedule that is stated in the indenture. The schedule is often referred to as the *coupon formula*. Thus, to find the new coupon rate, you would use the following coupon formula:

new coupon rate = reference rate ± quoted margin

Just as with a fixed-coupon bond, a semiannual coupon payment will be one-half the (annual) coupon *rate*.

An **inverse floater** is a floating-rate security with a coupon formula that actually increases the coupon rate when a reference interest rate decreases, and vice versa. A coupon formula such as coupon rate = 12% – reference rate accomplishes this.

Some floating-rate securities have coupon formulas based on inflation and are referred to as **inflation-indexed bonds**. A bond with a coupon formula of 3% + annual change in CPI is an example of such an inflation-linked security.

The parties to the bond contract can limit their exposure to extreme fluctuations in the reference rate by placing upper and lower limits on the coupon rate. The upper limit, which is called a **cap**, puts a maximum on the interest rate paid by the borrower/issuer. The lower limit, called a **floor**, puts a minimum on the periodic coupon interest payments received by the lender/security owner. When both limits are present simultaneously, the combination is called a **collar**.

Consider a floating-rate security (floater) with a coupon rate at issuance of 5%, a 7% cap, and a 3% floor. If the coupon rate (reference rate plus the margin) rises above 7%, the borrower will pay (lender will receive) only 7% for as long as the coupon rate, according to the formula, remains at or above 7%. If the coupon rate falls below 3%, the borrower will pay 3% for as long as the coupon rate, according to the formula, remains at or below 3%.

LOS 60.c: Define accrued interest, full price, and clean price.

When a bond trades between coupon dates, the seller is entitled to receive any interest earned from the previous coupon date through the date of the sale. This is known as **accrued interest** and is an amount that is payable by the buyer (new owner) of the bond. The new owner of the bond will receive all of the next coupon payment and will then recover any accrued interest paid on the date of purchase. The accrued interest is calculated as the fraction of the coupon period that has passed times the coupon.

In the United States, the convention is for the bond buyer to pay any accrued interest to the bond seller. The amount that the buyer pays to the seller is the agreed-upon price of the bond (the **clean price**) plus any accrued interest. In the United States, bonds trade with the next coupon attached, which is termed *cum coupon*. A bond traded without the right to the next coupon is said to be trading *ex-coupon*. The total amount paid, including accrued interest, is known as the **full (or dirty) price** of the bond. The full price = clean price + accrued interest.

If the issuer of the bond is in default (i.e., has not made periodic obligatory coupon payments), the bond will trade without accrued interest, and it is said to be trading *flat*.

LOS 60.d: Explain the provisions for redemption and retirement of bonds.

The redemption provisions for a bond refer to how, when, and under what circumstances the principal will be repaid.

Coupon Treasury bonds and most corporate bonds are **nonamortizing**; that is, they pay only interest until maturity, at which time the entire par or face value is repaid. This repayment structure is referred to as a *bullet bond* or *bullet maturity*. Alternatively, the bond terms may specify that the principal be repaid through a series of payments over time or all at once prior to maturity, at the option of either the bondholder or the issuer (putable and callable bonds).

Amortizing securities make periodic *interest and principal* payments over the life of the bond. A conventional mortgage is an example of an amortizing loan; the payments are all equal, and each payment consists of the periodic interest payment and the repayment of a portion of the original principal. For a fully amortizing loan, the final (level) payment at maturity retires the last remaining principal on the loan (e.g., a typical automobile loan).

Prepayment options give the issuer/borrower the right to accelerate the principal repayment on a loan. These options are present in mortgages and other amortizing loans. Amortizing loans require a series of equal payments that cover the periodic interest and reduce the outstanding principal each time a payment is made. When a person gets a home mortgage or an automobile loan, she often has the right to prepay it at any time, in whole or in part. If the borrower sells the home or auto, she is required to pay the loan off in full. The significance of a prepayment option to an investor in a mortgage or mortgage-backed security is that there is additional uncertainty about the cash flows to be received compared to a security that does not permit prepayment.

Call provisions give the issuer the right (but not the obligation) to retire all or a part of an issue prior to maturity. If the bonds are called, the bondholders have no choice but to surrender their bonds for the call price because the bonds quit paying interest when they are called. Call features give the issuer the opportunity to replace higher-than-market coupon bonds with lower-coupon issues.

Typically, there is a period of years after issuance during which the bonds cannot be called. This is termed the period of *call protection* because the bondholder is protected from a call over this period. After the period (if any) of call protection has passed, the bonds are referred to as *currently callable*.

There may be several call dates specified in the indenture, each with a lower call price. Customarily, when a bond is called on the first permissible call date, the call price is above the par value. If the bonds are not called entirely or not called at all, the call price declines over time according to a schedule. For example, a call schedule may specify that a 20-year bond can be called after five years at a price of 110 (110% of par), with the call price declining to 105 after ten years and 100 in the 15th year.

©2009 Kaplan, Inc.

Nonrefundable bonds prohibit the call of an issue using the proceeds from a lower coupon bond issue. Thus, a bond may be callable but not refundable. A bond that is *noncallable* has absolute protection against a call prior to maturity. In contrast, a callable but *nonrefundable* bond can be called for any reason other than refunding.

When bonds are called through a call option or through the provisions of a sinking fund, the bonds are said to be **redeemed**. If a lower coupon issue is sold to provide the funds to call the bonds, the bonds are said to be **refunded**.

Sinking fund provisions provide for the repayment of principal through a series of payments over the life of the issue. For example, a 20-year issue with a face amount of $300 million may require that the issuer retire $20 million of the principal every year beginning in the sixth year. This can be accomplished in one of two ways—*cash* or *delivery*:

- *Cash payment.* The issuer may deposit the required cash amount annually with the issue's trustee who will then retire the applicable proportion of bonds (1/15 in this example) by using a selection method such as a lottery. The bonds selected by the trustee are typically retired at par.
- *Delivery of securities.* The issuer may purchase bonds with a total par value equal to the amount that is to be retired in that year in the market and deliver them to the trustee who will retire them.

If the bonds are trading below par value, delivery of bonds purchased in the open market is the less expensive alternative. If the bonds are trading above the par value, delivering cash to the trustee to retire the bonds at par is the less expensive way to satisfy the sinking fund requirement.

An **accelerated sinking fund provision** allows the issuer the choice of retiring more than the amount of bonds specified in the sinking fund requirement. As an example, the issuer may be required to redeem $5 million par value of bonds each year but may choose to retire up to $10 million par value of the issue.

Regular and Special Redemption Prices

When bonds are redeemed under the call provisions specified in the bond indenture, these are known as regular redemptions, and the call prices are referred to as **regular redemption prices**. However, when bonds are redeemed to comply with a sinking fund provision or because of a property sale mandated by government authority, the redemption prices (typically par value) are referred to as **special redemption prices**. Asset sales may be forced by a regulatory authority (e.g., the forced divestiture of an operating division by antitrust authorities or through a governmental unit's right of eminent domain). Examples of sales forced through the government's right of eminent domain would be a forced sale of privately held land for erection of electric utility lines or for construction of a freeway.

LOS 60.e: Identify the common options embedded in a bond issue, explain the importance of embedded options, and state whether such options benefit the issuer or the bondholder.

The following are examples of *embedded options*, embedded in the sense that they are an integral part of the bond contract and are not a separate security. Some embedded options are exercisable at the option of the issuer of the bond, and some are exercisable at the option of the purchaser of the bond.

Security owner options. In the following cases, the option embedded in the fixed-income security is an option granted to the security holder (lender) and gives additional value to the security, compared to an otherwise-identical straight (option-free) security.

1. A *conversion option* grants the holder of a bond the right to convert the bond into a fixed number of common shares of the issuer. This choice/option has value for the bondholder. An exchange option is similar but allows conversion of the bond into a security other than the common stock of the issuer.

2. *Put provisions* give bondholders the right to sell (put) the bond to the issuer at a specified price prior to maturity. The put price is generally par if the bonds were originally issued at or close to par. If interest rates have risen and/or the creditworthiness of the issuer has deteriorated so that the market price of such bonds has fallen below par, the bondholder may choose to exercise the put option and require the issuer to redeem the bonds at the put price.

3. *Floors* set a minimum on the coupon rate for a floating-rate bond, a bond with a coupon rate that changes each period based on a reference rate, usually a short-term rate such as LIBOR or the T-bill rate.

Security issuer options. In these cases, the embedded option is exercisable at the option of the issuer of the fixed income security. Securities where the issuer chooses whether to exercise the embedded option will be priced less (or with a higher coupon) than otherwise identical securities that do not contain such an option.

1. *Call provisions* give the bond issuer the right to redeem (pay off) the issue prior to maturity. The details of a call feature are covered later in this topic review.

2. *Prepayment options* are included in many amortizing securities, such as those backed by mortgages or car loans. A prepayment option gives the borrower/issuer the right to prepay the loan balance prior to maturity, in whole or in part, without penalty. Loans may be prepaid for a variety of reasons, such as the refinancing of a mortgage due to a drop in interest rates or the sale of a home prior to its loan maturity date.

3. *Accelerated sinking fund provisions* are embedded options held by the issuer that allow the issuer to (annually) retire a larger proportion of the issue than is required by the sinking fund provision, up to a specified limit.

4. *Caps* set a maximum on the coupon rate for a floating-rate bond, a bond with a coupon rate that changes each period based on a reference rate, usually a short-term rate such as LIBOR or the T-bill rate.

©2009 Kaplan, Inc.

Professor's Note: Caps and floors do not need to be "exercised" by the issuer or bondholder. They are considered embedded options because a cap is equivalent to a series of interest rate call options and a floor is equivalent to a series of interest rate put options. This will be explained further in our topic review of Option Markets and Contracts in the Study Session covering derivatives.

To summarize, the following embedded options favor the issuer/borrower: (1) the right to call the issue, (2) an accelerated sinking fund provision, (3) a prepayment option, and (4) a cap on the floating coupon rate that limits the amount of interest payable by the borrower/issuer. Bonds with these options will tend to have higher market yields since bondholders will require a premium relative to otherwise identical option-free bonds.

The following embedded options favor the *bondholders*: (1) conversion provisions, (2) a floor that guarantees a minimum interest payment to the bondholder, and (3) a put option. The market yields on bonds with these options will tend to be lower than otherwise identical option-free bonds since bondholders will find these options attractive.

LOS 60.f: Describe methods used by institutional investors in the bond market to finance the purchase of a security (i.e., margin buying and repurchase agreements).

Margin buying involves borrowing funds from a broker or a bank to purchase securities where the securities themselves are the collateral for the margin loan. The margin amount (percentage of the bonds' value) is regulated by the Federal Reserve in the United States, under the Securities and Exchange Act of 1934.

A **repurchase (repo) agreement** is an arrangement by which an institution sells a security with a commitment to buy it back at a later date at a specified (higher) price. The *repurchase price* is greater than the selling price and accounts for the interest charged by the buyer, who is, in effect, lending funds to the seller. The interest rate implied by the two prices is called the *repo rate*, which is the annualized percentage difference between the two prices. A repurchase agreement for one day is called an *overnight repo*, and an agreement covering a longer period is called a *term repo*. The interest cost of a *repo* is customarily less than the rate a bank or brokerage would charge on a margin loan.

Most bond-dealer financing is achieved through repurchase agreements rather than through margin loans. Repurchase agreements are not regulated by the Federal Reserve, and the collateral position of the lender/buyer in a repo is better in the event of bankruptcy of the dealer, since the security is owned by the lender. The lender has only the obligation to sell it back at the price specified in the repurchase agreement, rather than simply having a claim against the assets of the dealer for the margin loan amount.

KEY CONCEPTS

LOS 60.a

A bond's indenture contains the obligations, rights, and any options available to the issuer or buyer of a bond.

Covenants are the specific conditions of the obligation:
- Affirmative covenants specify actions that the borrower/issuer must perform.
- Negative covenants prohibit certain actions by the borrower/issuer.

LOS 60.b

Bonds have the following features:
- Maturity—the term of the loan agreement.
- Par value (face value)—the principal amount of the fixed income security that the bond issuer promises to pay the bondholders over the life of the bond.
- Coupon rate—the rate used to determine the periodic interest to be paid on the principal amount. Interest can be paid annually or semiannually, depending on the terms. Coupon rates may be fixed or variable.

Types of coupon rate structures:
- Option-free (straight) bonds pay periodic interest and repay the par value at maturity.
- Zero-coupon bonds pay no explicit periodic interest and are sold at a discount to par value.
- Step-up notes have a coupon rate that increases over time according to a specified schedule.
- Deferred coupon bonds initially make no coupon payments (they are deferred for a period of time). At the end of the deferral period, the accrued (compound) interest is paid, and the bonds then make regular coupon payments until maturity.
- A floating (variable) rate bond has a coupon formula that is based on a reference rate (usually LIBOR) and a quoted margin. A cap is a maximum coupon rate the issuer must pay, and a floor is a minimum coupon rate the bondholder will receive on any coupon date.

LOS 60.c

Accrued interest is the interest earned since the last coupon payment date and is paid by a bond buyer to a bond seller.

Clean price is the quoted price of the bond without accrued interest.

Full price refers to the quoted price plus any accrued interest.

©2009 Kaplan, Inc.

LOS 60.d

Bond retirement (payoff) provisions:

- Amortizing securities make periodic payments that include both interest and principal payments so that the entire principal is paid off with the last payment unless prepayment occurs.
- A prepayment option is contained in some amortizing debt and allows the borrower to pay off principal at any time prior to maturity, in whole or in part.
- Sinking fund provisions require that a part of a bond issue be retired at specified dates, typically annually.
- Call provisions enable the borrower (issuer) to buy back the bonds from the investors (redeem them) at a call price(s) specified in the bond indenture.
- Callable but nonrefundable bonds can be called prior to maturity, but their redemption cannot be funded by the issuance of bonds with a lower coupon rate.

LOS 60.e

Embedded options that benefit the issuer reduce the bond's value (increase the yield) to a bond purchaser. Examples are:

- Call provisions.
- Accelerated sinking fund provisions.
- Caps (maximum interest rates) on floating-rate bonds.

Embedded options that benefit bondholders increase the bond's value (decrease the yield) to a bond purchaser. Examples are:

- Conversion options (the option of bondholders to convert their bonds into shares of the bond issuer's common stock).
- Put options (the option of bondholders to return their bonds to the issuer at a predetermined price).
- Floors (minimum interest rates) on floating-rate bonds.

LOS 60.f

Institutions can finance secondary market bond purchases by margin buying (borrowing some of the purchase price, using the securities as collateral) or, more commonly, by repurchase (repo) agreements, an arrangement in which an institution sells a security with a promise to buy it back at an agreed-upon higher price at a specified date in the future.

CONCEPT CHECKERS

1. A bond's indenture:
    A. contains its covenants.
    B. is the same as a debenture.
    C. relates only to its interest and principal payments.

2. A bond has a par value of $5,000 and a coupon rate of 8.5% payable semiannually. What is the dollar amount of the semiannual coupon payment?
    A. $212.50.
    B. $238.33.
    C. $425.00.

3. From the perspective of the bondholder, which of the following pairs of options would add value to a straight (option-free) bond?
    A. Call option and conversion option.
    B. Put option and conversion option.
    C. Prepayment option and put option.

4. A 10-year bond pays no interest for three years, then pays $229.25, followed by payments of $35 semiannually for seven years and an additional $1,000 at maturity. This bond is a:
    A. step-up bond.
    B. zero-coupon bond.
    C. deferred coupon bond.

5. Consider a $1 million semiannual-pay floating-rate issue where the rate is reset on January 1 and July 1 each year. The reference rate is 6-month LIBOR, and the stated margin is +1.25%. If 6-month LIBOR is 6.5% on July 1, what will the next semiannual coupon be on this issue?
    A. $38,750.
    B. $65,000.
    C. $77,500.

6. Which of the following statements is *most accurate* with regard to floating-rate issues that have caps and floors?
    A. A cap is an advantage to the bondholder, while a floor is an advantage to the issuer.
    B. A floor is an advantage to the bondholder, while a cap is an advantage to the issuer.
    C. A floor is an advantage to both the issuer and the bondholder, while a cap is a disadvantage to both the issuer and the bondholder.

7. An investor paid a full price of $1,059.04 each for 100 bonds. The purchase was between coupon dates, and accrued interest was $23.54 per bond. What is each bond's clean price?
    A. $1,000.00.
    B. $1,035.50.
    C. $1,082.58.

©2009 Kaplan, Inc.

8. Which of the following statements is *most accurate* with regard to a call provision?
   A. A call provision will benefit the issuer in times of declining interest rates.
   B. A callable bond will trade at a higher price than an identical noncallable bond.
   C. A nonrefundable bond provides more protection to the bondholder than a noncallable bond.

9. Which of the following *most accurately* describes the maximum price for a currently callable bond?
   A. Its par value.
   B. The call price.
   C. The present value of its par value.

Use the following information to answer Questions 10 and 11.

Consider $1,000,000 par value, 10-year, 6.5% coupon bonds issued on January 1, 2005. The bonds are callable and there is a sinking fund provision. The market rate for similar bonds is currently 5.7%. The main points of the prospectus are summarized as follows:

Call dates and prices:

- 2005 through 2009: 103.
- After January 1, 2010: 102.

Additional information:

- The bonds are non-refundable.
- The sinking fund provision requires that the company redeem $100,000 of the principal amount each year. Bonds called under the terms of the sinking fund provision will be redeemed at par.
- The credit rating of the bonds is currently the same as at issuance.

10. Using only the above information, Gould should conclude that:
    A. the bonds do not have call protection.
    B. the bonds were issued at and currently trade at a premium.
    C. given current rates, the bonds will likely be called and new bonds issued.

11. Which of the following statements about the sinking fund provisions for these bonds is *most accurate*?
    A. An investor would benefit from having his bonds called under the provision of the sinking fund.
    B. An investor will receive a premium if the bond is redeemed prior to maturity under the provision of the sinking fund.
    C. The bonds do not have an accelerated sinking fund provision.

12. An investor buying bonds on margin:
    A. must pay interest on a loan.
    B. is not restricted by government regulation of margin lending.
    C. actually lends the bonds to a bank or brokerage house.

13. Which of the following is *least likely* a provision for the early retirement of debt by the issuer?
   A. A conversion option.
   B. A call option.
   C. A sinking fund.

14. A mortgage is *least likely*:
   A. a collateralized loan.
   B. subject to early retirement.
   C. characterized by highly predictable cash flows.

©2009 Kaplan, Inc.

ANSWERS – CONCEPT CHECKERS

1. **A** An indenture is the contract between the company and its bondholders and contains the bond's covenants.

2. **A** The annual interest is 8.5% of the $5,000 par value, or $425. Each semiannual payment is one-half of that, or $212.50.

3. **B** A put option and a conversion option have positive value to the bondholder. The other options favor the issuer and result in a lower value than a straight bond.

4. **C** This pattern describes a deferred coupon bond. The first payment of $229.25 is the value of the accrued coupon payments for the first three years.

5. **A** The coupon rate is 6.5 + 1.25 = 7.75. The semiannual coupon payment equals (0.5)(0.0775)($1,000,000) = $38,750.

6. **B** A cap is a maximum on the coupon rate and is advantageous to the issuer. A floor is a minimum on the coupon rate and is, therefore, advantageous to the bondholder.

7. **B** The full price includes accrued interest, while the clean price does not. Therefore, the clean price is 1,059.04 − 23.54 = $1,035.50.

8. **A** A call provision gives the bond issuer the right to call the bond at a price specified in the bond indenture. A bond issuer may want to call a bond if interest rates have decreased so that borrowing costs can be decreased by replacing the bond with a lower coupon issue.

9. **B** Whenever the price of the bond increases above the strike price stipulated on the call option, it will be optimal for the issuer to call the bond. So theoretically, the price of a currently callable bond should never rise above its call price.

10. **A** The bonds are callable in 2005, indicating that there is no period of call protection. We have no information about the pricing of the bonds at issuance. The company may not *refund* the bonds (i.e., they cannot call the bonds with the proceeds of a new debt offering at the currently lower market yield).

11. **C** The sinking fund provision does not provide for an acceleration of the sinking fund redemptions. With rates currently below the coupon rate, the bonds will be trading at a premium to par value. Thus, a sinking fund call at par would not benefit a bondholder.

12. **A** Margin loans require the payment of interest, and the rate is typically higher than funding costs when repurchase agreements are used.

13. **A** A conversion option allows bondholders to exchange their bonds for common stock.

14. **C** A mortgage can typically be retired early in whole or in part (a prepayment option), and this makes the cash flows difficult to predict with any accuracy.

The following is a review of the Analysis of Fixed Income Investments principles designed to address the learning outcome statements set forth by CFA Institute®. This topic is also covered in:

RISKS ASSOCIATED WITH INVESTING IN BONDS

EXAM FOCUS

This topic review introduces various sources of risk that investors are exposed to when investing in fixed income securities. The key word here is "introduces." The most important source of risk, interest rate risk, has its own full topic review in Study Session 16 and is more fully developed after the material on the valuation of fixed income securities. Prepayment risk has its own topic review at Level 2, and credit risk and reinvestment risk are revisited to a significant extent in other parts of the Level 1 curriculum. In this review, we present some working definitions of the risk measures and identify the factors that will affect these risks. To avoid unnecessary repetition, some of the material is abbreviated here, but be assured that your understanding of this material will be complete by the time you work through this Study Session and the one that follows.

LOS 61.a: Explain the risks associated with investing in bonds.

Interest rate risk refers to the effect of changes in the prevailing market rate of interest on bond values. When interest rates rise, bond values fall. This is the source of interest rate risk which is approximated by a measure called **duration**.

Yield curve risk arises from the possibility of changes in the shape of the yield curve (which shows the relation between bond yields and maturity). While duration is a useful measure of interest rate risk for equal changes in yield at every maturity (parallel changes in the yield curve), changes in the shape of the yield curve mean that yields change by different amounts for bonds with different maturities.

Call risk arises from the fact that when interest rates fall, a callable bond investor's principal may be returned and must be reinvested at the new lower rates. Certainly bonds that are not callable have no call risk, and call protection reduces call risk. When interest rates are more volatile, callable bonds have relatively more call risk because of an increased probability of yields falling to a level where the bonds will be called.

Prepayment risk is similar to call risk. Prepayments are principal repayments in excess of those required on amortizing loans, such as residential mortgages. If rates fall, causing prepayments to increase, an investor must reinvest these prepayments at the new lower rate. Just as with call risk, an increase in interest rate volatility increases prepayment risk.

Reinvestment risk refers to the fact that when market rates fall, the cash flows (both interest and principal) from fixed-income securities must be reinvested at lower rates, reducing the returns an investor will earn. Note that reinvestment risk is related to call risk and prepayment risk. In both of these cases, it is the reinvestment of principal cash

©2009 Kaplan, Inc.

flows at lower rates than were expected that negatively impacts the investor. Coupon bonds that contain neither call nor prepayment provisions will also be subject to reinvestment risk, since the coupon interest payments must be reinvested as they are received.

Note that investors can be faced with a choice between reinvestment risk and price risk. A noncallable zero-coupon bond has no reinvestment risk over its life since there are no cash flows to reinvest, but a zero-coupon bond (as we will cover shortly) has more interest rate risk than a coupon bond of the same maturity. Therefore, the coupon bond will have more reinvestment risk and less price risk.

Credit risk is the risk that the creditworthiness of a fixed-income security's issuer will deteriorate, increasing the required return and decreasing the security's value.

Liquidity risk has to do with the risk that the sale of a fixed-income security must be made at a price less than fair market value because of a lack of liquidity for a particular issue. Treasury bonds have excellent liquidity, so selling a few million dollars worth at the prevailing market price can be easily and quickly accomplished. At the other end of the liquidity spectrum, a valuable painting, collectible antique automobile, or unique and expensive home may be quite difficult to sell quickly at fair-market value. Since investors prefer more liquidity to less, a decrease in a security's liquidity will decrease its price, as the required yield will be higher.

Exchange-rate risk arises from the uncertainty about the value of foreign currency cash flows to an investor in terms of his home-country currency. While a U.S. Treasury bill (T-bill) may be considered quite low risk or even risk-free to a U.S.-based investor, the value of the T-bill to a European investor will be reduced by a depreciation of the U.S. dollar's value relative to the euro.

Inflation risk might be better described as *unexpected* inflation risk and even more descriptively as purchasing-power risk. While a $10,000 zero-coupon Treasury bond can provide a payment of $10,000 in the future with near certainty, there is uncertainty about the amount of goods and services that $10,000 will buy at the future date. This uncertainty about the amount of goods and services that a security's cash flows will purchase is referred to here as inflation risk.

Volatility risk is present for fixed-income securities that have embedded options, such as call options, prepayment options, or put options. Changes in interest rate volatility affect the value of these options and, thus, affect the values of securities with embedded options.

Event risk encompasses the risks outside the risks of financial markets, such as the risks posed by natural disasters and corporate takeovers.

Sovereign risk refers to changes in governmental attitudes and policies toward the repayment and servicing of debt. Governments may impose restrictions on the outflows of foreign exchange to service debt even by private borrowers. Foreign municipalities may adopt different payment policies due to varying political priorities. A change in government may lead to a refusal to repay debt incurred by a prior regime. Remember, the quality of a debt obligation depends not only on the borrower's ability to repay but also on the borrower's desire or willingness to repay. This is true of sovereign debt as well, and we can think of sovereign risk as having two components: a change in a government's willingness to repay and a change in a country's ability to repay. The second component has been the important one in most defaults and downgrades of sovereign debt.

LOS 61.b: Identify the relations among a bond's coupon rate, the yield required by the market, and the bond's price relative to par value (i.e., discount, premium, or equal to par).

When the coupon rate on a bond is equal to its market yield, the bond will trade at its **par value**. When issued, the coupon rate on bonds is typically set at or near the prevailing market yield on similar bonds so that the bonds trade initially at or near their par value. If the yield required in the market for the bond subsequently rises, the price of the bond will fall and it will trade at a **discount** to (below) its par value. The required yield can increase because interest rates have increased, because the extra yield investors require to compensate for the bond's risk has increased, or because the risk of the bond has increased since it was issued. Conversely, if the required yield falls, the bond price will increase and the bond will trade at a **premium** to (above) its par value.

The relation is illustrated in Figure 1.

Figure 1: Market Yield vs. Bond Value for an 8% Coupon Bond

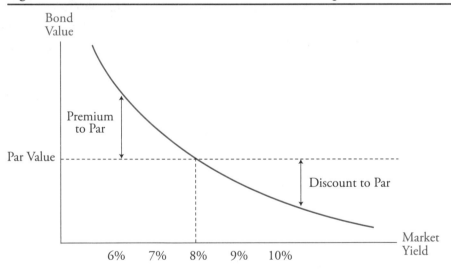

 Professor's Note: This is a crucial concept and the reasons underlying this relation will be clear after you cover the material on bond valuation methods in the next Study Session.

LOS 61.c: Explain how features of a bond (e.g., maturity, coupon, and embedded options) and the level of a bond's yield affect the bond's interest rate risk.

Interest rate risk, as we are using it here, refers to the sensitivity of a bond's value to changes in market interest rates/yields. Remember that there is an inverse relationship between yield and bond prices—when yields increase, bond prices decrease. The term we use for the measure of interest rate risk is **duration**, which gives us a good approximation of a bond's change in price for a given change in yield.

 Professor's Note: This is a very important concept. Notice that the terms "interest rate risk," "interest rate sensitivity," and "duration" are used interchangeably.

We introduce this concept by simply looking at how a bond's maturity and coupon affect its price sensitivity to interest rate changes.

- If two bonds are identical except for maturity, the one with the longer maturity has the greater duration since it will have a greater percentage change in value for a given change in yield.
- For two otherwise identical bonds, the one with the higher coupon rate has the lower duration. The price of the bond with the higher coupon rate will change less for a given change in yield than the price of the lower coupon bond will.

The presence of embedded options also affects the sensitivity of a bond's value to interest rate changes (its duration). Prices of putable and callable bonds will react differently to changes in yield than the prices of straight (option-free) bonds will.

- A call feature limits the upside price movement of a bond when interest rates decline; loosely speaking, the bond price will not rise above the call price. This leads to the conclusion that the value of a callable bond will be less sensitive to interest rate changes than an otherwise identical option-free bond.
- A put feature limits the downside price movement of a bond when interest rates rise; loosely speaking, the bond price will not fall below the put price. This leads to the conclusion that the value of a putable bond will be less sensitive to interest rate changes than an otherwise identical option-free bond.

The relations we have developed so far are summarized in Figure 2.

Figure 2: Bond Characteristics and Interest Rate Risk

Characteristic	Interest Rate Risk	Duration
Maturity up	Interest rate risk up	Duration up
Coupon up	Interest rate risk down	Duration down
Add a call	Interest rate risk down	Duration down
Add a put	Interest rate risk down	Duration down

Professor's Note: We have examined several factors that affect interest rate risk, but only maturity is positively related to interest rate risk (longer maturity, higher duration). To remember this, note that the words "maturity" and "duration" both have to do with time. The other factors, coupon rate, yield, and the presence of puts and calls, are all negatively related to interest rate risk (duration). Increasing coupons, higher yields, and "adding" options all decrease interest rate sensitivity (duration).

LOS 61.d: Identify the relationship among the price of a callable bond, the price of an option-free bond, and the price of the embedded call option.

As we noted earlier, a call option favors the issuer and decreases the value of a callable bond relative to an otherwise identical option-free bond. The issuer owns the call. Essentially, when you purchase a callable bond, you have purchased an option-free bond but have "given" a call option to the issuer. The value of the callable bond is less than the value of an option-free bond by an amount equal to the value of the call option.

This relation can be shown as:

callable bond value = value of option-free bond – value of embedded call option

Figure 3 shows this relationship. The value of the call option is greater at lower yields so that as the yield falls, the difference in price between a straight bond and a callable bond increases.

Figure 3: Price-Yield Curves for Callable and Noncallable Bonds

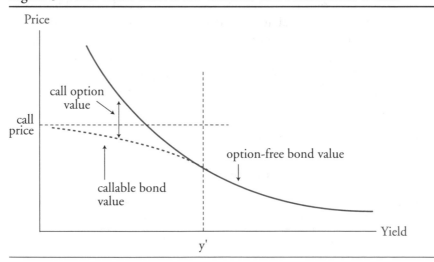

LOS 61.e: Explain the interest rate risk of a floating-rate security and why such a security's price may differ from par value.

Recall that floating-rate securities have a coupon rate that floats, in that it is periodically reset based on a market-determined reference rate. The objective of the resetting mechanism is to bring the coupon rate in line with the current market yield so the bond sells at or near its par value. This will make the price of a floating-rate security much less

©2009 Kaplan, Inc.

sensitive to changes in market yields than a fixed-coupon bond of equal maturity. That's the point of a floating-rate security, less interest rate risk.

Between coupon dates, there is a time lag between any change in market yield and a change in the coupon rate (which happens on the next *reset* date). The longer the time period between the two dates, the greater the amount of potential bond price fluctuation. In general, we can say that the longer (shorter) the reset period, the greater (less) the interest rate risk of a floating-rate security at any reset date.

As long as the required margin above the reference rate exactly compensates for the bond's risk, the price of a floating-rate security will return to par at each reset date. For this reason, the interest rate risk of a floating rate security is very small as the reset date approaches.

There are two primary reasons that a bond's price may differ from par at its coupon reset date. The presence of a **cap** (maximum coupon rate) can increase the interest rate risk of a floating-rate security. If the reference rate increases enough that the cap rate is reached, further increases in market yields will decrease the floater's price. When the market yield is above its capped coupon rate, a floating-rate security will trade at a discount. To the extent that the cap fixes the coupon rate on the floater, its price sensitivity to changes in market yield will be increased. This is sometimes referred to as **cap risk**.

A floater's price can also differ from par due to the fact that the margin is fixed at issuance. Consider a firm that has issued floating-rate debt with a coupon formula of LIBOR + 2%. This 2% margin should reflect the credit risk and liquidity risk of the security. If the firm's creditworthiness improves, the floater is less risky and will trade at a premium to par. Even if the firm's creditworthiness remains constant, a change in the market's required yield premium for the firm's risk level will cause the value of the floater to differ from par.

LOS 61.f: Compute and interpret the duration and dollar duration of a bond.

By now you know that duration is a measure of the price sensitivity of a security to changes in yield. Specifically, it can be interpreted as an approximation of the *percentage* change in the security price for a 1% change in yield. We can also interpret duration as the *ratio* of the percentage change in price to the change in yield in percent.

This relation is:

$$\text{duration} = -\frac{\text{percentage change in bond price}}{\text{yield change in percent}}$$

When calculating the direction of the price change, remember that yields and prices are inversely related. If you are given a rate decrease, your result should indicate a price increase. Also note that the duration of a zero-coupon bond is approximately equal to its years to maturity, and the duration of a floater is equal to the fraction of a year until the next reset date.

Let's consider some numerical examples.

Example 1: Approximate price change when yields increase

If a bond has a duration of 5 and the yield increases from 7% to 8%, calculate the approximate percentage change in the bond price.

Answer:

−5 × 1% = −5%, or a 5% decrease in price. Since the yield increased, the price decreased.

Example 2: Approximate price change when yields decrease

A bond has a duration of 7.2. If the yield decreases from 8.3% to 7.9%, calculate the approximate percentage change in the bond price.

Answer:

−7.2 × (−0.4%) = 2.88%. Here the yield decreased and the price increased.

The "official" formula for what we just did (because duration is always expressed as a positive number and because of the negative relation between yield and price) is:

$$\text{percentage price change} = -\text{duration} \times (\text{yield change in \%})$$

Sometimes the interest rate risk of a bond or portfolio is expressed as its **dollar duration**, which is simply the approximate price change in dollars in response to a change in yield of 100 basis points (1%). With a duration of 5.2 and a bond market value of $1.2 million, we can calculate the dollar duration as 5.2% × $1.2 million = $62,400.

Now let's do it in reverse and calculate the duration from the change in yield and the *percentage* change in the bond's price.

Example 3: Calculating duration given a yield increase

If a bond's yield rises from 7% to 8% and its price falls 5%, calculate the duration.

Answer:

$$\text{duration} = -\frac{\text{percentage change in price}}{\text{change in yield}} = -\frac{-5.0\%}{+1.0\%} = 5$$

©2009 Kaplan, Inc.

Example 4: Calculating duration given a yield decrease

If a bond's yield decreases by 0.1% and its price increases by 1.5%, calculate its duration.

Answer:

$$\text{duration} = -\frac{\text{percentage change in price}}{\text{change in yield}} = -\frac{1.5\%}{-0.1\%} = 15$$

 Professor's Note: Since bond price changes for yield increases and for yield decreases are typically different, duration is typically calculated using an average of the price changes for an increase and for a decrease in yield. In a subsequent reading on interest rate risk we cover this calculation of "effective duration." Here we simply illustrate the basic concept of duration as the approximate percentage price change for a change in yield of 1%.

Example 5: Calculating the new price of a bond

A bond is currently trading at $1,034.50, has a yield of 7.38%, and has a duration of 8.5. If the yield rises to 7.77%, calculate the new price of the bond.

Answer:

The change in yield is 7.77% – 7.38% = 0.39%.

The approximate price change is –8.5 × 0.39% = –3.315%.

Since the yield *increased*, the price will decrease by this *percentage*.

The new price is (1 – 0.03315) × $1,034.50 = $1,000.21.

LOS 61.g: Describe yield-curve risk and explain why duration does not account for yield-curve risk for a portfolio of bonds.

The duration for a portfolio of bonds has the same interpretation as for a single bond; it is the approximate percentage change in *portfolio* value for a 1% change in yields. Duration for a portfolio measures the sensitivity of a portfolio's value to an equal change in yield for all the bonds in the portfolio.

A graph of the relationship between maturity and yield is known as a **yield curve**. The yield curve can have any shape: upward sloping, downward sloping, flat, or some combination of these slopes. Changing yield curve shapes lead to **yield curve risk**, the interest rate risk of a portfolio of bonds that is not captured by the duration measure.

In Figure 4 we illustrate two ways that the yield curve might shift when interest rates increase, a parallel shift and a non-parallel shift.

Figure 4: Yield Curve Shifts

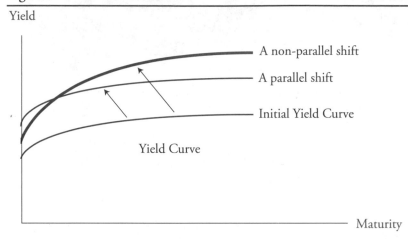

The duration of a bond portfolio can be calculated from the individual bond durations and the proportions of the total portfolio value invested in each of the bonds. That is, the portfolio duration is a market-weighted average of the individual bond's durations. If the yields on all the bonds in the portfolio change by the same absolute percent amount, we term that a **parallel shift**. Portfolio duration is an approximation of the price sensitivity of a portfolio to parallel shifts of the yield curve.

For a non-parallel shift in the yield curve, the yields on different bonds in a portfolio can change by different amounts, and duration alone cannot capture the effect of a "yield change" on the value of the portfolio. This risk of decreases in portfolio value from changes in the shape of the yield curve (i.e., from non-parallel shifts in the yield curve) is termed yield curve risk.

Considering the non-parallel yield curve shift in Figure 4, the yield on short maturity bonds has increased by a small amount, and they will have experienced only a small decrease in value as a consequence. Long maturity bonds have experienced a significant increase in yield and significant decreases in value as a result. Duration can be a poor approximation of the sensitivity of the value of a bond portfolio to non-parallel shifts in the yield curve.

To estimate the impact of non-parallel shifts, bond portfolio managers calculate **key rate durations**, which measure the sensitivity of the portfolio's value to changes in yields for specific maturities (or portions of the yield curve). Key rate duration is described in detail at Level 2.

©2009 Kaplan, Inc.

LOS 61.h: Explain the disadvantages of a callable or prepayable security to an investor.

Compared to an option-free bond, bonds with call provisions and securities with prepayment options offer a much less certain cash flow stream. This uncertainty about the timing of cash flows is one disadvantage of callable and prepayable securities.

A second disadvantage stems from the fact that the call of a bond and increased prepayments of amortizing securities are both more probable when interest rates have decreased. The disadvantage here is that more principal (all of the principal, in the case of a call) is returned when the opportunities for reinvestment of these principal repayments are less attractive. When rates are low, you get more principal back that must be reinvested at the new lower rates. When rates rise and opportunities for reinvestment are better, less principal is likely to be returned early.

A third disadvantage is that the potential price appreciation of callable and prepayable securities from decreases in market yields is less than that of option-free securities of like maturity. For a currently-callable bond, the call price puts an upper limit on the bond's price appreciation. While there is no equivalent price limit on a prepayable security, the effect of the prepayment option operates similarly to a call feature and reduces the appreciation potential of the securities in response to falling market yields.

Overall, the risks of early return of principal and the related uncertainty about the yields at which funds can be reinvested are termed *call risk* and *prepayment risk*, respectively.

LOS 61.i: Identify the factors that affect the reinvestment risk of a security and explain why prepayable amortizing securities expose investors to greater reinvestment risk than nonamortizing securities.

As noted in our earlier discussion of reinvestment risk, cash flows prior to stated maturity from coupon interest payments, bond calls, principal payments on amortizing securities, and prepayments all subject security holders to reinvestment risk. Remember a lower coupon increases duration (interest rate risk) but decreases reinvestment risk compared to an otherwise identical higher coupon issue.

A security has *more* reinvestment risk when:

*   The coupon is higher so that interest cash flows are higher.
*   It has a call feature.
*   It is an amortizing security.
*   It contains a prepayment option.

As noted earlier, when interest rates decline, there is an increased probability of the early return of principal for prepayable securities. The early return of principal increases the amount that must be reinvested at lower prevailing rates. With prepayable securities, the uncertainty about the bondholder's return due to early return of principal and the prevailing reinvestment rates when it is returned (i.e., reinvestment risk) is greater.

LOS 61.j: Describe the various forms of credit risk and describe the meaning and role of credit ratings.

A bond's *rating* is used to indicate its relative probability of default, which is the probability of its issuer not making timely interest and principal payments as promised in the bond indenture. A bond rating of AA is an indication that the expected probability of default over the life of the bond is less than that of an A rated bond, which has a lower expected probability of default than a BBB (triple B) rated bond, and so on through the lower ratings. We can say that lower-rated bonds have more **default risk**, the risk that a bond will fail to make promised/scheduled payments (either interest payments or principal payments). Since investors prefer less risk of default, a lower-rated issue must promise a higher yield to compensate investors for taking on a greater probability of default.

The difference between the yield on a Treasury security, which is assumed to be default risk free, and the yield on a similar maturity bond with a lower rating is termed the **credit spread**.

yield on a risky bond = yield on a default-free bond + credit spread

Credit spread risk refers to the fact that the default risk premium required in the market for a given rating can increase, even while the yield on Treasury securities of similar maturity remains unchanged. An increase in this credit spread increases the required yield and decreases the price of a bond.

Downgrade risk is the risk that a credit rating agency will lower a bond's rating. The resulting increase in the yield required by investors will lead to a decrease in the price of the bond. A rating increase is termed an **upgrade** and will have the opposite effect, decreasing the required yield and increasing the price.

Rating agencies give bonds ratings which are meant to give bond purchasers an indication of the risk of default. While the ratings are primarily based on the financial strength of the company, different bonds of the same company can have slightly different ratings depending on differences in collateral or differences in the priority of the bondholders' claim (e.g., junior or subordinated bonds may get lower ratings than senior bonds). Bond ratings are not absolute measures of default risk, but rather give an indication of the relative probability of default across the range of companies and bonds.

For ratings given by Standard and Poor's Corporation, a bond rated AAA (triple-A) has been judged to have the least risk of failing to make its promised interest and principal payments (defaulting) over its life. Bonds with greater risk of defaulting on promised payments have lower ratings such as AA (double-A), A (single-A), BBB, BB, and so on. U.S. Treasury securities and a small number of corporate bonds receive an AAA rating.

Pluses and minuses are used to indicate differences in default risk within categories, with AA+ a better rating than AA, which is better than AA-. Bonds rated AAA through BBB are considered *investment grade* and bonds rated BB and below are considered speculative and sometimes termed *junk bonds* or, more positively, *high-yield bonds*. Bonds rated CCC, CC, and C are highly speculative and bonds rated D are currently in default.

©2009 Kaplan, Inc.

Moody's Investor Services, Inc., another prominent issuer of bond ratings, classifies bonds similarly but uses Aa1 as S&P uses AA+, Aa2 as AA, Aa3 as AA-, and so on. Bonds with lower ratings carry higher promised yields in the market because investors exposed to more default risk require a higher promised return to compensate them for bearing greater default risk.

LOS 61.k: Explain liquidity risk and why it might be important to investors even if they expect to hold a security to the maturity date.

We described liquidity earlier and noted that investors prefer more liquidity to less. This means that investors will require a higher yield for less liquid securities, other things equal. The difference between the price that dealers are willing to pay for a security (the bid) and the price at which dealers are willing to sell a security (the ask) is called the **bid-ask spread**. The bid-ask spread is an indication of the liquidity of the market for a security. If trading activity in a particular security declines, the bid-ask spread will widen (increase), and the issue is considered to be less liquid.

If investors are planning to sell a security prior to maturity, a decrease in liquidity will increase the bid-ask spread, lead to a lower sale price, and can decrease the returns on the position. Even if an investor plans to hold the security until maturity rather than trade it, poor liquidity can have adverse consequences stemming from the need to periodically assign current values to portfolio securities. This periodic valuation is referred to as **marking to market**. When a security has little liquidity, the variation in dealers' bid prices or the absence of dealer bids altogether makes valuation difficult and may require that a valuation model or pricing service be used to establish current value. If this value is low, institutional investors may be hurt in two situations.

1. Institutional investors may need to mark their holdings to market to determine their portfolio's value for periodic reporting and performance measurement purposes. If the market is illiquid, the prevailing market price may misstate the true value of the security and can reduce returns/performance.

2. Marking to market is also necessary with repurchase agreements to ensure that the collateral value is adequate to support the funds being borrowed. A lower valuation can lead to a higher cost of funds and decreasing portfolio returns.

 Professor's Note: CFA Institute seems to use "low liquidity" and "high liquidity risk" interchangeably. I believe you can treat these (liquidity and liquidity risk) as the same concept on the exam, although you should remember that low liquidity means high liquidity risk.

LOS 61.l: Describe the exchange rate risk an investor faces when a bond makes payments in a foreign currency.

If a U.S. investor purchases a bond that makes payments in a foreign currency, dollar returns on the investment will depend on the exchange rate between the dollar and the foreign currency. A depreciation (decrease in value) of the foreign currency will reduce the returns to a dollar-based investor. **Exchange rate risk** is the risk that the actual cash flows from the investment may be worth less in domestic currency than was expected when the bond was purchased.

LOS 61.m: Explain inflation risk.

Inflation risk refers to the possibility that prices of goods and services in general will increase more than expected. Since fixed-coupon bonds pay a constant periodic stream of interest income, an increasing price level decreases the amount of real goods and services that bond payments will purchase. For this reason, inflation risk is sometimes referred to as purchasing power risk. When expected inflation increases, the resulting increase in nominal rates and required yields will decrease the values of previously issued fixed-income securities.

LOS 61.n: Explain how yield volatility affects the price of a bond with an embedded option and how changes in volatility affect the value of a callable bond and a putable bond.

Without any volatility in interest rates, a call provision and a put provision have little value, if any, assuming no changes in credit quality that affect market values. In general, an increase in the yield/price volatility of a bond increases the values of both put options and call options.

We already saw that the value of a callable bond is less than the value of an otherwise-identical option-free (straight) bond by the value of the call option because the call option is retained by the issuer, not owned by the bondholder. The relation is:

value of a callable bond = value of an option-free bond – value of the call

An increase in yield volatility increases the value of the call option and decreases the market value of a callable bond.

A put option is owned by the bondholder, and the price relation can be described as:

value of a putable bond = value of an option-free bond + value of the put

An increase in yield volatility increases the value of the put option and increases the value of a putable bond.

©2009 Kaplan, Inc.

Therefore, we conclude that increases in interest rate volatility affect the prices of callable bonds and putable bonds in opposite ways. **Volatility risk** for callable bonds is the risk that volatility will increase, and volatility risk for putable bonds is the risk that volatility will decrease.

LOS 61.o: Describe the various forms of event risk.

Event risk occurs when something significant happens to a company (or segment of the market) that has a sudden and substantial impact on its financial condition and on the underlying value of an investment. Event risk, with respect to bonds, can take many forms:

- *Disasters* (e.g., hurricanes, earthquakes, or industrial accidents) impair the ability of a corporation to meet its debt obligations if the disaster reduces cash flow. For example, an insurance company's ability to make debt payments may be affected by property/casualty insurance payments in the event of a disaster.
- *Corporate restructurings* [e.g., spin-offs, leveraged buyouts (LBOs), and mergers] may have an impact on the value of a company's debt obligations by affecting the firm's cash flows and/or the underlying assets that serve as collateral. This may result in bond-rating downgrades and may also affect similar companies in the same industry.
- *Regulatory issues*, such as changes in clean air requirements, may cause companies to incur large cash expenditures to meet new regulations. This may reduce the cash available to bondholders and result in a ratings downgrade. A change in the regulations for some financial institutions prohibiting them from holding certain types of security, such as junk bonds (those rated below BBB), can lead to a volume of sales that decreases prices for the whole sector of the market.

KEY CONCEPTS

LOS 61.a

There are many types of risk associated with fixed income securities:

- *Interest rate risk*—uncertainty about bond prices due to changes in market interest rates.
- *Call risk*—the risk that a bond will be called (redeemed) prior to maturity under the terms of the call provision and that the funds must then be reinvested at the then-current (lower) yield.
- *Prepayment risk*—the uncertainty about the amount of bond principal that will be repaid prior to maturity.
- *Yield curve risk*—the risk that changes in the shape of the yield curve will reduce bond values.
- *Credit risk*—includes the risk of default, the risk of a decrease in bond value due to a ratings downgrade, and the risk that the credit spread for a particular rating will increase.
- *Liquidity risk*—the risk that an immediate sale will result in a price below fair value (the prevailing market price).
- *Exchange rate risk*—the risk that the domestic currency value of bond payments in a foreign currency will decrease due to exchange rate changes.
- *Volatility risk*—the risk that changes in expected interest rate volatility will affect the values of bonds with embedded options.
- *Inflation risk*—the risk that inflation will be higher than expected, eroding the purchasing power of the cash flows from a fixed income security.
- *Event risk*—the risk of decreases in a security's value from disasters, corporate restructurings, or regulatory changes that negatively affect the firm.
- *Sovereign risk*—the risk that governments may repudiate debt, prohibit debt repayment by private borrowers, or impose general restrictions on currency flows.

LOS 61.b

When a bond's coupon rate is less than its market yield, the bond will trade at a discount to its par value.

When a bond's coupon rate is greater than its market yield, the bond will trade at a premium to its par value.

LOS 61.c

The level of a bond's interest rate risk (duration) is:

- Positively related to its maturity.
- Negatively related to its coupon rate.
- Negatively related to its market YTM.
- Less over some ranges for bonds with embedded options.

LOS 61.d

The price of a callable bond equals the price of an identical option-free bond minus the value of the embedded call.

©2009 Kaplan, Inc.

LOS 61.e

Floating-rate bonds have interest rate risk between reset dates and their prices can differ from their par values, even at reset dates, due to changes in liquidity or in credit risk after they have been issued.

LOS 61.f

The duration of a bond is the approximate percentage price change for a 1% change in yield.

The dollar duration of a bond is the approximate dollar price change for a 1% change in yield.

LOS 61.g

Yield curve risk of a bond portfolio is the risk (in addition to interest rate risk) that the portfolio's value may decrease due to a non-parallel shift in the yield curve (change in its shape).

When yield curve shifts are not parallel, the duration of a bond portfolio does not capture the true price effects because yields on the various bonds in the portfolio may change by different amounts.

LOS 61.h

Disadvantages to an investor of a callable or prepayable security:
- Timing of cash flows is uncertain.
- Principal is most likely to be returned early when interest rates available for reinvestment are low.
- Potential price appreciation is less than that of option-free bonds.

LOS 61.i

A security has more reinvestment risk when it has a higher coupon, is callable, is an amortizing security, or has a prepayment option.

A prepayable amortizing security has greater reinvestment risk because of the probability of accelerated principal payments when interest rates, including reinvestment rates, fall.

LOS 61.j

Credit risk includes:
- Default risk—the probability of default.
- Downgrade risk—the probability of a reduction in the bond rating.
- Credit spread risk—uncertainty about the bond's yield spread to Treasuries based on its bond rating.

Credit ratings are designed to indicate to investors a bond's relative probability of default. Bonds with the lowest probability of default receive ratings of AAA. Bonds rated AA, A, and BBB are also considered investment grade bonds. Speculative or high yield bonds are rated BB or lower.

LOS 61.k

Lack of liquidity can have adverse effects on calculated portfolio values and, therefore, on performance measures for a portfolio. This makes liquidity a concern for a manager even though sale of the bonds is not anticipated.

LOS 61.l

An investor who buys a bond with cash flows denominated in a foreign currency will see the value of the bond decrease if the foreign currency depreciates (the exchange value of the foreign currency declines) relative to the investor's home currency.

LOS 61.m

If inflation increases unexpectedly, the purchasing power of a bond's future cash flows is decreased and bond values fall.

LOS 61.n

Increases in yield volatility increase the value of put and call options embedded in bonds, decreasing the value of a callable bond (because the bondholder is short the call) and increasing the value of putable bonds (because the bondholder is long the put).

LOS 61.o

Event risk encompasses non-financial events that can hurt the value of a bond, including disasters that reduce the issuer's earnings or diminish asset values; takeovers or restructurings that can have negative effects on the priority of bondholders' claims; and changes in regulation that can decrease the issuer's earnings or narrow the market for a particular class of bonds.

©2009 Kaplan, Inc.

CONCEPT CHECKERS

1. A bond with a 7.3% yield has a duration of 5.4 and is trading at $985. If the yield decreases to 7.1%, the new bond price is *closest* to:
    A. $974.40.
    B. $995.60.
    C. $1091.40.

2. If interest rate volatility *increases*, which of the following bonds will experience a price *decrease*?
    A. A callable bond.
    B. A putable bond.
    C. A zero-coupon, option-free bond.

3. A noncallable, AA-rated, 5-year zero-coupon bond with a yield of 6% is *least likely* to have:
    A. interest rate risk.
    B. reinvestment risk.
    C. default risk.

4. The current price of a bond is 102.50. If interest rates change by 0.5%, the value of the bond price changes by 2.50. What is the duration of the bond?
    A. 2.44.
    B. 2.50.
    C. 4.88.

5. Which of the following bonds has the *greatest* interest rate risk?
    A. 5% 10-year callable bond.
    B. 5% 10-year putable bond.
    C. 5% 10-year option-free bond.

6. A floating-rate security will have the greatest duration:
    A. the day before the reset date.
    B. the day after the reset date.
    C. never—floating-rate securities have a duration of zero.

7. The duration of a bond is 5.47, and its current price is $986.30. Which of the following is the *best* estimate of the bond price change if interest rates *increase* by 2%?
    A. −$109.40.
    B. −$107.90.
    C. $109.40.

8. A straight 5% bond has two years remaining to maturity and is priced at $981.67. A callable bond that is the same in every respect as the straight bond, except for the call feature, is priced at $917.60. With the yield curve flat at 6%, what is the value of the embedded call option?
    A. $45.80.
    B. $64.07.
    C. $101.00.

9.   A straight 5% coupon bond has two years remaining to maturity and is priced at $981.67 ($1,000 par value). A putable bond, which is the same in every respect as the straight bond except for the put provision, is priced at 101.76 (percent of par value). With the yield curve flat at 6%, what is the value of the embedded put option?
   A. $17.60.
   B. $26.77.
   C. $35.93.

10.   Which of the following is *least likely* to fall under the heading of event risk with respect to fixed-income securities?
   A. A change in rate regulation.
   B. One firm's acquisition by another.
   C. A Federal Reserve decrease in money supply.

11.   Which of the following 5-year bonds has the *highest* interest rate risk?
   A. A floating-rate bond.
   B. A zero-coupon bond.
   C. A 5% fixed-coupon bond.

12.   An investor is concerned about interest rate risk. Which of the following three bonds (similar except for yield and maturity) has the *least* interest rate risk? The bond with:
   A. 5% yield and 10-year maturity.
   B. 5% yield and 20-year maturity.
   C. 6% yield and 10-year maturity.

13.   Which of the following statements about the risks of bond investing is *most accurate*?
   A. A bond rated AAA has no credit risk.
   B. A bond with call protection has volatility risk.
   C. A U.S. Treasury bond has no reinvestment risk.

14.   Which of the following securities will have the *least* reinvestment risk for a long-term investor?
   A. A 10-year, zero-coupon bond.
   B. A 6-month T-bill.
   C. A 30-year, prepayable amortizing bond.

15.   A 2-year, zero-coupon U.S. Treasury note is *least likely* to have:
   A. inflation risk.
   B. currency risk.
   C. volatility risk.

©2009 Kaplan, Inc.

ANSWERS – CONCEPT CHECKERS

1. **B** The percentage price change, based on duration is equal to $-5.4 \times (-0.2\%) = 1.08\%$. The new price is $1.0108 \times 985 = \$995.64$.

2. **A** An increase in volatility will increase the value of the call option and decrease the value of a callable bond. A putable bond will increase in value. The value of option-free bonds will be unaffected.

3. **B** A zero-coupon bond, as a security, has no reinvestment risk because there are no cash flows prior to maturity that must be reinvested. A double-A bond has some (small) default risk. Zero-coupon bonds have the most interest rate risk for a given maturity.

4. **C** The duration is computed as follows:

$$\text{duration} = \frac{\text{percentage change in price}}{\text{change in yield as a decimal}} = \frac{2.50/102.5}{0.005} = \frac{2.44\%}{0.5\%} = 4.88$$

5. **C** Embedded options reduce duration/interest rate risk.

6. **B** The duration of a floating-rate bond is higher the greater the time lag until the next coupon payment/reset date. The greatest duration/interest rate risk is, therefore, immediately after the coupon has been reset.

7. **B** The approximate dollar change in price is computed as follows:

dollar price change = $-5.47 \times 0.02 \times 986.30 = -\$107.90$

8. **B** The option value is the difference between the value of an option-free bond and the corresponding price of the callable bond. Its value is computed as:

call option value = $\$981.67 - \$917.60 = \$64.07$

9. **C** The value of the embedded put option is the difference between the price of the putable bond and the price of the straight bond. So it is computed as:

option value = $\$1,017.60 - \$981.67 = \$35.93$

10. **C** Event risk refers to events that can impact a firm's ability to pay its debt obligations that are separate from market risks. The Fed's actions can impact interest rates, but this is a market risk factor, not event risk.

11. **B** The zero-coupon bond will have the greatest duration of any of the three bonds and, as such, will be subject to the greatest interest rate risk.

12. **C** Interest rate risk is *inversely* related to the yield and directly related to maturity. All else equal, the lower the yield, the greater the interest rate risk. All else equal, the longer the maturity, the greater the interest rate risk. This bond has the higher yield and the shorter maturity, and, thus, has the lowest interest rate risk.

13. **B** A Treasury bond pays semiannual coupon interest and, therefore, has reinvestment risk. A triple-A rated bond can lose its AAA rating, so it has downgrade risk, a component of credit risk. A bond with a call feature has volatility risk even when the call cannot be exercised immediately. The call feature still has value (to the issuer), and its value will be affected by volatility changes.

14. **A** A 10-year, zero-coupon bond has no cash flows prior to maturity to reinvest while the entire amount invested in 6-month bills must be reinvested twice each year.

15. **C** It will have inflation (purchasing power) risk. It will have currency risk to non-U.S. dollar investors. Volatility risk only applies to bonds with embedded options.

©2009 Kaplan, Inc.

The following is a review of the Analysis of Fixed Income Investments principles designed to address the learning outcome statements set forth by CFA Institute®. This topic is also covered in:

OVERVIEW OF BOND SECTORS AND INSTRUMENTS

Study Session 15

EXAM FOCUS

This review introduces the various types of fixed income securities and a fair amount of terminology relating to fixed income securities. Pay special attention to the mechanics of these securities; that is, how they pay, when they pay, and what they pay. The additional information is nice, but likely not crucial. Try to gain enough understanding of the terms listed in the learning outcome statements so that you will understand them when they are used in a question. Much of this material is unlikely to be tested by itself; however, knowing the basics about Treasury securities, mortgage-backed securities, and municipal securities is important as a foundation for much of the material on debt securities that follows, as well as for the more detailed material on fixed income valuation and risk that is contained in the Level 2 and Level 3 curriculum.

LOS 62.a: Describe the features, credit risk characteristics, and distribution methods for government securities.

Bonds issued by a country's central government are referred to as **sovereign bonds** or sovereign debt. The sovereign debt of the U.S. government consists of U.S. Treasury securities, which are considered to be essentially free of default risk. The sovereign debt of other countries is considered to have varying degrees of credit risk. Sovereign debt can be issued in a country's own domestic market, another country's foreign bond market, or in the Eurobond market.

Sovereign debt is typically issued in the currency of the issuing country, but can be issued in other currencies as well. Bond rating agencies, such as Standard and Poor's, rate sovereign debt based on its perceived credit risk, often giving different ratings to sovereign debt denominated in the home currency (local currency) and to the sovereign debt of the same country denominated in foreign currency.

Professor's Note: Remember that it is often easier for a country to print currency (expand the money supply) in order to meet obligations denominated in the home currency than it is to exchange the local currency for a fixed amount of foreign currency. Thus, local currency sovereign debt often receives a higher rating than the foreign currency denominated debt of the same country.

There are four primary methods used by central governments to issue sovereign debt.

1. **Regular cycle auction—single price**. Under this method the debt is auctioned periodically according to a cycle and the highest price (lowest yield) at which the entire issue to be auctioned can be sold is awarded to all bidders. This is the system used by the U.S. Treasury.

2. **Regular cycle auction—multiple price**. Under this method, winning bidders receive the bonds at the price(s) that they bid.

3. An **ad hoc auction system** refers to a method where the central government auctions new securities when it determines market conditions are advantageous.

4. A **tap system** refers to the issuance and auction of bonds identical to previously issued bonds. Under this system, bonds are sold periodically, not according to a regular cycle.

LOS 62.b: Describe the types of securities issued by the U.S. Department of the Treasury (e.g. bills, notes, bonds, and inflation protection securities), and differentiate between on-the-run and off-the-run Treasury securities.

Treasury securities (Treasuries) are issued by the U.S. Treasury. Because they are backed by the full faith and credit of the U.S. government, they are considered to be free from credit risk (though they're still subject to interest rate/price risk). The Treasury issues three distinct types of securities: (1) bills, (2) notes and bonds, and (3) inflation-protected securities.

Treasury bills (T-bills) have maturities of less than one year and do not make explicit interest payments, paying only the face (par) value at the maturity date. T-bills are sold at a discount to par value and interest is received when the par value is paid at maturity (like zero-coupon bonds). The interest on T-bills is sometimes called *implicit interest* since the interest (difference between the purchase price and the par value) is not made in a separate "explicit" payment, as it is on bonds and notes. Securities of this type are known as *pure discount* securities.

• There are *three maturity cycles*: 28, 91, and 182 days, adjustable by one day (up or down) due to holidays. They are also known as 4-week, 3-month, and 6-month T-bills, respectively.
• Periodically, the Treasury also issues *cash management* bills with maturities ranging from a few days to six months to help overcome temporary cash shortages prior to the quarterly receipt of tax payments.

Treasury notes and **Treasury bonds** pay semiannual coupon interest at a rate that is fixed at issuance. Notes have original maturities of 2, 3, 5, and 10 years. Bonds have original maturities of 20 or 30 years.

Prior to 1984, some Treasury bonds were issued that are callable at par five years prior to maturity. The Treasury has not issued callable bonds since 1984.

©2009 Kaplan, Inc.

Treasury bond and note prices in the secondary market are quoted in percent and 32nds of 1% of face value. A quote of 102-5 (sometimes 102:5) is 102% plus $\frac{5}{32}$% of par, which for a $100,000 face value T-bond, translates to a price of:

$$\left[102 + \frac{5}{32}\right]\% \times \$100,000 = 1.0215625 \times \$100,000 = \$102,156.25$$

Since 1997, the U.S. Treasury has issued **Treasury Inflation-Protected Securities** (TIPS). Currently, inflation-protected 5- and 10-year notes and 20-year bonds are offered by the Treasury. The details of how TIPS work are:

- TIPS make semiannual coupon interest payments at a rate fixed at issuance, just like notes and bonds.
- The par value of TIPS begins at $1,000 and is adjusted semiannually for changes in the Consumer Price Index (CPI). If there is deflation (falling price levels), the adjusted par value is reduced for that period. The fixed coupon rate is paid semiannually as a percentage of the *inflation adjusted par value.*
- Any increase in the par value from the inflation adjustment is taxed as income in the year of the adjustment:

$$\text{TIPS coupon payment} = \text{inflation-adjusted par value} \times \frac{\text{stated coupon rate}}{2}$$

For example, consider a $100,000 par value TIPS with a 3% coupon rate, set at issuance. Six months later the *annual* rate of inflation (CPI) is 4%. The par value will be increased by one-half of the 4% (i.e., 2%) and will be 1.02 × 100,000 = $102,000.

The first *semiannual* coupon will be one-half of the 3% coupon rate times the inflation adjusted par value: 1.5% × 102,000 = $1,530. Any percentage change in the CPI over the next 6-month period will be used to adjust the par value from $102,000 to a new inflation-adjusted value, which will be multiplied by 1.5% to compute the next coupon payment.

If the adjusted par value (per bond) is greater than $1,000 at maturity, the holder receives the adjusted par value as the maturity payment. If the adjusted par value is less than $1,000 (due to deflation), holders receive $1,000 at maturity as this is the minimum repayment amount.

On-the-Run and Off-the-Run Treasury Securities

Treasury issues are divided into two categories based on their vintage:

1. **On-the-run issues** are the most recently auctioned Treasury issues.

2. **Off-the-run issues** are older issues that have been replaced (as the most traded issue) by a more recently auctioned issue. Issues replaced by several more recent issues are known as *well off-the-run* issues.

The distinction is that the on-the-run issues are more actively traded and therefore more liquid than off-the-run issues. Market prices of on-the-run issues provide better information about current market yields.

LOS 62.c: Describe how stripped Treasury securities are created and distinguish between coupon strips and principal strips.

Since *the U.S. Treasury does not issue zero-coupon notes and bonds*, investment bankers began stripping the coupons from Treasuries to create zero-coupon securities of various maturities to meet investor demand. These securities are termed **stripped Treasuries or Treasury strips.** In 1985, the Treasury introduced the Separate Trading of Registered Interest and Principal Securities (STRIPS) program. Under this program, the Treasury issues coupon-bearing notes and bonds as it normally does, but then it allows certain government securities dealers to buy large amounts of these issues, strip the coupons from the principal, repackage the cash flows, and sell them separately as zero-coupon bonds, at discounts to par value.

For example, a 10-year T-note has 20 coupons and one principal payment; these 21 cash flows can be repackaged and sold as 21 different zero-coupon securities. The stripped securities (Treasury strips) are divided into two groups:

1. **Coupon strips** (denoted as ci) refers to strips created from coupon payments stripped from the original security.

2. **Principal strips** refers to bond and note principal payments with the coupons stripped off. Those derived from stripped bonds are denoted bp and those from stripped notes np.

 Professor's Note: While the payments on coupon strips and principal strips with the same maturity date are identical, certain countries treat them differently for tax purposes, and they often trade at slightly different prices.

STRIPS are taxed by the IRS on their implicit interest (movement toward par value), which, for fully taxable investors, results in negative cash flows in years prior to maturity. The Treasury STRIPS program also created a procedure for *reconstituting* Treasury notes and bonds from the individual pieces.

LOS 62.d: Describe the types and characteristics of securities issued by U.S. federal agencies.

Agency bonds are debt securities issued by various agencies and organizations of the U.S. government, such as the Federal Home Loan Bank (FHLB). Most agency issues are *not* obligations of the U.S. Treasury and technically should not be considered the same as Treasury securities.

Even so, they are very high quality securities that have almost no risk of default.

©2009 Kaplan, Inc.

There are two types of federal agencies:

1. *Federally related institutions,* such as the Government National Mortgage Association (Ginnie Mae) and the Tennessee Valley Authority (TVA), which are owned by the U.S. government and are exempt from Securities and Exchange Commission (SEC) registration. In general, these securities are backed by the full faith and credit of the U.S. government, except in the case of the TVA and Private Export Funding Corporation. Essentially, these securities are free from credit risk.

2. *Government sponsored enterprises* (GSEs) include the Federal Farm Credit System, the Federal Home Loan Bank System, the Federal National Mortgage Association (Fannie Mae), the Federal Home Loan Bank Corporation (Freddie Mac), and the Student Loan Marketing Association (Sallie Mae). These are privately owned, but publicly chartered organizations, and were created by the U.S. Congress. They issue their securities directly in the marketplace and expose investors to some (albeit very little) credit risk.

Debentures are securities that are not backed by collateral (i.e., they are unsecured). GSEs commonly issue debentures. These are of many maturity structures and can be coupon interest paying securities or discount securities (referred to as bills).

LOS 62.e: Describe the types and characteristics of mortgage-backed securities and explain the cash flow, prepayments, and prepayment risk for each type.

Mortgage-backed securities (MBSs) are backed (secured) by pools of mortgage loans, which not only provide *collateral* but also the *cash flows* to service the debt. A mortgage-backed security is any security where the collateral for the issued security is a pool of mortgages.

The cash flows from a mortgage are different from the cash flows of a coupon bond. Mortgage loans are amortizing loans in that they make a series of equal payments consisting of the periodic interest on the outstanding principal and a partial repayment of the principal amount. Residential real estate mortgages are typically for 30 years and consist of 360 equal monthly payments. In the early years, the greater portion of the payment is interest, and the final payment, after 30 years, is almost all principal.

 Professor's Note: Amortizing loans and amortization schedules are covered in the Study Session on Quantitative Methods.

The Government National Mortgage Association (GNMA), the Federal National Mortgage Association (FNMA), and the Federal Home Loan Mortgage Corporation (FHLMC) all issue mortgage-backed securities. All three are sponsored by the U.S. government and they are known now by the names Ginnie Mae, Fannie Mae, and Freddie Mac. Each purchases mortgages from lenders to provide funds for mortgage loans. The agencies issue three types of mortgage-backed securities: mortgage passthrough securities, collateralized mortgage obligations, and stripped mortgage-backed securities. This process of combining many similar debt obligations as the collateral for issuing securities is called *securitization*. The primary reason for mortgage securitization is to increase the debt's attractiveness to investors and to decrease investor required rates of return, increasing the availability of funds for home mortgages.

There are three types of cash flows from a mortgage: (1) periodic interest, (2) scheduled repayments of principal, and (3) principal repayments in excess of scheduled principal payments. Borrowers (issuers of mortgages) typically have the right to pay additional principal amounts without penalty, reducing the outstanding principal amount and thereby reducing future interest cash flows. If the borrower sells the property backing the mortgage, the entire principal amount is repaid at one time. Because the borrower can accelerate principal repayment, the owner of a mortgage has *prepayment risk*. Prepayment risk is similar to call risk except that prepayments may be part of or all of the outstanding principal amount. This, in turn, subjects the mortgage holder to reinvestment risk, as principal may be repaid when yields for reinvestment are low.

Ginnie Mae, Fannie Mae, and Freddie Mac all guarantee the timely payment of scheduled interest and principal payments from their mortgage-backed securities. They are able to do this because they only purchase or underwrite loans that conform to certain standards regarding borrower credit ratings, loan size, and the ratio of each loan to the value of the property securing it.

A **mortgage passthrough security** passes the payments made on a pool of mortgages through proportionally to each security holder. A holder of a mortgage passthrough security that owns a 1% portion of the issue will receive a 1% share of all the monthly cash flows from all the mortgages, after a small percentage fee for administration is deducted. Each monthly payment consists of interest, scheduled principal payments, and prepayments of principal in excess of the scheduled amount. Since each holder receives a percentage of all cash flows, a mortgage passthrough security has prepayment risk as a single mortgage would, but there is some diversification benefit from the pooling of hundreds or thousands of mortgages. Since prepayments tend to accelerate when interest rates fall, due to the refinancing and early payoff of existing mortgage loans, security holders can expect to receive greater principal payments when mortgage rates have decreased since the mortgages in the pool were issued.

Collateralized mortgage obligations (CMOs) are created from mortgage passthrough certificates and referred to as derivative mortgage-backed securities, since they are derived from a simpler MBS structure. CMOs have a more complex structure than mortgage passthroughs. A CMO issue has different "tranches," each of which has a different type of claim to the cash flows from the pool of mortgages (i.e., their claims are not just a proportional claim on the total cash flows from the pool).

 Professor's Note: Tranche is from the French word for "slice." In finance, when a security issue consists of different classes of securities with differing claims and especially with differing risks, the different classes of securities are called tranches. You will likely run into this term only in reference to the different classes of securities that make up a CMO.

An example of a simple *sequential* CMO structure with three tranches will help to illustrate a CMO structure. Assume that three tranches are created out of a passthrough security. Let's call them Tranches I, II, and III. They receive interest on the basis of their outstanding par values. The following are the details of the payments to each of the three tranches.

1. Tranche I (the *short*-term segment of the issue) receives net interest on outstanding principal and all of the principal payments from the mortgage pool until it is completely paid off.

2. Tranche II (the *intermediate*-term) receives its share of net interest and starts receiving all of the principal payments after Tranche I has been completely paid off. Prior to that, it only receives interest payments.

3. Tranche III (the *long*-term) receives monthly net interest and starts receiving all principal repayments after Tranches I and II have been completely paid off. Prior to that it only receives interest payments.

Tranche I has the shortest expected maturity and may appeal to an investor with a preference for securities with a shorter time horizon, who previously could not participate in the mortgage-backed securities market. Other structures, with prepayments primarily affecting only some of the tranches, are used to redistribute prepayment risk. The tranches with less prepayment risk will become more attractive to some investors. Investors better able to bear prepayment risk will find the tranches with higher prepayment risk attractive.

Stripped mortgage-backed securities are either the principal or interest portions of a mortgage passthrough security. Prepayments affect the values of interest-only (IO) strips and principal-only (PO) strips differently. The holder of a principal-only strip will gain from prepayments because the face value of the security is received sooner rather than later. The holder of an interest-only strip will receive less total payments when prepayment rates are higher since interest is only paid on the outstanding principal amount, which is decreased by prepayments.

LOS 62.f: State the motivation for creating a collateralized mortgage obligation.

The **motivation for creating CMOs** is to *redistribute the prepayment risk* inherent in mortgage passthrough securities and/or *create securities with various maturity ranges*. The CMO structure takes the cash flows from the mortgage pool and, in a simple structure, allocates any principal payments (both scheduled payments and prepayments) sequentially over time to holders of different CMO tranches, rather than equally to all security holders. Creating a CMO does not alter the *overall* risk of prepayment, it redistributes prepayment risk.

As a general rule, CMOs are created to satisfy a broader range of investor risk/return preferences—making investing in mortgage-backed securities more appealing to a wider audience and decreasing overall borrowing costs.

LOS 62.g: Describe the types of securities issued by municipalities in the United States and distinguish between tax-backed debt and revenue bonds.

Debt securities issued by state and local governments in the United States are known as *municipal bonds* (or "munis" for short). *Municipal bonds* are issued by states, counties, cities, and other political subdivisions (such as school, water, or sewer districts). These bonds are often issued as *serial bonds*, that is, a larger issue is divided into a series of smaller issues, each with its own maturity date and coupon rate.

Municipal bonds are often referred to as *tax-exempt* or *tax-free* bonds, since the coupon interest is exempt from federal income taxes. Note that, while interest income may be tax free, realized capital gains are not. They are subject to normal capital gains taxes at the federal level. However, not all municipal bonds are tax exempt; some are taxable:

- *Tax exempt.* Different states tax municipal securities differently; the vast majority of states treat *their own bonds* (i.e., those issued within the state) as tax exempt, but consider the interest income earned on out-of-state bonds as fully taxable. Thus, the interest income earned on most in-state bonds held by a resident of that state is free from *both* state and federal income tax. Such bonds are referred to as *double tax free.*
- *Taxable.* A municipal bond must meet certain federal standards in order to qualify for the tax-exempt status. If they don't, the bonds are considered "taxable" and the *interest income on these bonds is subject to federal income tax* (they could still be exempt from state taxes). *Taxable municipal bonds are the exception* rather than the rule, as most municipal issues are exempt from federal taxes.

An opinion as to the tax-exempt status of the bonds, typically by a well-respected law firm specializing in municipal bond issues, is provided to purchasers when the bonds are issued.

Tax-Backed Debt and Revenue Bonds

Tax-backed bonds, also called general obligation (GO) bonds, are backed by the full faith, credit, and *taxing power* of the issuer. Tax-backed debt is issued by school districts, towns, cities, counties, states, and special districts, and include the following types:

- *Limited tax GO debt* is subject to a statutory limit on taxes that may be raised to pay off the obligation.
- *Unlimited tax GO debt*, the most common type of GO bond, is secured by the full faith and credit of the borrower and backed by its unlimited taxing authority, which includes the ability to impose individual income tax, sales tax, property tax, and corporate tax. This is the more secure form of GO.
- *Double-barreled* bonds, a special class of GOs, are backed not only by the issuing authority's taxing power, but also by additional resources that could include fees, grants, and special charges that fall outside the general fund.
- *Appropriation-backed obligations* are also known as *moral obligation bonds*. States sometimes act as a back up source of funds for issuers during times of shortfall. However, the state's obligation is not legally binding, but is a "moral obligation." The state may appropriate funds from its general fund. This *moral pledge* enhances the security of such bonds.

©2009 Kaplan, Inc.

- Debt supported by *public credit enhancement* programs possess a guarantee by the state or federal government, which is a legally enforceable contract and is used normally to assist the state's school system.

Revenue bonds are supported only through revenues generated by projects that are funded with the help of the original bond issue. For example, revenue bonds can be issued to fund transportation systems, housing projects, higher education, health care, sports arenas, harbors, and ports. These bonds fall outside GO debt limits and do not require voter approval.

The distinction between a general obligation and a revenue bond is important for a bondholder, because the issuer of a revenue bond is obligated to pay principal and interest *only if a sufficient level of revenue is generated* by the project. If the funds aren't there, the issuer does not make payments on the bond. In contrast, general obligation bonds are required to be serviced in a timely fashion irrespective of the level of tax income generated by the municipality. At issuance, revenue bonds typically involve more risk than general obligation bonds and, therefore, provide higher yields.

Insured Bonds and Prefunded Bonds

Insured bonds carry the guarantee of a third party that all principal and interest payments will be made in a timely manner. The third-party guarantee (insurance) typically cannot be canceled; it is good for the life of the bond. There are several firms that specialize in providing insurance for municipal bond issues. Municipal bond insurance results in higher ratings, usually AAA, which reduces the required yield and improves the liquidity of the bonds. Insured bonds are especially common in the revenue bond market but the general obligation bonds of smaller municipal issuers are often insured to broaden their appeal to investors.

Prefunded bonds are bonds for which Treasury securities have been purchased and placed in a special escrow account in an amount sufficient to make all the remaining required bond payments. The Treasury securities' income and principal payments must be sufficient to fund the municipal bond's required payments until maturity or through the first call date. Bonds that are prefunded have little or no credit risk and are likely to receive a rating of AAA.

LOS 62.h: Describe the characteristics and motivation for the various types of debt issued by corporations (including corporate bonds, medium-term notes, structured notes, commercial paper, negotiable CDs, and bankers acceptances).

Rating Agencies and Credit Ratings

Rating agencies, such as Moody's and S&P, rate specific debt issues of corporations. Some of the factors they consider are quantitative, but many are qualitative. Even quantitative factors can be somewhat subjective. The ratings are issued to indicate the relative probability that all promised payments on the debt will be made over the life of the security and, therefore, must be forward looking. Ratings on long-term bonds will consider factors that may come into play over at least one full economic cycle.

Some of the *firm-specific* factors considered are:

- Past repayment history.
- Quality of management, ability to adapt to changing conditions.
- The industry outlook and firm strategy.
- Overall debt level of the firm.
- Operating cash flow, ability to service debt.
- Other sources of liquidity (cash, salable assets).
- Competitive position, regulatory environment, and union contracts/history.
- Financial management and controls.
- Susceptibility to event risk and political risk.

Some factors *specific to a particular debt issue* are:

- Priority of the claim being rated.
- Value/quality of any collateral pledged to secure the debt.
- The covenants of the debt issue.
- Any guarantees or obligations for parent company support.

 Professor's Note: It may help to remember the primary factors as all Cs: Character of the issuer, Capacity to repay, the Collateral provided, and the Covenants of the debt issue.

Secured Debt, Unsecured Debt, and Credit Enhancements for Corporate Bonds

Secured debt is backed by the pledge of assets/collateral, which can take the following forms:

- *Personal property* (e.g., machinery, vehicles, patents).
- *Real property* (e.g., land and buildings).
- *Financial assets* (e.g., stocks, bonds, notes). These assets are marked to market from time to time to monitor their liquidation values. Covenants may require a pledge of more assets if values are insufficient. Bonds backed by financial assets are called *collateral trust bonds*.

In all of these cases, the bondholder holds a lien on the pledged property. In the case of default, the lien holder can sell the property and use the proceeds to satisfy the obligations of the borrower. In most cases of default, some mutual agreement will be reached for a new structure, but the bondholders' claim on the pledged assets significantly strengthens their position in renegotiation.

Unsecured debt is not backed by any pledge of specific collateral. Unsecured bonds are referred to as *debentures*. They represent a general claim on any assets of the issuer that have not been pledged to secure other debt. If pledged assets generate funds upon liquidation in excess of the obligation, then these excess funds are available for satisfying the claims of unsecured debt holders. *Subordinated debentures* have claims that are satisfied after (subordinate to) the claims of *senior debt*.

Credit enhancements are the guarantees of others that the corporate debt obligation will be paid in a timely manner. Typically, they take one of the following forms:

- *Third-party* guarantees that the debt obligations will be met. Often, parent companies guarantee the loans of their affiliates and subsidiaries.

©2009 Kaplan, Inc.

- *Letters of credit* are issued by banks and guarantee that the bank will advance the funds to service the corporation's debt.
- *Bond insurance* can be obtained from firms that specialize in providing it.

When analyzing credit-enhanced debt, analysts should focus on the financial strength of both the corporation issuing the debt and the financial strength of the party providing credit enhancement. The protection to the bond holder is no better than the promise of the entity offering the credit enhancement. A decrease in the creditworthiness of the guarantor (enhancer) can lead to a rating downgrade of the debt issue.

Medium-Term Notes

 Professor's Note: Be careful here. Medium-term notes are not necessarily medium-term or notes!

Corporate bond issues typically (1) are sold all at once, (2) are sold on a firm-commitment basis whereby an underwriting syndicate guarantees the sale of the whole issue, and (3) consist of bonds with a single coupon rate and maturity.

Medium-term notes (MTNs) differ from a regular corporate bond offering in all of these characteristics.

MTNs are registered under SEC Rule 415 (*shelf registration*) which means that they need not be sold all at once. Once registered, such securities can be "placed on the shelf" and sold in the market over time at the discretion of the issuer. MTNs are sold over time, with each sale satisfying some minimum dollar amount set by the issuer, typically $1 million and up.

MTNs are issued in various maturities, ranging from 9 months to periods as long as 100 years. Issuers provide *maturity ranges* (e.g., 18 months to 2 years) for MTNs that they wish to sell and provide yield quotes for those ranges, typically as a spread to comparable maturity Treasury issues. Investors interested in purchasing the notes make an offer to the issuer's agent, specifying the face value and an exact maturity within one of the ranges offered. The agent then confirms the issuer's willingness to sell those MTNs and effects the transaction.

The offering is done by the issuer's agent on a *best-efforts* basis. There is no firm commitment on the agent's part to sell a specific amount of bonds.

MTNs can have fixed or floating-rate coupons, can be denominated in any currency, and can have special features, such as calls, caps, floors, and non-interest rate indexed coupons. The notes issued can be combined with derivative instruments to create the special features that an investor requires. The combination of the derivative and notes is called a *structured security*.

Structured Notes

A **structured note** is a debt security created when the issuer combines a typical bond or note with a derivative. This is done to create a security that has special appeal to some institutional investors. The targeted institutional investors face restrictions on the types of securities they can purchase. Structured securities allow them to avoid these restrictions. As with any innovative debt security, the motivation to issue them is to lower overall borrowing costs.

As an example, consider an institutional investor that is prohibited from owning equity or derivative securities. An issuer could create a structured note where the periodic coupon payments were based on the performance of an equity security or an equity index. This structured note would still be a debt security, but would produce returns closer to holding the equity index itself. The mechanics of creating this security would be to issue a debt security and combine it with an *equity swap*. An equity swap is a derivative that requires the payment of a fixed rate of interest (the coupon rate on the bond here), and pays its owner the rate of return on the equity or equity index each period. By combining the bond with the equity swap, a structured note is created that pays the percentage rate of return on the equity semiannually instead of paying a fixed coupon payment.

Types of structured medium-term notes include:

- *Step-up notes*—Coupon rate increases over time on a preset schedule.
- *Inverse floaters*—Coupon rate increases when the reference rate decreases and decreases when the reference rate increases.
- *Deleveraged floaters*—Coupon rate equals a fraction of the reference rate plus a constant margin.
- *Dual-indexed floaters*—Coupon rate is based on the difference between two reference rates.
- *Range notes*—Coupon rate equals the reference rate if the reference rate falls within a specified range, or zero if the reference rate falls outside that range.
- *Index amortizing notes*—Coupon rate is fixed but some principal is repaid before maturity, with the amount of principal prepaid based on the level of the reference rate.

We will cover equity swaps, interest rate swaps, and other derivatives commonly used to create structured notes in a subsequent study session. For our purposes here, it is sufficient that you understand that structured notes are created by combining regular debt with derivative securities to make a "debt security" that allows certain institutional investors to get around restrictions they face and thereby reduce the borrowing costs of the company creating the structured note.

Commercial Paper: Directly-Placed and Dealer-Placed Paper

Commercial paper is a short-term, unsecured debt instrument used by corporations to borrow money at rates lower than bank rates. Commercial paper is issued with maturities of 270 days or less, since debt securities with maturities of 270 days or less are exempt from SEC registration. It is issued with maturities as short as two days, with most issues being in the 2-day to 90-day range.

©2009 Kaplan, Inc.

Like T-bills, commercial paper is typically issued as a pure discount security and makes a single payment equal to the face value at maturity. There is no active secondary market in commercial paper and most buyers hold commercial paper until maturity.

Commercial paper is generally issued by corporations with relatively strong credit and the proceeds are often used to finance credit given to the firm's customers or to finance inventories. Finance subsidiaries of manufacturing firms issue commercial paper to fund customers' purchases of the parent company's products. Issuers often keep unused bank lines of credit in place to use in case new paper cannot be issued to generate the funds needed to pay off maturing paper.

Directly-placed paper is commercial paper that is sold to large investors without going through an agent or broker-dealer. Large issuers will deal with a select group of regular commercial paper buyers who customarily buy very large amounts.

Dealer-placed paper is sold to purchasers through a commercial-paper dealer. Most large investment firms have commercial paper desks to serve their customers' needs for short-term cash-management products.

Negotiable CDs and Bankers Acceptances

Certificates of deposit (CDs) are issued by banks and sold to their customers. They represent a promise by the bank to repay a certain amount plus interest and, in that way, are similar to other bank deposits. In contrast to regular bank deposits, CDs are issued in specific denominations and for specified periods of time that can be of any length. In the United States, CDs are insured by the Federal Deposit Insurance Corporation (FDIC) for up to $100,000 in the event the issuing bank becomes insolvent. Amounts above $100,000 are not insured and are, therefore, only as secure as the bank that issues the CD.

Typical bank CDs in the United States carry a penalty to the CD owner if the funds are withdrawn earlier than the maturity date of the CD. **Negotiable CDs**, however, permit the owner to sell the CD in the secondary market at any time. Negotiable CDs issued in the United States by U.S. banks are termed domestic CDs, whereas U.S. dollar denominated CDs issued by foreign banks and branches of U.S. banks outside the United States are termed Eurodollar CDs. Negotiable CDs have maturities ranging from days up to five years. The interest rate paid on them is called the London Interbank Offering Rate because they are primarily issued by banks' London branches.

Bankers acceptances are essentially guarantees by a bank that a loan will be repaid. They are created as part of commercial transactions, especially international trade. As an example, consider an importer who agrees to pay for goods shipped to him by an exporter, 45 days after the goods are shipped. The importer goes to his bank and gets a letter of credit stating that the bank will guarantee the payment, say $1 million. This letter must be sent to the bank of the exporter before the exporter will actually ship the goods. When the exporter delivers the shipping documents to her bank, she will receive the present value of the $1 million, discounted because the payment will not be made for 45 days.

The final step in the creation of a bankers acceptance is that the exporter's bank presents the evidence of shipment to the issuing bank (the importer's bank) which then "accepts" the evidence of shipment. It is this accepted promise to pay $1 million in 45 days that is the bankers acceptance. The importer will sign documents evidencing his obligation to his bank and becomes the borrower of the funds. When this final step is completed, the importer receives the documents necessary to receive the shipment of goods.

The exporter's bank can either continue to hold the acceptance or sell it to an investor, often a money market fund interested in short-term paper. The acceptance is a discount instrument and sells for the present value of the single $1 million payment to be made 45 days from the shipping date. The secondary market for bankers acceptances is limited so their liquidity is limited and most purchasers intend to hold them until their maturity dates.

The credit risk of a bankers acceptance is the risk that the importer (the initial borrower of the funds) and the accepting bank will both fail to make the promised payment.

LOS 62.i: Define an asset-backed security, describe the role of a special purpose vehicle in an asset-backed security's transaction, state the motivation for a corporation to issue an asset-backed security, and describe the types of external credit enhancements for asset-backed securities.

Credit card debt, auto loans, bank loans, and corporate receivables are often securitized in the same way as mortgages are in the MBS structure. These financial assets are the underlying collateral for bonds which are also **asset-backed securities** (ABSs). While the above types of underlying assets are the most common, innovative ABSs have also been created. In one case, singer David Bowie sold a $55 million dollar ABS issue where the underlying assets were the royalties from 25 of his albums released prior to 1990.

Role of a Special Purpose Vehicle

A **special purpose vehicle** or *special purpose corporation* is a separate legal entity to which a corporation transfers the financial assets for an ABS issue. The importance of this is that a legal transfer of the assets is made to the special purpose vehicle. This shields the assets from the claims of the corporation's general creditors, making it possible for the ABS issue to receive a higher credit rating than the corporation as a whole. Because the assets are sold to the special purpose vehicle, they are highly unlikely to be subject to any claims arising from the bankruptcy of the corporation, and the special purpose vehicle is termed a *bankruptcy remote* entity.

The **motivation for a corporation to issue asset-backed securities** is to reduce borrowing costs. By transferring the assets into a separate entity, the entity can issue the bonds and receive a higher rating than the unsecured debt of the corporation. The higher rating reduces the required yield on the (ABS) debt.

©2009 Kaplan, Inc.

External Credit Enhancements

Since asset-backed securities, on their own, may not receive the highest possible credit rating, the issuer may choose to enhance the credit rating by providing additional guarantees or security. Credit quality can be enhanced either externally or internally. **External credit enhancement** commonly takes the following forms:

- *Corporate guarantees*, which may be provided by the corporation creating the ABS or its parent.
- *Letters of credit*, which may be obtained from a bank for a fee.
- *Bond insurance*, which may be obtained from an insurance company or a provider specializing in underwriting such structures. This is also referred to as an *insurance wrap*.

None of these enhancements come without cost. The decision of how much enhancement to provide involves a tradeoff between the cost of enhancement and the resulting decrease in the market yield required on the bonds.

Note that the quality of a credit-enhanced security is only as good as the quality of the guarantor, and the credit rating of the security can reflect any deterioration in the guarantor's rating.

LOS 62.j: Describe collateralized debt obligations.

A **collateralized debt obligation** (CDO) is a debt instrument where the collateral for the promise to pay is an underlying pool of other debt obligations and even other CDOs. These underlying debt obligations can be business loans, mortgages, debt of developing countries, corporate bonds of various ratings, asset-backed securities, or even problem/non-performing loans. Tranches of the CDO are created based on the seniority of the claims to the cash flows of the underlying assets, and these are given separate credit ratings depending on the seniority of the claim, as well as the creditworthiness of the underlying pool of debt securities.

CDOs may be created by a sponsor that seeks to profit on the spread between the rate to be earned on the underlying assets and the rate promised to the CDO holder (an arbitrage CDO), or created by a bank or insurance company seeking to reduce its loan exposure on its balance sheet (a balance sheet CDO).

LOS 62.k: Describe the mechanisms available for placing bonds in the primary market and differentiate the primary and secondary markets in bonds.

The **primary market** for debt (newly created debt securities) functions in a manner similar to the primary market for equities. Typically, an investment banker is involved in advising the debt issuer and in distributing (selling) the debt securities to investors. When the investment banker actually purchases the entire issue and resells it, they are said to have "underwritten" the issue. This arrangement is termed a *firm commitment* while the deal is termed a *bought deal*. In an underwritten offering of debt securities, the underwriter will typically put together a syndicate of other investment bankers to aid in distributing the securities. The underwriters can reduce their risk by preselling as much of the offering as possible to their institutional clients and hedging the interest rate risk exposure of the issue for the period they anticipate owning the securities. An alternative is for the investment banker to agree to sell all of the issue that they can and this is termed doing the offering on a *best efforts* basis.

In the above described process, since the price paid for the issue and the anticipated sale price is determined between the (lead) investment bank and the issuing company, the offering is termed a *negotiated offering*. Another approach is an *auction process* where an issuer of debt securities determines the size and terms of the issue and several investment banks, or underwriting syndicates of multiple investment banks, bid on what interest rate they require to sell it. The syndicate with the lowest interest rate bid will be awarded the deal.

In the United States, securities to be offered to public investors must be registered with the SEC. When a new issue of debt securities is not registered for sale to the public, it still may be sold to a small number of investors. This is called a *private placement* or Rule 144A offering (after the rule that allows such transactions). Avoidance of the registration process is valuable to the issuer and, since a private placement involves a sale to a small number of investors/institutions, the issue can be tailored to the needs and preferences of the buyers. Since the issue cannot be sold to the public unless it is subsequently registered, the buyers will require a slightly higher interest rate to compensate them for the lack of liquidity of securities that are sold though a private placement.

The **secondary market** for debt securities includes exchanges, an over-the-counter dealer market, and electronic trading networks. Traditionally, most secondary trading in debt securities was transacted in a dealer market, with broker/dealers buying and selling bonds for and from their inventories (i.e., acting as market makers). More recently, the costs and risks of supplying the capital necessary to adequately fund bond trading operations have increased and spreads have decreased. Because of this, electronic trading has become a more important part of the secondary market for debt securities. These electronic networks can be bids and offers by a single dealer, bids and offers by multiple dealers, or simply anonymous customer bids and offers posted on an electronic trading system with a trade clearing system.

©2009 Kaplan, Inc.

KEY CONCEPTS

LOS 62.a

Sovereign debt refers to the debt obligations of governments. U.S. Treasury securities are sovereign debt of the U.S. government and are considered free of credit risk. Sovereign debt of other countries has varying degrees of credit risk.

Sovereign debt is typically issued using one of four methods:
- Regular auction cycle with the entire issue sold at a single price.
- Regular auction cycle with bonds issued at multiple prices.
- Ad hoc auction system with no regular cycle.
- Tap system, auctioning new bonds identical to previously issued bonds.

LOS 62.b

Securities issued by the U.S. Treasury include:
- Bills—pure-discount securities maturing in four weeks, three months, or six months.
- Notes—coupon securities maturing in two, five, and ten years.
- Bonds—coupon securities maturing in 20 or 30 years.

Treasury Inflation Protected Securities (TIPS) are U.S. Treasury issues in which the coupon rate is fixed but the par value is adjusted periodically for inflation, based on changes in the CPI.

U.S. Treasuries from the most recent auction are referred to as on-the-run issues, while Treasuries from previous auctions are referred to as off-the-run issues.

LOS 62.c

Stripped Treasury securities are created by bond dealers who buy Treasury securities, separate each of their scheduled coupon and principal payments, and resell these as zero-coupon securities.

Treasury strips are traded in two forms—coupon strips and principal strips—and are taxed by the IRS on the basis of accrued interest, like other zero-coupon securities.

LOS 62.d

Agencies of the U.S. government, including federally related institutions and government sponsored enterprises, issue bonds that are not obligations of the U.S. Treasury but are considered to be almost default risk free.

LOS 62.e

A mortgage passthrough security is backed by a pool of amortizing mortgage loans (the collateral) and has monthly cash flows that include interest payments, scheduled principal payments, and prepayments of principal.

Prepayment risk is significant for investors in passthrough securities, since most mortgage loans contain a prepayment option, which allows the issuer (borrower) to make additional principal payments at any time.

Collateralized mortgage obligations (CMOs) are customized claims to the principal and/or interest payments of mortgage passthrough securities and redistribute the prepayment risk and/or maturity risk of the securities.

LOS 62.f

CMOs are created to decrease borrowing costs by redistributing prepayment risk or altering the maturity structure to better suit investor preferences.

LOS 62.g

Interest payments on state and local government securities (municipal securities, or munis) are usually exempt from U.S. federal taxes, and from state taxes in the state of issuance.

Municipal bonds include:
- Tax-backed (general obligation) bonds backed by the taxing authority of the governmental unit issuing the securities.
- Revenue bonds, backed only by the revenues from the project specifically financed by the bond issue.

LOS 62.h

Corporate debt securities include bonds, medium-term notes, and commercial paper. Bond rating agencies rate corporate bonds on capacity to repay (liquid assets and cash flow), management quality, industry prospects, corporate strategy, financial policies, credit history, overall debt levels, the collateral for the issue, and the nature of the covenants.

Corporate bonds may be secured or unsecured (called debentures). Security can be in the form of real property, financial assets, or personal property/equipment.

Medium-term notes (MTN) are issued periodically by corporations under a shelf registration, sold by agents on a best-efforts basis, and have maturities ranging from 9 months to more than 30 years.

Structured notes combine a bond with a derivative to create a security that fills a need for particular institutional investors.

Commercial paper is a short-term corporate financing vehicle and does not require registration with the SEC if its maturity is less than 270 days. CP comes in two forms:
- Directly-placed paper sold directly by the issuer.
- Dealer-placed paper sold to investors through agents/brokers.

Negotiable CDs are issued in a wide range of maturities by banks, trade in a secondary market, are backed by bank assets, and are termed Eurodollar CDs when denominated in U.S. dollars and issued outside the United States.

Bankers acceptances are issued by banks to guarantee a future payment for goods shipped, sold at a discount to the future payment they promise, short-term, and have limited liquidity.

  ©2009 Kaplan, Inc.

LOS 62.i

Asset-backed securities (ABS) are debt that is supported by the cash flows from an underlying pool of mortgages, auto loans, credit card receivables, commercial loans, or other financial assets.

A special purpose vehicle is an entity to which the assets that back an ABS are legally transferred. If the corporation transferring these assets goes bankrupt, the assets are not subject to claims from its creditors. As a result, the ABS can receive a higher credit rating than the corporation and reduce the corporation's funding costs.

External credit enhancement for an ABS can include corporate guarantees, letters of credit, or third-party bond insurance.

LOS 62.j

Collateralized debt obligations (CDOs) are backed by an underlying pool of debt securities which may be any one of a number of types: corporate bonds, loans, emerging markets debt, mortgage-backed securities, or other CDOs.

LOS 62.k

The primary market in bonds includes underwritten and best-efforts public offerings, as well as private placements.

The secondary market in bonds includes some trading on exchanges, a much larger volume of trading in a dealer market, and electronic trading networks which are an increasingly important part of the secondary market for bonds.

CONCEPT CHECKERS

1. A Treasury security is quoted at 97-17 and has a par value of $100,000. Which of the following is its quoted dollar price?
    A. $97,170.00.
    B. $97,531.25.
    C. $100,000.00.

2. An investor holds $100,000 (par value) worth of Treasury Inflation Protected Securities (TIPS) that carry a 2.5% semiannual pay coupon. If the annual inflation rate is 3%, what is the inflation-adjusted principal value of the bond after six months?
    A. $101,500.
    B. $102,500.
    C. $103,000.

3. An investor holds $100,000 (par value) worth of TIPS currently trading at par. The coupon rate of 4% is paid semiannually, and the annual inflation rate is 2.5%. What coupon payment will the investor receive at the end of the first six months?
    A. $2,000.
    B. $2,025.
    C. $2,050.

4. A Treasury note (T-note) principal strip has six months remaining to maturity. How is its price likely to compare to a 6-month Treasury bill (T-bill) that has just been issued? The T-note price should be:
    A. lower.
    B. higher.
    C. the same.

5. Which of the following statements about Treasury securities is *most* accurate?
    A. Treasury principal strips are usually created from Treasury bills.
    B. Treasury bonds may be used to create Treasury coupon strips.
    C. Treasury coupon strips make lower coupon payments than Treasury principal strips.

6. Which of the following municipal bonds typically has the *greater* risk and is issued with *higher* yields?
    A. Revenue bonds.
    B. Limited tax general obligation bonds.
    C. Unlimited tax general obligation bonds.

7. A bond issue that is serviced with the earnings from a pool of Treasury securities that have been placed in escrow is called a(n):
    A. insured bond.
    B. prerefunded bond.
    C. credit-enhanced obligation.

©2009 Kaplan, Inc.

8. Of the following, the debt securities that are most often registered according to the requirements of SEC Rule 415 (shelf registration) are:
    A. corporate bonds.
    B. medium-term notes.
    C. mortgage-backed securities.

9. A corporation issuing asset-backed securities can often improve the credit rating of the securities to above that of the issuing company by transferring the assets to a(n):
    A. asset trust.
    B. bond insurer.
    C. special purpose vehicle.

10. Which of the following is a *difference* between an on-the-run and an off-the-run issue? An on-the-run issue:
    A. is the most recently issued security of that type.
    B. has a shorter maturity than an off-the-run issue.
    C. is publicly traded whereas an off-the-run issue is not.

11. Compared to a public offering, a private placement of debt securities *likely* has:
    A. more liquidity and a lower yield.
    B. less liquidity and a lower yield.
    C. less liquidity and a higher yield.

12. Compared to negotiable CDs, bankers acceptances:
    A. are more liquid.
    B. have shorter maturities on average.
    C. are more likely to pay periodic interest.

13. A debt security that is collateralized by a pool of the sovereign debt of several developing countries is *most likely* a(n):
    A. CMO.
    B. CDO.
    C. ABS.

14. Activities in the primary market for debt securities would *least likely* include:
    A. market making.
    B. a best-efforts offering.
    C. a firm commitment.

ANSWERS – CONCEPT CHECKERS

1. **B**   This value is computed as follows: dollar price =
$$97\frac{17}{32}\% \times \$100,000 = 0.9753125 \times \$100,000 = \$97,531.25.$$

2. **A**   The annual inflation rate is 3%, which corresponds to 1.5% semiannually. Therefore, the principal value has increased by 1.5%. So we have: new principal = $100,000 × 1.015 = $101,500.

3. **B**   This coupon payment is computed as follows:
$$\text{coupon payment} = (\$100,000 \times 1.0125)\left(\frac{0.04}{2}\right) = \$2,025$$

4. **C**   The T-note principal strip has exactly the same cash flows (the principal) as the T-bill. Therefore, the prices of the two securities should be (about) equal. However, market imperfections, such as illiquidity, may lead to differences.

5. **B**   Treasury coupon and principal strips are created by separating (stripping) the principal and coupons from Treasury notes and bonds and selling packages of these single-maturity cash flows as individual zero-coupon securities. Treasury bills cannot be used because they are already zero-coupon securities.

6. **A**   Revenue bond issues are only obligated to pay principal and interest if revenue from the project that they helped fund is sufficient to service the issue. When issued, revenue bonds typically are riskier than general obligation bonds and, consequently, have higher yields.

7. **B**   The cash flows generated by an escrow pool of Treasury securities are used to service prerefunded bonds. Insured bonds carry third-party guarantees. There are no securities formally known as absolute priority bonds or credit enhanced obligations (yet).

8. **B**   Shelf registration is used with medium-term notes. This permits the issue to be held in inventory (on the "shelf") and sold in parcels at the discretion of the issuer. Corporate bonds and MBS are usually sold all at once.

9. **C**   The assets are sold to a special purpose vehicle to protect them from general claims against the issuing corporation.

10. **A**   On-the-run issues are the most recently issued securities.

11. **C**   Investors require a higher yield to compensate for the fact that privately placed debt is not registered for public sale and is therefore less liquid than debt registered for public sale.

12. **B**   Bankers acceptances are short-term and pay no periodic interest. Like negotiable CDs, they are as good as the credit of the issuing bank but have a very limited secondary market.

13. **B**   A CDO or collateralized debt obligation is backed by an underlying pool of debt securities which may be emerging markets debt. A CMO is backed by a pool of mortgages, and an ABS is backed by financial assets.

14. **A**   Market making refers to a dealer that trades in the secondary market for its own account from inventory.

©2009 Kaplan, Inc.

The following is a review of the Analysis of Fixed Income Investments principles designed to address the learning outcome statements set forth by CFA Institute®. This topic is also covered in:

UNDERSTANDING YIELD SPREADS

Study Session 15

EXAM FOCUS

Yield spreads are simply differences between the yields of any two debt securities or types of debt securities. Try to get a good grip on the spread terminology in this review and the characteristics that drive yield spreads. You should know all three theories of the term structure, not only their implications for the shape of the yield curve but also what the yield curve shape can tell us under each of the three theories. Learn the relationships between taxable and after-tax yields and between tax-free and taxable equivalent yields well. Calculations of these relations are almost sure to be worth some points come exam day.

LOS 63.a: Identify the interest rate policy tools available to a central bank (e.g., the U.S. Federal Reserve).

While interest rates are determined by a variety of economic conditions, in the United States the Federal Reserve (Fed) attempts to manage short-term rates through its *monetary policy tools*. The **four interest rate tools of the Fed** are as follows:

1. **The discount rate** is the rate at which banks can borrow reserves from the Fed. A lower rate tends to increase bank reserves, encourage lending, and decrease interest rates. A higher discount rate has the opposite effect, raising rates.

2. **Open market operations** refers to the buying or selling of Treasury securities by the Fed in the open market. When the Fed buys securities, cash replaces securities in investor accounts, more funds are available for lending, and interest rates decrease. Sales of securities by the Fed have the opposite effect, reducing cash balances and funds available for lending as well as increasing rates.

3. **Bank reserve requirements** are the percentage of deposits that banks must retain (not loan out). By increasing the percentage of deposits banks are required to retain as *reserves,* the Fed effectively decreases the funds that are available for lending. This decrease in amounts available for lending will tend to increase interest rates. A decrease in the percentage reserve requirement will increase the funds available for loans and tends to decrease interest rates.

4. **Persuading banks to tighten or loosen their credit policies**. By asking banks to alter their lending policies, the Fed attempts to affect their willingness to lend. Encouraging lending will tend to decrease rates and vice versa.

The most commonly used policy tool is *open market operations.*

LOS 63.b: Describe a yield curve and the various shapes of the yield curve.

We have mentioned yield curves previously as just a plot of yields by years to maturity. For a view of a current Treasury yield curve and related information, you can look at www.bloomberg.com/markets/rates/index.html. The Treasury yield curve shows the yields for U.S. Treasury securities (bills, notes, and bonds) with maturities from three months to 30 years.

There are four general shapes that we use to describe yield curves:

1. Normal or upward sloping.

2. Inverted or downward sloping.

3. Flat.

4. Humped.

These four shapes are illustrated in Figure 1.

Figure 1: Yield Curve Shapes

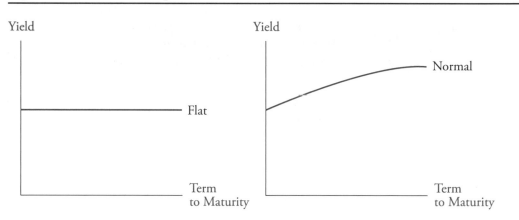

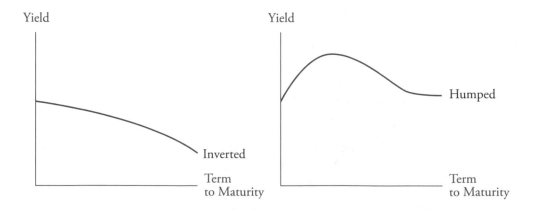

Yield curves can take on just about any shape, so don't think these examples are the only ones observed. These four are representative of general types, and you need to be familiar with what is meant by an "upward sloping" or "normal" yield curve and by an

©2009 Kaplan, Inc.

"inverted" or "downward sloping" yield curve. Humped and flat yield curves usually go by just those descriptive names and shouldn't present any problem. Just remember that a flat yield curve means that yields are all equal at every maturity.

LOS 63.c: Explain the basic theories of the term structure of interest rates and describe the implications of each theory for the shape of the yield curve.

The **pure expectations theory** states that the yield for a particular maturity is an average (not a simple average) of the short-term rates that are expected in the future. If short-term rates are expected to rise in the future, interest rate yields on longer maturities will be higher than those on shorter maturities, and the yield curve will be upward sloping. If short-term rates are expected to fall over time, longer maturity bonds will be offered at lower yields.

Proponents of the **liquidity preference theory** believe that, in addition to expectations about future short-term rates, investors require a risk premium for holding longer term bonds. This is consistent with the fact that interest rate risk is greater for longer maturity bonds.

Under this theory, the size of the liquidity premium will depend on how much additional compensation investors require to induce them to take on the greater risk of longer maturity bonds or, alternatively, how strong their preference for the greater liquidity of shorter term debt is. An illustration of the effect of a liquidity premium on a yield curve, where expected future short-term rates are constant, is presented in Figure 2.

Figure 2: Liquidity Premium

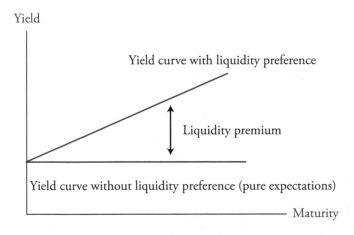

The **market segmentation theory** is based on the idea that investors and borrowers have preferences for different *maturity ranges*. Under this theory, the supply of bonds (desire to borrow) and the demand for bonds (desire to lend) determine equilibrium yields for the various maturity ranges. Institutional investors may have strong preferences for maturity ranges that closely match their liabilities. Life insurers and pension funds may prefer long maturities due to the long-term nature of the liabilities they must fund. A commercial bank that has liabilities of a relatively short maturity may prefer to invest in shorter-term debt securities. Another argument for the market segmentation theory is that there are legal or institutional policy restrictions that prevent investors from purchasing securities with maturities outside a particular maturity range. The determination of yields for various maturity ranges of the yield curve is illustrated in Figure 3.

Figure 3: Market Segmentation Theory and the Yield Curve

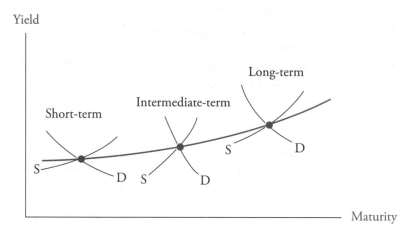

A somewhat weaker version of the market segmentation theory is the *preferred habitat theory*. Under this theory, yields also depend on supply and demand for various maturity ranges, but investors can be induced to move from their preferred maturity ranges when yields are sufficiently higher in other (non-preferred) maturity ranges.

Term Structure Theories and the Shape of the Yield Curve

The **pure expectations theory** by itself has no implications for the shape of the yield curve. The various expectations and the shapes that are consistent with them are:

Short-term rates expected to rise in the future → upward sloping yield curve
Short-term rates are expected fall in the future → downward sloping yield curve
Short-term rates expected to rise then fall → humped yield curve
Short-term rates expected to remain constant → flat yield curve

The shape of the yield curve, under the pure expectations theory, provides us with information about investor expectations about future short-term rates.

Under the **liquidity preference theory**, the yield curve may take on any of the shapes we have identified. If rates are expected to fall a great deal in the future, even adding a liquidity premium to the resulting negatively sloped yield curve can result in a downward sloping yield curve. A humped yield curve could still be humped even with a liquidity premium added to all the yields. Also note that, under the liquidity preference theory, an upward sloping yield curve can be consistent with expectations of declining short term rates in the future. This case is illustrated in Figure 4.

©2009 Kaplan, Inc.

Figure 4: Liquidity Premium Added to Decreasing Expected Rates

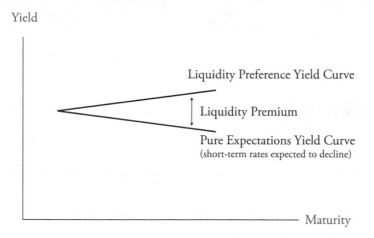

The **market segmentation theory** of the term structure is consistent with any yield curve shape. Under this theory, it is supply and demand for debt securities at each maturity range that determines the yield for that maturity range. There is no specific linkage among the yields at different maturities, although, under the *preferred habitat theory*, higher rates at an adjacent maturity range can induce investors to purchase bonds with maturities outside their preferred range of maturities.

LOS 63.d: Define a spot rate.

Yield to maturity is the single discount rate that makes the present value of a bond's promised cash flows equal to its market price. Actually, the appropriate discount rates for cash flows that come at different points in time are typically not all the same. The discount rate for a payment that comes one year from now is not necessarily the same discount rate that should be applied to a payment that comes five or ten years from now. That is, the spot-rate yield curve is not *flat* (horizontal).

The appropriate discount rates for individual future payments are called **spot rates**. The spot rates for different time periods that correctly value (produce a value equal to market price) the cash flows from a Treasury bond are called **arbitrage-free** Treasury spot rates, or the *theoretical Treasury spot-rate curve*. We will examine the methodology for estimating these rates and why they are called "arbitrage-free" spot rates a bit later. Here we just introduce the idea of spot rates to differentiate them from coupon bond yields (YTMs). Conceptually, spot rates are the discount rates for (yields on) zero-coupon bonds, securities that have only a single cash flow at a future date. A simple example (with annual rather than semiannual payments) will illustrate this concept as applied to coupon bonds.

Consider an annual-pay bond with a 10% coupon rate and three years to maturity. This bond will make three payments. For a $1,000 bond these payments will be $100 in one year, $100 at the end of two years, and $1,100 three years from now. Suppose we are given the following spot rates:

1 year = 8%

2 year = 9%

3 year = 10%

Discounting each promised payment by its corresponding spot rate, we can value the bond as:

$$\frac{100}{1.08} + \frac{100}{1.09^2} + \frac{1,100}{1.10^3} = 1,003.21$$

LOS 63.e: Compute, compare, and contrast the various yield spread measures.

A yield spread is simply the difference between the yields on two bonds or two types of bonds. Three different yield spread measures are as follows:

1. The **absolute yield spread** is simply the difference between yields on two bonds. This simple measure is sometimes called the *nominal spread*. Absolute yield spreads are usually expressed in basis points (100ths of 1%).

   absolute yield spread = yield on the higher-yield bond − yield on the lower-yield bond

2. The **relative yield spread** is the absolute yield spread expressed as a percentage of the yield on the benchmark bond.

   $$\text{relative yield spread} = \frac{\text{absolute yield spread}}{\text{yield on the benchmark bond}}$$

3. The **yield ratio** is the ratio of the yield on the subject bond to the yield on the benchmark bond.

   $$\text{yield ratio} = \frac{\text{subject bond yield}}{\text{benchmark bond yield}}$$

Note that the yield ratio is simply one plus the relative yield spread. The calculation of these yield spread measures is illustrated in the following example.

Example: Computing yield spreads

Consider two bonds, X and Y. Their respective yields are 6.50% and 6.75%. Using bond X as the benchmark bond, compute the absolute yield spread, the relative yield spread, and the yield ratio for these bonds.

Answer:

      absolute yield spread = 6.75% − 6.50% = 0.25% or 25 basis points
      relative yield spread = 0.25% / 6.50% = 0.038 = 3.8%
      yield ratio = 6.75% / 6.50% = 1.038

©2009 Kaplan, Inc.

The most commonly used yield spread is the *absolute* yield spread, even though it is the most simplistic. A shortcoming of the absolute yield spread is that it may remain constant, even though overall rates rise or fall. In this case, the effect of rising or falling rates on spreads is captured by the relative yield spread or the yield ratio.

For example, consider two yields that rise from 6.5% and 7.0% to 7.0% and 7.5%, respectively. The absolute yield spread remains constant at 50 basis points, while the relative spread falls from 7.69% to 7.14% and the yield ratio decreases from 1.077 to 1.071.

LOS 63.f: Describe a credit spread and discuss the suggested relation between credit spreads and the well-being of the economy.

A **credit (or quality) spread** is the difference in yields between two issues that are similar in all respects except for credit rating. An example of a credit spread is the difference in yields between long AA rated general obligation (GO) municipal bonds and long A rated GO munis (an intramarket spread as well). Obviously, these spreads show the effect of credit quality on yields and reveal the risk-return tradeoff the investor can expect (i.e., how much added return an investor can earn by investing in issues with higher perceived credit risk).

Credit spreads are related to the state of the economy. During an expanding economy, credit spreads decline as corporations are expected to have stronger cash flows. On the other hand, during economic contractions, cash flows are pressured, leading to a greater probability of default and higher yields on lower-quality issues. When investors anticipate an economic downturn, they often sell low-quality issues and buy high-quality issues, including Treasuries. This "flight to quality" puts downward pressure on the prices of low-quality issues, raising their yields.

LOS 63.g: Identify how embedded options affect yield spreads.

A call option on a bond is an option the bond issuer holds and will only be exercised if it is advantageous to the issuer to do so. From the bondholder's perspective, a noncallable bond is preferred to a bond that is otherwise identical but callable. Investors will require a higher yield on a callable bond, compared to the same bond without the call feature. Therefore, yield spreads to a benchmark bond, such as a similar maturity Treasury issue, are higher for the callable bond. By the same reasoning, yield spreads must be greater to compensate bondholders for the prepayment option embedded in mortgage passthrough securities.

The inclusion of a put provision or a conversion option with a bond will have the opposite effect; the choice of whether to exercise either of these options is the bondholder's. Compared to an identical option-free bond, a putable bond will have a lower yield spread to Treasuries due to the value of the put feature "included" with the bond.

The fact that option provisions affect yield spreads is important because this tells us that spreads for bonds with embedded options are not purely premiums for credit risk, liquidity differences, and maturity (duration) risk.

LOS 63.h: Explain how the liquidity or issue-size of a bond affects its yield spread relative to risk-free securities and relative to other securities.

Bonds that have *less liquidity have higher spreads* to Treasuries. Investors prefer more liquidity to less and will pay a premium for greater liquidity. A higher price for a bond that is identical to another in all aspects except that it is more actively traded—and therefore more liquid—translates into a lower yield compared to the less liquid bond.

Liquidity is affected by the size of an issue. *Larger issues normally have greater liquidity* because they are more actively traded in the secondary market. Empirical evidence suggests that issues with *greater size have lower yield spreads*. When compared with identical but smaller issues, larger-size issues have lower yields due to their greater liquidity.

LOS 63.i: Compute the after-tax yield of a taxable security and the tax-equivalent yield of a tax-exempt security.

The **after-tax yield** on a taxable security can be calculated as:

$$\text{after-tax yield} = \text{taxable yield} \times (1 - \text{marginal tax rate})$$

Example: Computing after-tax yield

What is the after-tax yield on a corporate bond with a yield of 10% for an investor with a 40% marginal tax rate?

Answer:

Investors are concerned with after-tax returns. The marginal tax rate is the percentage that must be paid in taxes on one additional dollar of income, in this case interest income.

For an investor with a marginal tax rate of 40%, 40 cents of every additional dollar of taxable interest income must be paid in taxes. For a taxable bond that yields 10%, the after-tax yield to an investor with a 40% marginal tax rate will be:

$$10\%(1 - 0.4) = 6.0\% \text{ after tax}$$

©2009 Kaplan, Inc.

Tax-exempt securities can offer lower yields compared to taxable securities because the yields they offer are after-tax yields. The higher an investor's marginal tax rate, the greater the attractiveness of a tax exempt issue compared to a taxable issue. The **taxable-equivalent yield** is the yield a particular investor must earn on a taxable bond to have the same after-tax return they would receive from a particular tax-exempt issue. The calculation is just a rearrangement of the after-tax yield formula listed previously.

$$\text{taxable-equivalent yield} = \frac{\text{tax-free yield}}{(1 - \text{marginal tax rate})}$$

Example: Taxable-equivalent yield

Consider a municipal bond that offers a yield of 4.5%. If an investor is considering buying a fully taxable Treasury security offering a 6.75% yield, should she buy the Treasury security or the municipal bond, given that her marginal tax rate is 35%?

Answer:

We can approach this problem from two perspectives. First, the taxable equivalent yield on the municipal bond is $\frac{4.5\%}{(1-0.35)} = 6.92\%$, which is higher than the taxable yield, so the municipal bond is preferred.

Alternatively, the after-tax return on the taxable bond is $0.0675 \times (1 - 0.35) = 4.39\%$.

Thus, the after-tax return on the municipal bond (4.5%) is greater than the after-tax yield on the taxable bond (4.39%), and the municipal bond is preferred.

Either approach gives the same answer; she should buy the municipal bond.

LOS 63.j: Define LIBOR and explain its importance to funded investors who borrow short term.

We previously mentioned **LIBOR** (London Interbank Offered Rate) in reference to the rates paid on negotiable CDs by banks and bank branches located in London. LIBOR has become the most important benchmark or reference rate for floating-rate debt securities and short-term lending. LIBOR is determined each day and published by the British Bankers' Association for several currencies, including the U.S., Canadian, and Australian dollars, the Euro, Japanese yen, British pounds, and Swiss francs, among others. While the maturity of the CDs that banks invest in can range from overnight to five years, LIBOR is most important for short-term rates of one year or less.

A **funded investor** is one who borrows to finance an investment position. The importance of LIBOR in this context is as a measure of the funding costs because the loans to finance the investment are most often floating-rate loans or short-term loans where the reference rate is published LIBOR. Recall that floating-rate loans are based on a reference rate plus a margin. A funded investor with a borrowing rate of 2-month (60-day) LIBOR + 40 basis points would have a borrowing cost (annualized) of 2.6% when 2-month LIBOR is quoted at 2.2%. The profits of such a funded investor would depend on his or her ability to earn greater than a 2.6% annual rate on the investments funded in such a manner.

©2009 Kaplan, Inc.

KEY CONCEPTS

LOS 63.a
The Federal Reserve Board's tools for affecting short-term interest rates are the discount rate, open-market operations, the reserve requirement, and persuasion to influence banks' lending policies.

LOS 63.b
Yield curves represent the plot of yield against maturity.

The general yield curve shapes are upward or downward sloping, flat, or humped.

LOS 63.c
Theories of the yield curve and their implications for the shape of the yield curve are:
- The *pure expectations theory* argues that rates at longer maturities depend only on expectations of future short-term rates and is consistent with any yield curve shape.
- The *liquidity preference theory* of the term structure states that longer-term rates reflect investors' expectations about future short-term rates and an increasing liquidity premium to compensate investors for exposure to greater amounts of interest rate risk at longer maturities. The liquidity preference theory can be consistent with a downward sloping curve if an expected decrease in short-term rates outweighs the liquidity premium.
- The *market segmentation theory* argues that lenders and borrowers have preferred maturity ranges and that the shape of the yield curve is determined by the supply and demand for securities within each maturity range, independent of the yield in other maturity ranges. It is consistent with any yield curve shape and in a somewhat weaker form is known as the preferred habitat theory.

LOS 63.d
Treasury spot rates are the appropriate discount rates for single cash flows (coupon or principal payments) from a U.S. Treasury security, given the time until the payment is to be received.

LOS 63.e
Types of yield spreads:
- The *absolute yield spread* is the difference between the yield on a particular security or sector and the yield of a reference (benchmark) security or sector, which is often on-the-run Treasury securities of like maturity.
- The *relative yield spread* is the absolute yield spread expressed as a percentage of the benchmark yield. This is arguably a superior measure to the absolute spread, since it will reflect changes in the level of interest rates even when the absolute spread remains constant.
- The *yield ratio* is the ratio of the yield on a security or sector to the yield on a benchmark security or sector; it is simply one plus the relative yield spread.

LOS 63.f

A credit spread is the yield difference between two bond issues due to differences in their credit ratings.

Credit spreads narrow when the economy is healthy and expanding, while they increase during contractions/recessions reflecting a "flight to (higher) quality" by investors.

LOS 63.g

Call options and prepayment options increase yields and yield spreads compared to option-free bonds.

Put options and conversion options decrease yields and yield spreads compared to comparable option-free bonds.

LOS 63.h

Bonds with less liquidity are less desirable and must offer a higher yield. Larger bond issues are more liquid and, other things equal, will have lower yield spreads.

LOS 63.i

To compare a tax-exempt bond with a taxable issue, use either of the following:
- After-tax yield = taxable yield × (1 − marginal tax rate), and compare it to tax-exempt yield.
- Taxable-equivalent yield $= \dfrac{\text{tax-free yield}}{(1-\text{marginal tax rate})}$, and compare it to a taxable yield.

LOS 63.j

LIBOR for various currencies is determined from rates at which large London banks loan money to each other and is the most important reference rate globally for floating-rate debt and short-term loans of various maturities.

©2009 Kaplan, Inc.

CONCEPT CHECKERS

1. Under the pure expectations theory, an inverted yield curve is interpreted as evidence that:
   A. demand for long-term bonds is falling.
   B. short-term rates are expected to fall in the future.
   C. investors have very little demand for liquidity.

2. According to the liquidity preference theory, which of the following statements is *least accurate*?
   A. All else equal, investors prefer short-term securities over long-term securities.
   B. Investors perceive little risk differential between short-term and long-term securities.
   C. Borrowers will pay a premium for long-term funds to avoid having to roll over short-term debt.

3. With respect to the term structure of interest rates, the market segmentation theory holds that:
   A. an increase in demand for long-term borrowings could lead to an inverted yield curve.
   B. expectations about the future of short-term interest rates are the major determinants of the shape of the yield curve.
   C. the yield curve reflects the maturity demands of financial institutions and investors.

4. The most commonly used tool of the Fed to control interest rates is:
   A. the discount rate.
   B. the bank reserve requirement.
   C. open market operations.

5. For two bonds that are alike in all respects except maturity, the relative yield spread is 7.14%. The yield ratio is *closest* to:
   A. 0.714.
   B. 1.0714.
   C. 107.14.

6. Assume the following yields for different bonds issued by a corporation:
   - 1-year bond: 5.50%.
   - 2-year bond: 6.00%.
   - 3-year bond: 7.00%.

   If a 3-year U.S. Treasury is yielding 5%, then what is the *absolute* yield spread on the 3-year corporate issue?
   A. 0.40.
   B. 100 bp.
   C. 200 bp.

7. Assume the following corporate yield curve:
    - 1-year bond: 5.00%.
    - 2-year bond: 6.00%.
    - 3-year bond: 7.00%.

    If a 3-year U.S. Treasury yielding 6% is the benchmark bond, the *relative* yield spread on the 3-year corporate is:
    A. 16.67%.
    B. 1.167.
    C. 14.28%.

8. If a U.S. investor is forecasting that the yield spread between U.S. Treasury bonds and U.S. corporate bonds is going to widen, which of the following beliefs would he be also *most likely* to hold?
    A. The economy is going to expand.
    B. The economy is going to contract.
    C. There will be no change in the economy.

9. For two bonds that are alike in all respects except credit risk, the yield ratio is 1.0833. If the yield on the higher yield bond is 6.5%, the lower yield bond yield is *closest* to:
    A. 5.50%.
    B. 6.00%.
    C. 8.33%.

10. Given two bonds that are equivalent in all respects except tax status, the marginal tax rate that will make an investor indifferent between an 8.2% taxable bond and a 6.2% tax-exempt bond is *closest* to:
    A. 24.39%.
    B. 37.04%.
    C. 43.47%.

11. Which of the following statements *most accurately* describes the relationship between the economic health of a nation and credit spreads?
    A. Credit spreads and economic well-being are not correlated.
    B. Credit spreads decrease during an expanding economy because corporate cash flows are expected to rise.
    C. Credit spreads increase during an expanding economy because corporations invest in more speculative projects.

12. Which of the following *most accurately* describes the relationship between liquidity and yield spreads relative to Treasury issues? All else being equal, bonds with:
    A. less liquidity have lower yield spreads to Treasuries.
    B. greater liquidity have higher yield spreads to Treasuries.
    C. less liquidity have higher yield spreads to Treasuries.

©2009 Kaplan, Inc.

13.   A narrowing of credit spreads would have the *least* impact on the value of which
       of the following investments?
       A. AAA corporate bond.
       B. 30-year Treasury bond.
       C. BB+ rated corporate bond.

14.   Assume an investor is in the 31% marginal tax bracket. She is considering the
       purchase of either a 7.5% corporate bond that is selling at par or a 5.25% tax-
       exempt municipal bond that is also selling at par. Given that the two bonds are
       comparable in all respects except their tax status, the investor should buy the:
       A. corporate bond, since it has the higher yield of 7.50%.
       B. municipal bond, since its taxable-equivalent yield is 7.61%.
       C. corporate bond, since its after-tax yield is higher.

ANSWERS – CONCEPT CHECKERS

1. **B**   An inverted or downward-sloping yield curve, under the pure expectations theory, indicates that short-term rates are expected to decline in the future.

2. **B**   Rational investors feel that long-term bonds have more risk exposure than short-term securities (i.e., long-term securities are less liquid and subject to more price volatility). The other statements are correct.

3. **C**   The market segmentation theory holds that certain types of financial institutions and investors prefer to confine (most of) their investment activity to certain maturity ranges of the fixed-income market and that supply and demand forces within each segment ultimately determine the shape of the yield curve.

4. **C**   Open market operations are carried on frequently. The Fed's selling of Treasuries in the open market takes money out of the economy, reducing the amount of loanable funds and increasing interest rates. The opposite occurs when the Fed buys Treasuries in the open market.

5. **B**   The yield ratio is 1 + relative yield spread, or 1 + 0.0714 = 1.0714.

6. **C**   Absolute yield spread = yield on the 3-year corporate issue – yield on the on-the-run 3-year Treasury issue = 7.00% – 5.00% = 2.00% or 200 bp.

7. **A**   The yield on the corporate is 7%, so the relative yield spread is $\frac{7\% - 6\%}{6\%}$, which is 1/6 or 16.67% of the 3-year Treasury yield.

8. **B**   A contracting economy means lower corporate earnings which increases the probability of default on debt and increases yield spreads between corporate issues and Treasuries at a particular maturity.

9. **B**   yield ratio $= \dfrac{\text{higher yield bond}}{\text{lower yield bond}} = 1.0833.$ Given the higher yield is 6.5%, the lower yield can be calculated as: $\dfrac{6.5\%}{1.0833} = \text{lower yield bond} = 6.0\%.$

10. **A**   The tax rate that makes investors indifferent between two otherwise equivalent bonds is determined by solving for the tax rate in the equation: tax-exempt yield = (1 – tax rate) × taxable yield. Rearranging this relationship, we have:

    $$\text{marginal tax rate} = 1 - \frac{\text{tax-exempt rate}}{\text{taxable rate}} = 1 - \frac{6.2}{8.2} = 24.39\%.$$

11. **B**   As an economy expands, credit spreads decline as expected corporate earnings rise. This is because, with stronger earnings, corporations are less likely to default on their debt.

12. **C**   The less liquidity a bond has, the higher its yield spread relative to Treasuries. This is because investors require a higher yield to compensate them for giving up liquidity, which results in a greater spread over Treasury issues, which are very liquid.

13. **B**   Since we usually speak of credit spreads as yield spreads to Treasuries, a change in the yield spread does not imply any change in the values of Treasuries.

©2009 Kaplan, Inc.

14. **B** The taxable-equivalent yield on this municipal bond is $\dfrac{5.25}{(1-0.31)} = \dfrac{5.25}{0.69} = 7.61\%$.

Since this is higher than the yield on the (taxable) corporate bond, the municipal bond is preferred. Alternatively, the after-tax yield on the corporate is 7.5% (1 – 0.31) = 5.175%, which is less than the tax-exempt yield, leading to the same decision.

The following is a review of the Analysis of Fixed Income Investments principles designed to address the learning outcome statements set forth by CFA Institute®. This topic is also covered in:

INTRODUCTION TO THE VALUATION OF DEBT SECURITIES

Study Session 16

EXAM FOCUS

Bond valuation is all about calculating the present value of the promised cash flows. If your time-value-of-money (TVM) skills are not up to speed, take the time now to revisit the Study Session 2 review of TVM concepts. The material in this topic review is very important. Calculating the value of a bond by discounting expected cash flows should become an easy exercise. The final material, on discounting a bond's expected cash flows using spot rates and the idea of "arbitrage-free" bond valuation, is quite important as well. A good understanding here will just make what follows easier to understand.

LOS 64.a: Explain the steps in the bond valuation process.

The general procedure for valuing fixed-income securities (or any security) is to take the present values of all the expected cash flows and add them up to get the value of the security.

There are three steps in the bond valuation process:

Step 1: **Estimate the cash flows** over the life of the security. For a bond, there are two types of cash flows: (1) the coupon payments and (2) the return of principal.

Step 2: **Determine the appropriate discount rate** based on the risk of (uncertainty about) the receipt of the estimated cash flows.

Step 3: **Calculate the present value of the estimated cash flows** by multiplying the bond's expected cash flows by the appropriate discount factors.

LOS 64.b: Identify the types of bonds for which estimating the expected cash flows is difficult and explain the problems encountered when estimating the cash flows for these bonds.

Certainly, one problem in estimating future cash flows for bonds is predicting defaults and any potential credit problems that make the receipt of future cash flows uncertain. Aside from credit risk, however, we can identify three situations where estimating future cash flows poses additional difficulties.

1. **The principal repayment stream is not known with certainty.** This category includes bonds with embedded options (puts, calls, prepayment options, and accelerated sinking fund provisions). For these bonds, the future stream of principal payments is uncertain and will depend to a large extent on the future path of interest rates. For example, lower rates will increase prepayments of mortgage passthrough securities, and principal will be repaid earlier.

©2009 Kaplan, Inc.

2. **The coupon payments are not known with certainty.** With floating-rate securities, future coupon payments depend on the path of interest rates. With some floating-rate securities, the coupon payments may depend on the price of a commodity or the rate of inflation over some future period.

3. **The bond is convertible or exchangeable into another security.** Without information about future stock prices and interest rates, we don't know when the cash flows will come or how large they will be.

LOS 64.c: Compute the value of a bond and the change in value that is attributable to a change in the discount rate.

For a Treasury bond, the appropriate rate used to value the promised cash flows is the risk-free rate. This may be a single rate, used to discount all of the cash flows, or a series of discount rates that correspond to the times until each cash flow arrives.

For non-Treasury securities, we must add a risk premium to the risk-free (Treasury) rate to determine the appropriate discount rate. This risk premium is one of the yield spread measures covered in the previous review and is the added yield to compensate for greater risk (credit risk, liquidity risk, call risk, prepayment risk, and so on). When using a single discount rate to value bonds, the risk premium is added to the risk-free rate to get the appropriate discount rate for all of the expected cash flows.

yield on a risky bond = yield on a default-free bond + risk premium

Other things being equal, the riskier the security, the higher the yield differential (or risk premium) we need to add to the on-the-run Treasury yields.

Computing the Value of a Bond

Valuation with a single yield (discount rate). Recall that we valued an annuity using the time value of money keys on the calculator. For an option-free coupon bond, the coupon payments can be valued as an annuity. In order to take into account the payment of the par value at maturity, we will enter this final payment as the future value. This is the basic difference between valuing a coupon bond and valuing an annuity.

For simplicity, consider a security that will pay $100 per year for ten years and make a single $1,000 payment at maturity (in ten years). If the appropriate discount rate is 8% for all the cash flows, the value is:

$$\frac{100}{1.08} + \frac{100}{1.08^2} + \frac{100}{1.08^3} + \frac{100}{1.08^4} + ... + \frac{100}{1.08^{10}} + \frac{1,000}{1.08^{10}}$$

$= \$1,134.20 =$ present value of expected cash flows

This is simply the sum of the present values of the future cash flows, $100 per year for ten years and $1,000 (the principal repayment) to be received at the end of the tenth year, at the same time as the final coupon payment.

The calculator solution is:

N = 10; PMT = 100; FV = 1,000; I/Y = 8; CPT → PV = –$1,134.20

where:
N = number of years
PMT = the *annual* coupon payment
I/Y = the *annual* discount rate
FV = the par value or selling price at the end of an assumed holding period

Professor's Note: Take note of a couple of points here. The discount rate is entered as a whole number in percent, 8, not 0.08. The ten coupon payments of $100 each are taken care of in the N = 10 entry, the principal repayment is in the FV = 1,000 entry. Lastly, note that the PV is negative; it will be the opposite sign to the sign of PMT and FV. The calculator is just "thinking" that if you receive the payments and future value (you own the bond), you must pay the present value of the bond today (you must buy the bond). That's why the PV amount is negative; it is a cash outflow to a bond buyer. Just make sure that you give the payments and future value the same sign, and then you can ignore the sign on the answer (PV).

The Change in Value When Interest Rates Change

Bond values and bond yields are inversely related. An *increase* in the discount rate will *decrease* the present value of a bond's expected cash flows; a decrease in the discount rate will increase the present value of a bond's expected cash flows. The change in bond value in response to a change in the discount rate can be calculated as the difference between the present values of the cash flows at the two different discount rates.

©2009 Kaplan, Inc.

Example: Changes in required yield

A bond has a par value of $1,000, a 6% semiannual coupon, and three years to maturity. Compute the bond values when the yield to maturity is 3%, 6%, and 12%.

Answer:

$$\text{At } I/Y = \frac{3}{2}; \; N = 3 \times 2; \; FV = 1,000; \; PMT = \frac{60}{2}; \; CPT \to PV = -1,085.458$$

$$\text{At } I/Y = \frac{6}{2}; \; N = 3 \times 2; \; FV = 1,000; \; PMT = \frac{60}{2}; \; CPT \to PV = -1,000.000$$

$$\text{At } I/Y = \frac{12}{2}; \; N = 3 \times 2; \; FV = 1,000; \; PMT = \frac{60}{2}; \; CPT \to PV = -852.480$$

We have illustrated here a point covered earlier; if the yield to maturity equals the coupon rate, the bond value is equal to par. If the yield to maturity is higher (lower) than the coupon rate, the bond is trading at a discount (premium) to par.

We can now calculate the percentage change in price for changes in yield. If the required yield decreases from 6% to 3%, the value of the bond increases by:

$$\frac{1,085.46}{1,000.00} - 1 = 8.546\%.$$

If the yield increases from 6% to 12%, the bond value decreases by:

$$\frac{852.48}{1,000.00} - 1 = -14.752\%.$$

Professor's Note: Notice that in these calculations, you only need to change the interest rate (I/Y) and then compute PV once the values of N, PMT, and FV have been entered. The TVM keys "remember" the values for these inputs even after the calculator has been turned off!

Price-yield profile. If you plot a bond's yield to its corresponding value, you'll get a graph like the one shown in Figure 1. Here we see that higher prices are associated with lower yields. This graph is called the *price-yield curve*. Note that it is not a straight line but is curved. For option-free bonds, the price-yield curve is convex toward the origin, meaning it looks like half of a smile.

Figure 1: The Price-Yield Profile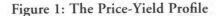

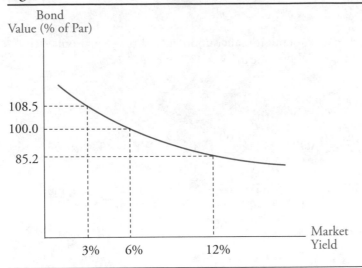

LOS 64.d: Explain how the price of a bond changes as the bond approaches its maturity date and compute the change in value that is attributable to the passage of time.

Prior to maturity, a bond can be selling at a significant discount or premium to par value. However, regardless of its required yield, the price will converge to par value as maturity approaches. Consider the bond in the previous example ($1,000 par value, 3-year life, paying 6% semiannual coupons). The bond values corresponding to required yields of 3, 6, and 12% as the bond approaches maturity are presented in Figure 2.

Figure 2: Bond Values and the Passage of Time

Time to Maturity	YTM = 3%	YTM = 6%	YTM = 12%
3.0 years	$1,085.40	$1,000.00	$852.48
2.5	1,071.74	1,000.00	873.63
2.0	1,057.82	1,000.00	896.05
1.5	1,043.68	1,000.00	919.81
1.0	1,029.34	1,000.00	945.00
0.5	1,014.78	1,000.00	971.69
0.0	1,000.00	1,000.00	1,000.00

To compute the change in bond value due to the passage of time, just revalue the bond with the number of periods (remaining until maturity) reduced. Note that in the preceding example, the value of a 6% bond with three years until maturity and a yield to maturity of 3% is FV = 1,000; PMT = 30; N = 6; I/Y = 1.5; CPT → PV = $1,085.46. To see the effect of the passage of time (with the yield to maturity held constant) just enter N = 5 CPT → PV to get the value one period (six months) from

©2009 Kaplan, Inc.

now of $1,071.74, or N = 4 CPT → PV to get the value two periods (one year) from now of $1,057.82.

The change in value associated with the passage of time for the three bonds represented in Figure 2 is presented graphically in Figure 3.

Figure 3: Premium, Par, and Discount Bonds

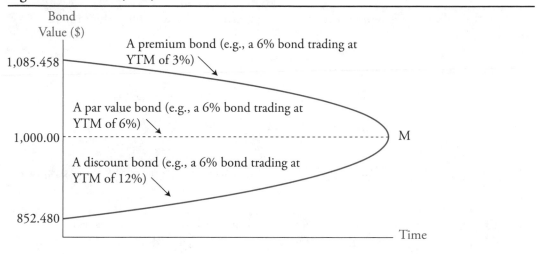

LOS 64.e: Compute the value of a zero-coupon bond.

Since a zero-coupon bond has only a single payment at maturity, the value of a zero is simply the present value of the par or face value. Given the yield to maturity, the calculation is:

$$\text{bond value} = \frac{\text{maturity value}}{(1+i)^{\text{number of years} \times 2}}$$

Note that this valuation model requires just three pieces of information:

1. The bond's maturity value, assumed to be $1,000.
2. The semiannual discount rate, i.
3. The life of the bond, N years.

Alternatively, using the TVM keys, we enter:

PMT = 0; FV = par; N = # years × 2; I/Y = YTM/2 = semiannual discount rate; CPT → PV

Although zero-coupon bonds do not pay coupons, it is customary to value zero-coupon bonds using semiannual discount rates. Note that N is now two times the number of years to maturity and that the semiannual discount rate is one-half the yield to maturity expressed as a BEY.

Example: Valuing a zero-coupon bond

Compute the value of a 10-year, $1,000 face value zero-coupon bond with a yield to maturity of 8%.

Answer:

To find the value of this bond given its yield to maturity of 8% (a 4% semiannual rate), we can calculate:

$$\text{bond value} = \frac{1,000}{\left(1 + \frac{0.08}{2}\right)^{10 \times 2}} = \frac{1,000}{(1.04)^{20}} = \$456.39$$

Or, using a calculator, use the following inputs:

$$N = 10 \times 2 = 20; \text{ FV} = 1,000; \text{ I/Y} = \frac{8}{2} = 4; \text{ PMT} = 0; \text{ CPT} \rightarrow \text{PV} = -\$456.39$$

The difference between the current price of the bond ($456.39) and its par value ($1,000) is the amount of compound interest that will be earned over the 10-year life of the issue.

 Professor's Note: Exam questions will likely specify whether annual or semiannual discounting should be used. Just be prepared to value a zero-coupon bond either way.

LOS 64.f: Explain the arbitrage-free valuation approach and the market process that forces the price of a bond toward its arbitrage-free value and explain how a dealer can generate an arbitrage profit if a bond is mispriced.

Yield to maturity is a summary measure and is essentially an internal rate of return based on a bond's cash flows and its market price. In the traditional valuation approach, we get the yield to maturity of bonds with maturity and risk characteristics similar to those of the bond we wish to value. Then we use this rate to discount the cash flows of the bond to be valued.

With the **arbitrage-free valuation approach**, we *discount each cash flow using a discount rate that is specific to the maturity of each cash flow.* Again, these discount rates are called **spot rates** and can be thought of as the required rates of return on zero-coupon bonds maturing at various times in the future.

The arbitrage-free valuation approach simply says that the value of a Treasury bond based on (Treasury) spot rates must be equal to the value of the parts (i.e., the sum of the present values of all of the expected cash flows). If this is not the case, there must be an arbitrage opportunity. If a bond is selling for less than the sum of the present values of its expected cash flows, an arbitrageur will buy the bond and sell the pieces. If the bond is selling for more than the sum of the values of the pieces (individual cash flows), one could buy the pieces, package them to make a bond, and then sell the bond package to earn an arbitrage profit.

The first step in checking for arbitrage-free valuation is to value a coupon bond using the appropriate spot rates. The second step is to compare this value to the market price of the bond. If the computed value is not equal to the market price, there is an arbitrage profit to be earned by buying the lower-priced alternative (either the bond or the individual cash flows) and selling the higher-priced alternative. Of course, this assumes that there are zero-coupon bonds available that correspond to the coupon bond's cash flows.

> **Example: Arbitrage-free valuation**
>
> Consider a 6% Treasury note with 1.5 years to maturity. Spot rates (expressed as semiannual yields to maturity) are: 6 months = 5%, 1 year = 6%, and 1.5 years = 7%. If the note is selling for $992, compute the arbitrage profit, and explain how a dealer would perform the arbitrage.
>
> **Answer:**
>
> To value the note, note that the cash flows (per $1,000 par value) will be $30, $30, and $1,030 and that the semiannual discount rates are half the stated yield to maturity.
>
> Using the semiannual spot rates, the present value of the expected cash flows is:
>
> $$\text{present value using spot rates} = \frac{30}{1.025} + \frac{30}{1.03^2} + \frac{1,030}{1.035^3} = \$986.55$$
>
> This value is less than the market price of the note, so we will buy the individual cash flows (zero-coupon bonds), combine them into a 1.5-year note package, and sell the package for the market price of the note. This will result in an immediate and riskless profit of 992.00 – 986.55 = $5.45 per bond.

Determining whether a bond is over- or undervalued is a 2-step process. First, compute the value of the bond using either the spot rates or yield to maturity, remembering that both are often given as two times the semiannual discount rate(s). Second, compare this value to the market price given in the problem to see which is higher.

How a Dealer Can Generate an Arbitrage Profit

Recall that the Treasury STRIPS program allows dealers to divide Treasury bonds into their coupon payments (by date) and their maturity payments in order to create zero-coupon securities. The program also allows reconstitution of Treasury bonds/notes by putting the individual cash flows back together to create Treasury securities. Ignoring any costs of performing these transformations, the ability to separate and reconstitute Treasury securities will insure that the arbitrage-free valuation condition is met.

The STRIPS program allows for just the arbitrage we outlined previously. If the price of the bond is greater than its arbitrage-free value, a dealer could buy the individual cash flows and sell the package for the market price of the bond. If the price of the bond is less than its arbitrage-free value, an arbitrageur can make an immediate and riskless profit by purchasing the bond and selling the parts for more than the cost of the bond.

Such arbitrage opportunities and the related buying of bonds priced too low and sales of bonds priced too high will force the bond prices toward equality with their arbitrage-free values, eliminating further arbitrage opportunities.

©2009 Kaplan, Inc.

KEY CONCEPTS

LOS 64.a

To value a bond, one must:
- Estimate the amount and timing of the bond's future payments of interest and principal.
- Determine the appropriate discount rate(s).
- Calculate the sum of the present values of the bond's cash flows.

LOS 64.b

Certain bond features, including embedded options, convertibility, or floating rates, can make the estimation of future cash flows uncertain, which adds complexity to the estimation of bond values.

LOS 64.c

To compute the value of an option-free coupon bond, value the coupon payments as an annuity and add the present value of the principal repayment at maturity.

The change in value that is attributable to a change in the discount rate can be calculated as the change in the bond's present value based on the new discount rate (yield).

LOS 64.d

When interest rates (yields) do not change, a bond's price will move toward its par value as time passes and the maturity date approaches.

To compute the change in value that is attributable to the passage of time, revalue the bond with a smaller number of periods to maturity.

LOS 64.e

The value of a zero-coupon bond calculated using a semiannual discount rate, i (one-half its annual yield to maturity), is:

$$\text{bond value} = \frac{\text{maturity value}}{(1 + i)^{\text{number of years} \times 2}}$$

LOS 64.f

A Treasury spot yield curve is considered "arbitrage-free" if the present values of Treasury securities calculated using these rates are equal to equilibrium market prices.

If bond prices are not equal to their arbitrage-free values, dealers can generate arbitrage profits by buying the lower-priced alternative (either the bond or the individual cash flows) and selling the higher-priced alternative (either the individual cash flows or a package of the individual cash flows equivalent to the bond).

CONCEPT CHECKERS

1. An analyst observes a 5-year, 10% coupon bond with semiannual payments. The
    face value is £1,000. How much is each coupon payment?
    A. £25.
    B. £50.
    C. £100.

2. A 20-year, 10% annual-pay bond has a par value of $1,000. What would this
    bond be trading for if it were being priced to yield 15% as an annual rate?
    A. $685.14.
    B. $687.03.
    C. $828.39.

3. An analyst observes a 5-year, 10% semiannual-pay bond. The face amount is
    £1,000. The analyst believes that the yield to maturity for this bond should be
    15%. Based on this yield estimate, the price of this bond would be:
    A. £828.40.
    B. £1,189.53.
    C. £1,193.04.

4. Two bonds have par values of $1,000. Bond A is a 5% annual-pay, 15-year bond
    priced to yield 8% as an annual rate; the other (Bond B) is a 7.5% annual-pay,
    20-year bond priced to yield 6% as an annual rate. The values of these two
    bonds would be:

	Bond A	Bond B
A.	$740.61	$847.08
B.	$740.61	$1,172.04
C.	$743.22	$1,172.04

5. Bond A is a 15-year, 10.5% semiannual-pay bond priced with a yield to
    maturity of 8%, while Bond B is a 15-year, 7% semiannual-pay bond priced
    with the same yield to maturity. Given that both bonds have par values of
    $1,000, the prices of these two bonds would be:

	Bond A	Bond B
A.	$1,216.15	$913.54
B.	$1,216.15	$944.41
C.	$746.61	$913.54

Use the following data to answer Questions 6 through 8.

An analyst observes a 20-year, 8% option-free bond with semiannual coupons. The
required semiannual-pay yield to maturity on this bond was 8%, but suddenly it drops to
7.25%.

6. As a result of the drop, the price of this bond:
    A. will increase.
    B. will decrease.
    C. will stay the same.

©2009 Kaplan, Inc.

7.   Prior to the change in the required yield, what was the price of the bond?
     A. 92.64.
     B. 100.00.
     C. 107.85.

8.   The percentage change in the price of this bond when the rate decreased is *closest* to:
     A. 7.86%.
     B. 7.79%.
     C. 8.00%.

9.   Treasury spot rates (expressed as semiannual-pay yields to maturity) are as follows: 6 months = 4%, 1 year = 5%, 1.5 years = 6%. A 1.5-year, 4% Treasury note is trading at $965. The arbitrage trade and arbitrage profit are:
     A. buy the bond, sell the pieces, earn $7.09 per bond.
     B. sell the bond, buy the pieces, earn $7.09 per bond.
     C. sell the bond, buy the pieces, earn $7.91 per bond.

10. A $1,000, 5%, 20-year annual-pay bond has a yield of 6.5%. If the yield remains unchanged, how much will the bond value increase over the next three years?
     A. $13.62.
     B. $13.78.
     C. $13.96.

11. The value of a 17-year, zero-coupon bond with a maturity value of $100,000 and a semiannual-pay yield of 8.22% is *closest* to:
     A. $24,618.
     B. $25,425.
     C. $26,108.

ANSWERS – CONCEPT CHECKERS

1. **B** $CPN = 1,000 \times \dfrac{0.10}{2} = £50$

2. **B**   bond value $= \displaystyle\sum_{t=1}^{20} \dfrac{100}{(1+0.15)^t} + \dfrac{1,000}{(1+0.15)^{20}} = \$687.03$

   N = 20; I/Y = 15; FV = 1,000; PMT = 100; CPT → PV = –$687.03

3. **A**   N = 10; I/Y = 7.5; FV = 1,000; PMT = 50; CPT → PV = –$828.40

4. **C**   Bond A: N = 15; I/Y = 8; FV = 1,000; PMT = 50; CPT → PV = –$743.22

   Bond B: N = 20; I/Y = 6; FV = 1,000; PMT = 75; CPT → PV = –$1,172.04

   Because the coupon on Bond A is less than its required yield, the bond will sell at a discount; conversely, because the coupon on Bond B is greater than its required yield, the bond will sell at a premium.

5. **A**   Bond A: N = 15 × 2 = 30; I/Y = $\dfrac{8}{2}$ = 4; FV = 1,000; PMT = $\dfrac{105}{2}$ = 52.50;

   CPT → PV = – $1,216.15

   Bond B: N = 15 × 2 = 30; I/Y = $\dfrac{8}{2}$ = 4; FV = 1,000; PMT = $\dfrac{70}{2}$ = 35;

   CPT → PV = – $913.54

6. **A**   The price-yield relationship is inverse. If the required yield falls, the bond's price will rise, and vice versa.

7. **B**   If YTM = stated coupon rate ⇒ bond price = 100 or par value.

8. **A**   The new value is 40 = N, $\dfrac{7.25}{2}$ = I / Y, 40 = PMT, 1,000 = FV

   CPT → PV = –1,078.55, an increase of 7.855%

9. **A**   arbitrage-free value = $\dfrac{20}{1.02} + \dfrac{20}{1.025^2} + \dfrac{1020}{1.03^3} = \$972.09$

   Since the bond price ($965) is less, buy the bond and sell the pieces for an arbitrage profit of $7.09 per bond.

10. **A**   With 20 years to maturity, the value of the bond with an annual-pay yield of 6.5% is 20 = N, 50 = PMT, 1,000 = FV, 6.5 = I/Y, CPT – PV = –834.72. With 17 = N, CPT → PV = –848.34, so the value will increase $13.62.

©2009 Kaplan, Inc.

11. **B** $PMT = 0, \ N = 2 \times 17 = 34, \ I/Y = \dfrac{8.22}{2} = 4.11, \ FV = 100,000$

$CPT \rightarrow PV = -25,424.75, \ or$

$\dfrac{100,000}{(1.0411)^{34}} = \$25,424.76$

The following is a review of the Analysis of Fixed Income Investments principles designed to address the learning outcome statements set forth by CFA Institute®. This topic is also covered in:

YIELD MEASURES, SPOT RATES, AND FORWARD RATES

EXAM FOCUS

This topic review gets a little more specific about yield measures and introduces some yield measures that you will (almost certainly) need to know for the exam: current yield, yield to maturity, and yield to call. Please pay particular attention to the concept of a bond equivalent yield and how to convert various yields to a bond equivalent basis. The other important thing about the yield measures here is to understand what they are telling you so that you understand their limitations. The Level 1 exam may place as much emphasis on these issues as on actual yield calculations.

The final section of this review introduces forward rates. The relationship between forward rates and spot rates is an important one. At a minimum, you should be prepared to solve for spot rates given forward rates and to solve for an unknown forward rate given two spot rates. You should also get a firm grip on the concept of an option-adjusted spread, when it is used and how to interpret it, as well as how and when it differs from a zero-volatility spread.

LOS 65.a: Explain the sources of return from investing in a bond.

Debt securities that make explicit interest payments have **three sources of return**:

1. The periodic *coupon interest payments* made by the issuer.

2. The *recovery of principal, along with any capital gain or loss* that occurs when the bond matures, is called, or is sold.

3. *Reinvestment income*, or the income earned from reinvesting the periodic coupon payments (i.e., the compound interest on reinvested coupon payments).

The interest earned on reinvested income is an important source of return to bond investors. The uncertainty about how much reinvestment income a bondholder will realize is what we have previously addressed as *reinvestment risk*.

LOS 65.b: Compute and interpret the traditional yield measures for fixed-rate bonds and explain their limitations and assumptions.

Current yield is the simplest of all return measures, but it offers limited information. This measure looks at just one source of return: *a bond's annual interest income*—it does not consider capital gains/losses or reinvestment income. The formula for the current yield is:

$$\text{current yield} = \frac{\text{annual cash coupon payment}}{\text{bond price}}$$

©2009 Kaplan, Inc.

Example: Computing current yield

Consider a 20-year, $1,000 par value, 6% *semiannual-pay* bond that is currently trading at $802.07. Calculate the current yield.

Answer:

The *annual* cash coupon payments total:

annual cash coupon payment = par value $\times$ stated coupon rate = $1,000 $\times$ 0.06 = $60

Since the bond is trading at $802.07, the current yield is:

$$\text{current yield} = \frac{60}{802.07} = 0.0748, \text{ or } 7.48\%.$$

Note that current yield is based on *annual* coupon interest so that it is the same for a semiannual-pay and annual-pay bond with the same coupon rate and price.

Yield to maturity (YTM) is an annualized internal rate of return, based on a bond's price and its promised cash flows. For a bond with semiannual coupon payments, the yield to maturity is stated as two times the semiannual internal rate of return implied by the bond's price. The formula that relates the bond price (including accrued interest) to YTM for a semiannual coupon bond is:

$$\text{bond price} = \frac{CPN_1}{\left(1 + \frac{YTM}{2}\right)} + \frac{CPN_2}{\left(1 + \frac{YTM}{2}\right)^2} + \cdots + \frac{CPN_{2N} + Par}{\left(1 + \frac{YTM}{2}\right)^{2N}}$$

where:
bond price = full price including accrued interest
CPN_t = the (semiannual) coupon payment received after t semiannual periods
N = number of years to maturity
YTM = yield to maturity

YTM and price contain the same information. That is, given the YTM, you can calculate the price and given the price, you can calculate the YTM.

We cannot easily solve for YTM from the bond price. Given a bond price and the coupon payment amount, we could solve it by trial and error, trying different values of YTM until the present value of the expected cash flows is equal to price. Fortunately, your calculator will do exactly the same thing, only faster. It uses a trial and error algorithm to find the discount rate that makes the two sides of the pricing formula equal.

Study Session 16

Example: Computing YTM

Consider a 20-year, $1,000 par value bond, with a 6% coupon rate (semiannual payments) with a full price of $802.07. Calculate the YTM.

Answer:

Using a financial calculator, you'd find the YTM on this bond as follows:

$PV = -802.07$; $N = 20 \times 2 = 40$; $FV = 1{,}000$; $PMT = 60/2 = 30$; $CPT \rightarrow I/Y = 4.00$

4% is the semiannual discount rate, $\dfrac{YTM}{2}$ in the formula, so the YTM = $2 \times 4\% = 8\%$.

Note that the signs of PMT and FV are positive, and the sign of PV is negative; you must do this to avoid the dreaded "Error 5" message on the TI calculator. If you get the "Error 5" message, you can assume you have not assigned a negative value to the price (PV) of the bond and a positive sign to the cash flows to be received from the bond.

There are certain relationships that exist between different yield measures, depending on whether a bond is trading at par, at a discount, or at a premium. These relationships are shown in Figure 1.

Figure 1: Par, Discount, and Premium Bond

Bond Selling at:	Relationship
Par	coupon rate = current yield = yield to maturity
Discount	coupon rate < current yield < yield to maturity
Premium	coupon rate > current yield > yield to maturity

These conditions will hold in all cases; every discount bond will have a nominal yield (coupon rate) that is less than its current yield and a current yield that is less than its YTM.

The yield to maturity calculated in the previous example (2 × the semiannual discount rate) is referred to as a **bond equivalent yield** (BEY), and we will also refer to it as a semiannual YTM or semiannual-pay YTM. If you are given yields that are identified as BEY, you will know that you must divide by two to get the semiannual discount rate. With bonds that make annual coupon payments, we can calculate an **annual-pay yield to maturity**, which is simply the internal rate of return for the expected annual cash flows.

©2009 Kaplan, Inc.

Example: Calculating YTM for annual coupon bonds

Consider an annual-pay 20-year, $1,000 par value, with a 6% coupon rate and a full price of $802.07. Calculate the *annual-pay YTM*.

Answer:

The relation between the price and the annual-pay YTM on this bond is:

$$802.07 = \sum_{t=1}^{20} \frac{60}{(1+\text{YTM})^t} + \frac{1,000}{(1+\text{YTM})^{20}} \Rightarrow \text{YTM} = 8.019\%.$$

Here we have separated the coupon cash flows and the principal repayment.

The calculator solution is:

PV = −802.07; N = 20; FV = 1,000; PMT = 60; CPT → I/Y = 8.019; 8.019% is the annual-pay YTM.

Use a discount rate of 8.019%, and you'll find the present value of the bond's future cash flows (annual coupon payments and the recovery of principal) will equal the current market price of the bond. *The discount rate is the bond's YTM.*

For zero-coupon Treasury bonds, the convention is to quote the yields as BEYs (semiannual-pay YTMs).

Example: Calculating YTM for zero-coupon bonds

A 5-year Treasury STRIP is priced at $768. Calculate the semiannual-pay YTM and annual-pay YTM.

Answer:

The direct calculation method, based on the geometric mean covered in Quantitative Methods, is:

$$\text{the semiannual-pay YTM or BEY} = \left[\left(\frac{1,000}{768} \right)^{\frac{1}{10}} - 1 \right] \times 2 = 5.35\%.$$

$$\text{the annual-pay YTM} = \left(\frac{1,000}{768} \right)^{\frac{1}{5}} - 1 = 5.42\%.$$

Using the TVM calculator functions:

PV = –768; FV = 1,000; PMT = 0; N = 10; CPT → I/Y = 2.675% × 2 = 5.35% for the semiannual-pay YTM, and PV = –768; FV = 1,000; PMT = 0; N = 5; CPT → I/Y = 5.42% for the annual-pay YTM.

The annual-pay YTM of 5.42% means that $768 earning compound interest of 5.42%/year would grow to $1,000 in five years.

The **yield to call** is used to calculate the yield on callable bonds that are selling at a premium to par. For bonds trading at a premium to par, the *yield to call* may be less than the yield to maturity. This can be the case when the call price is below the current market price.

The calculation of the yield to call is the same as the calculation of yield to maturity, except that the *call price is substituted* for the par value in FV and the *number of semiannual periods until the call date is substituted* for periods to maturity, N. When a bond has a period of call protection, we calculate the **yield to first call** over the period until the bond may first be called, and use the first call price in the calculation as FV. In a similar manner, we can calculate the yield to any subsequent call date using the appropriate call price.

If the bond contains a provision for a call at *par* at some time in the future, we can calculate the *yield to first par call* using the number of years until the par call date and par for the maturity payment. If you have a good understanding of the yield to maturity measure, the YTC is not a difficult calculation; just be very careful about the number of years to the call and the call price for that date. An example will illustrate the calculation of these yield measures.

Example: Computing the YTM, YTC, and yield to first par call

Consider a 20-year, 10% semiannual-pay bond with a full price of 112 that can be called in five years at 102 and called at par in seven years. Calculate the YTM, YTC, and yield to first par call.

 Professor's Note: Bond prices are often expressed as a percent of par (e.g., 100 = par).

Answer:

The **YTM** can be calculated as: N = 40; PV = –112; PMT = 5; FV = 100; CPT → I/Y = 4.361% × 2 = 8.72% = YTM.

To compute the **yield to first call** (YTFC), we substitute the number of semiannual periods until the first call date (10) for N, and the first call price (102) for FV, as follows:

N = **10**; PV = –112; PMT = 5; **FV = 102**;

CPT → I/Y = 3.71% and 2 × 3.71 = 7.42% = YTFC

To calculate the **yield to first par call** (YTFPC), we will substitute the number of semiannual periods until the first par call date (14) for N and par (100) for FV as follows:

N = **14**; PV = –112; PMT = 5; **FV = 100**;

CPT → I/Y = 3.873% × 2 = 7.746% = YTFPC

Note that the yield to call, 7.42%, is significantly lower than the yield to maturity, 8.72%. If the bond were trading at a discount to par value, there would be no reason to calculate the yield to call. For a discount bond, the YTC will be higher than the YTM since the bond will appreciate more rapidly with the call to at least par and, perhaps, an even greater call price. Bond yields are quoted on a yield to call basis when the YTC is less than the YTM, which can only be the case for bonds trading at a premium to the call price.

The **yield to worst** is the worst yield outcome of any that are possible given the call provisions of the bond. In the above example, the yield to first call is less than the YTM and less than the yield to first par call. So the worst possible outcome is a yield of 7.42%; the yield to first call is the *yield to worst*.

The **yield to refunding** refers to a specific situation where a bond is currently callable and current rates make calling the issue attractive to the issuer, but where the bond covenants contain provisions giving protection from refunding until some future date. The calculation of the yield to refunding is just like that of YTM or YTC. The difference here is that the yield to refunding would use the call price, but the date (and therefore the number of periods used in the calculation) is the date when refunding protection ends. Recall that bonds that are callable, but not currently refundable, can be called using funds from sources other than the issuance of a lower coupon bond.

The **yield to put** (YTP) is used if a bond has a put feature and is selling at a discount. The yield to put will likely be higher than the yield to maturity. The yield to put calculation is just like the yield to maturity with the number of semiannual periods until the put date as N, and the put price as FV.

Example: Computing YTM and YTP

Consider a 3-year, 6%, $1,000 *semiannual-pay* bond. The bond is selling for a full price of $925.40. The first put opportunity is at par in two years. Calculate the YTM and the YTP.

Answer:

Yield to maturity is calculated as:

N = 6; FV = 1,000; PMT = 30; PV = –925.40; CPT → I/Y = 4.44 × 2 = 8.88% = YTM

Yield to put is calculated as:

N = 4; FV = 1,000; PMT = 30; PV = –925.40; CPT → I/Y = 5.11 × 2 = 10.22% = YTP

In this example, the yield to put is higher than the YTM and, therefore, would be the appropriate yield to look at for this bond.

The **cash flow yield** (CFY) is used for mortgage-backed securities and other amortizing asset-backed securities that have monthly cash flows. In many cases, the amount of the principal repayment can be greater than the amount required to amortize the loan over its original life. Cash flow yield (CFY) incorporates an assumed schedule of monthly cash flows based on assumptions as to how prepayments are likely to occur. Once we have projected the monthly cash flows, we can calculate CFY as a *monthly* internal rate of return based on the market price of the security.

Professor's Note: It is unlikely that you will be required to actually calculate a CFY on the exam and more likely that you could be required to interpret one. If you need to calculate a CFY, just use the cash flow keys, put the price of the security as a negative value as CF_0, enter the monthly cash flows sequentially as CFn's, and solve for IRR, which will be a monthly rate.

The following formula is used to convert a (monthly) CFY into bond equivalent form:

$$\text{bond equivalent yield} = \left[\left(1 + \text{monthly CFY} \right)^6 - 1 \right] \times 2$$

Here, we have converted the monthly yield into a semiannual yield and then doubled it to make it equivalent to a semiannual-pay YTM or bond equivalent yield.

A limitation of the CFY measure is that actual prepayment rates may differ from those assumed in the calculation of CFY.

©2009 Kaplan, Inc.

The Assumptions and Limitations of Traditional Yield Measures

The primary *limitation of the yield to maturity measure* is that it does not tell us the compound rate of return that we will realize on a fixed-income investment over its life. This is because we do not know the rate of interest we will realize on the reinvested coupon payments (the reinvestment rate). Reinvestment income can be a significant part of the overall return on a bond. As noted earlier, the uncertainty about the return on reinvested cash flows is referred to as *reinvestment risk*. It is higher for bonds with higher coupon rates, other things equal, and potentially higher for callable bonds as well.

The realized yield on a bond is the actual compound return that was earned on the initial investment. It is usually computed at the end of the investment horizon. For a bond to have a *realized yield* equal to its YTM, all cash flows prior to maturity must be reinvested at the YTM, and the bond must be held until maturity. If the "average" reinvestment rate is below the YTM, the realized yield will be below the YTM. For this reason, it is often stated that: *The yield to maturity assumes cash flows will be reinvested at the YTM and assumes that the bond will be held until maturity.*

The other internal rate of return measures, YTC and YTP, suffer from the same shortcomings since they are calculated like YTMs and do not account for reinvestment income. The CFY measure is also an internal rate of return measure and can differ greatly from the realized yield if reinvestment rates are low, since scheduled principal payments and prepayments must be reinvested along with the interest payments.

LOS 65.c: Explain the importance of reinvestment income in generating the yield computed at the time of purchase, calculate the amount of income required to generate that yield, and discuss the factors that affect reinvestment risk.

Reinvestment income is important because if the reinvestment rate is less than the YTM, the realized yield on the bond will be less than the YTM. The realized yield will always be between the YTM and the assumed reinvestment rate.

If a bondholder holds a bond until maturity and reinvests all coupon interest payments, the total amount generated by the bond over its life has three components:

1. Bond principal.

2. Coupon interest.

3. Interest on reinvested coupons.

Once we calculate the total amount needed for a particular level of compound return over a bond's life, we can subtract the principal and coupon payments to determine the amount of reinvestment income necessary to achieve the target yield. An example will illustrate this calculation.

Example: Calculating required reinvestment income for a bond

If you purchase a 6%, 10-year Treasury bond at par, how much reinvestment income must be generated over its life to provide the investor with a compound return of 6% on a semiannual basis?

Answer:

Assuming the bond has a par value of $100, we first calculate the total value that must be generated ten years (20 semiannual periods) from now as:

$$100(1.03)^{20} = \$180.61$$

There are 20 bond coupons of $3 each, totaling $60, and a payment of $100 of principal at maturity.

Therefore, the required reinvestment income over the life of the bond is:

$$180.61 - 100 - 60 = \$20.61$$

Professor's Note: If we had purchased the bond at a premium or discount, we would still use the purchase price (which would not equal 100) and the required compound return to calculate the total future dollars required, and then subtract the maturity value and the total coupon payments to get the required reinvestment income.

Factors That Affect Reinvestment Risk

Other things being equal, a coupon bond's **reinvestment risk** will *increase* with:

- *Higher coupons*—because there's more cash flow to reinvest.
- *Longer maturities*—because more of the total value of the investment is in the coupon cash flows (and interest on coupon cash flows).

In both cases, the amount of reinvested income will play a bigger role in determining the bond's total return and, therefore, introduce more reinvestment risk. A noncallable zero-coupon bond has no reinvestment risk over its life because there are no cash flows to reinvest prior to maturity.

©2009 Kaplan, Inc.

LOS 65.d: Compute and interpret the bond equivalent yield of an annual-pay bond and the annual-pay yield of a semiannual-pay bond.

This LOS requires that you be able to turn a semiannual return into an annual return, and an annual return into a semiannual return.

> **Example: Comparing bonds with different coupon frequencies**
>
> Suppose that a corporation has a semiannual coupon bond trading in the United States with a YTM of 6.25%, and an annual coupon bond trading in Europe with a YTM = 6.30%. Which bond has the greater yield?
>
> **Answer:**
>
> To determine the answer, we can convert the yield on *the annual-pay bond* to a (semiannual-pay) bond equivalent yield. That is:
>
> $$\text{BEY of an annual-pay bond} = [(1 + \text{annual YTM})^{\frac{1}{2}} - 1] \times 2$$
>
> Thus, the BEY of the 6.30% annual-pay bond is:
>
> $$[(1 + 0.0630)^{0.5} - 1] \times 2 = [1.031 - 1] \times 2 = 0.031 \times 2 = 0.062 = 6.2\%$$
>
> The 6.25% semiannual-pay bond provides the better (bond equivalent) yield.
>
> Alternatively, we could convert the YTM of the semiannual-pay bond (which is a bond equivalent yield) to an equivalent annual-pay basis. The equivalent annual yield (EAY—*sometimes known as the effective annual yield*) to the 6.25% semiannual-pay YTM is:
>
> $$\text{equivalent annual yield} = \left(1 + \frac{0.0625}{2}\right)^{2} - 1 = 0.0635 \rightarrow 6.35\%$$

The EAY of the semiannual-pay bond is 6.35%, which is greater than the 6.3% for the annual-pay bond. Therefore, the semiannual-pay bond has a greater yield as long as we put the yields on an equivalent basis, calculating both as annual yields or calculating both as bond equivalent yields (semiannual yields × 2).

LOS 65.e: Describe the methodology for computing the theoretical Treasury spot rate curve and compute the value of a bond using spot rates.

The par yield curve gives the YTMs of bonds currently trading near their par values (YTM ≈ coupon rate) for various maturities. Here, we need to use these yields to get the theoretical Treasury spot rate curve by a process called **bootstrapping**.

The method of bootstrapping can be a little confusing, so let's first get the main idea and then go through a more realistic and detailed example. The general idea is that we will solve for spot rates by knowing the prices of coupon bonds. We always know one spot rate to begin with and then calculate the spot rate for the next longer period. When we know two spot rates, we can get the third based on the market price of a bond with three cash flows by using the spot rates to get the present values of the first two cash flows.

As an example of this method, consider that we know the prices and yields of three annual-pay bonds as shown in Figure 2. All three bonds are trading at par or $1,000.

Figure 2: Prices and Yield for Three Annual-Pay Bonds

Maturity	Coupon	Yield	Price
1 year	3%	3%	$1,000
2 years	4%	4%	$1,000
3 years	5%	5%	$1,000

Since the 1-year bond makes only one payment (it's an annual-pay bond) of $1,030 at maturity, the 1-year spot rate is 3%, the yield on this single payment. The 2-year bond makes two payments, a $40 coupon in one year and a $1,040 payment at maturity in two years. Since the spot rate to discount the 2-year bond's first cash flow is 3%, and since we know that the sum of the present values of the bond's cash flows must equal its (no-arbitrage) price of $1,000, we can write:

$$\frac{40}{1.03} + \frac{1,040}{(1 + \text{2-year spot rate})^2} = \$1,000$$

Based on this we can solve for the 2-year spot rate as follows:

1. $\dfrac{1,040}{(1 + \text{2-year spot})^2} = 1,000 - \dfrac{40}{1.03} = 1,000 - 38.83 = 961.17$

2. $\dfrac{1,040}{961.17} = (1 + \text{2-year spot})^2 = 1.082$

3. $\text{2-year spot} = (1.082)^{\frac{1}{2}} - 1 = 0.04019 = 4.019\%$

©2009 Kaplan, Inc.

Now that we have both the 1-year and 2-year spot rates, we can use the cash flows and price of the 3-year bond to write:

$$\frac{50}{1.03} + \frac{50}{(1.04019)^2} + \frac{1,050}{(1 + 3\text{-year spot})^3} = 1,000$$

And solve for the 3-year spot rate:

$$1,000 - \frac{50}{1.03} - \frac{50}{(1.04019)^2} = \frac{1,050}{(1 + 3\text{-year spot})^3}$$

$$1,000 - 48.54 - 46.21 = \frac{1,050}{(1 + 3\text{-year spot})^3}$$

$$905.25 = \frac{1,050}{(1 + 3\text{-year spot})^3}$$

$$\left(\frac{1,050}{905.25}\right)^{\frac{1}{3}} - 1 = 3\text{-year spot} = 0.05069 = 5.069\%$$

So we can state that:

$$\frac{50}{1.03} + \frac{50}{(1.04019)^2} + \frac{1,050}{(1.05069)^3} = \$1,000$$

We have just solved for the 2-year and 3-year spot rates by the method of bootstrapping.

In practice, Treasury bonds pay semiannually, and their YTMs are semiannual-pay YTMs. The next example illustrates the method of bootstrapping when coupons are paid semiannually.

Consider the yields on coupon Treasury bonds trading at par given in Figure 3. YTM for the bonds is expressed as a bond equivalent yield (semiannual-pay YTM).

Figure 3: Par Yields for Three Semiannual-Pay Bonds

Maturity	YTM	Coupon	Price
6 months	5%	5%	100
1 year	6%	6%	100
18 months	7%	7%	100

The bond with six months left to maturity has a semiannual discount rate of $0.05/2 = 0.025 = 2.5\%$ or 5% on an annual BEY basis. Since this bond will only make one payment of 102.5 in six months, the YTM is the spot rate for cash flows to be received six months from now.

The bootstrapping process proceeds from this point using the fact that the 6-month annualized spot rate is 5% together with the price/YTM information on the 1-year bond. We will use the formula for valuing a bond using spot rates that we covered earlier.

Noting that the 1-year bond will make two payments, one in six months of 3.0 and one in one year of 103.0, and that the appropriate spot rate to discount the coupon payment (which comes six months from now), we can write:

$$\frac{3}{1.025} + \frac{103}{\left(1 + \frac{S_{1.0}}{2}\right)^2} = 100, \text{ where } S_{1.0} \text{ is the annualized 1-year spot rate,}$$

and solve for $\frac{S_{1.0}}{2}$ as: $\dfrac{103}{\left(1 + \frac{S_{1.0}}{2}\right)^2} = 100 - \dfrac{3}{1.025} = 100 - 2.927 = 97.073$

$$\frac{103}{97.073} = \left(1 + \frac{S_{1.0}}{2}\right)^2, \text{ so } \sqrt{\frac{103}{97.073}} - 1 = \frac{S_{1.0}}{2}$$

$$= 0.030076 \text{ and } S_{1.0} = 2 \times 0.030076 = 0.060152 = 6.0152\%$$

Now that we have the 6-month and 1-year spot rates, we can use this information and the price of the 18-month bond to set the bond price equal to the value of the bond's cash flows as:

$$\frac{3.5}{1.025} + \frac{3.5}{(1.030076)^2} + \frac{103.5}{\left(1 + \frac{S_{1.5}}{2}\right)^3} = 100,$$

where $S_{1.5}$ is the annualized 1.5-year spot rate, and solve for $\frac{S_{1.5}}{2}$

$$\frac{103.5}{\left(1 + \frac{S_{1.5}}{2}\right)^3} = 100 - \frac{3.5}{1.025} - \frac{3.5}{(1.030076)^2} = 100 - 3.415 - 3.30 = 93.285$$

$$\frac{103.5}{93.285} = \left(1 + \frac{S_{1.5}}{2}\right)^3, \text{ so } \left(\frac{103.5}{93.285}\right)^{\frac{1}{3}} - 1 = \frac{S_{1.5}}{2}$$

©2009 Kaplan, Inc.

To summarize the method of bootstrapping spot rates from the par yield curve:

1. Begin with the 6-month spot rate.

2. Set the value of the 1-year bond equal to the present value of the cash flows with the 1-year spot rate divided by two as the only unknown.

3. Solve for the 1-year spot rate.

4. Use the 6-month and 1-year spot rates and equate the present value of the cash flows of the 1.5 year bond equal to its price, with the 1.5 year spot rate as the only unknown.

5. Solve for the 1.5-year spot rate.

 Professor's Note: You are responsible for "describing" this methodology, not for "computing" theoretical spot rates.

Example: Valuing a bond using spot rates

Given the following spot rates (in BEY form):

> 0.5 years = 4%
> 1.0 years = 5%
> 1.5 years = 6%

Calculate the value of a 1.5 year, 8% Treasury bond.

Answer:

Simply lay out the cash flows and discount by the spot rates, which are one-half the quoted rates since they are quoted in BEY form.

$$\frac{4}{\left(1+\frac{0.04}{2}\right)^1} + \frac{4}{\left(1+\frac{0.05}{2}\right)^2} + \frac{104}{\left(1+\frac{0.06}{2}\right)^3} = 102.9$$

or, with the TVM function:

N = 1; PMT = 0; I/Y = 2; FV = 4; CPT → PV = –3.92
N = 2; PMT = 0; I/Y = 2.5; FV = 4; CPT → PV = –3.81
N = 3; PMT = 0; I/Y = 3; FV = 104; CPT → PV = –95.17

Add these values together to get 102.9.

LOS 65.f: Differentiate between the nominal spread, the zero-volatility spread, and the option-adjusted spread.

The **nominal spread** is the simplest of the spread measures to use and to understand. It is simply an issue's YTM minus the YTM of a Treasury security of similar maturity. Therefore, the use of the nominal spread suffers from the same limitations as the YTM. YTM uses a single discount rate to value the cash flows, so it *ignores the shape of the spot yield curve.* In fact, YTM for a coupon bond is theoretically correct only to the extent that the spot rate curve is flat.

The Zero-Volatility Spread

One way to get a bond's nominal spread to Treasuries would be to add different amounts to the yield of a comparable Treasury bond, and value the bond with those YTMs. The amount added to the Treasury yield that produces a bond value equal to the market price of the bond must be the nominal yield spread.

This may seem like an odd way to get the spread, but it makes sense when you see how the **zero-volatility spread**, or static spread, is calculated. The zero-volatility spread (*Z*-spread) is the equal amount that we must add to each rate on the Treasury spot yield curve in order to make the present value of the risky bond's cash flows equal to its market price. Instead of measuring the spread to YTM, the zero-volatility spread measures the spread to Treasury spot rates necessary to produce a spot rate curve that "correctly" prices a risky bond (i.e., produces its market price).

For a risky bond, the value obtained from discounting the expected cash flows at Treasury spot rates will be too high because the Treasury spot rates are lower than those appropriate for a risky bond. In order to value it correctly, we have to increase each of the Treasury spot rates by some equal amount so that the present value of the risky bond's cash flows discounted at the (increased) spot rates equals the market value of the bond. The following example will illustrate the process for calculating the *Z*-spread.

©2009 Kaplan, Inc.

Example: Zero-volatility spread

1-, 2-, and 3-year spot rates on Treasuries are 4%, 8.167%, and 12.377%, respectively. Consider a 3-year, 9% annual coupon corporate bond trading at 89.464. The YTM is 13.50%, and the YTM of a 3-year Treasury is 12%. Compute the nominal spread and the zero-volatility spread of the corporate bond.

Answer:

The *nominal spread* is:

$$\text{nominal spread} = \text{YTM}_{\text{Bond}} - \text{YTM}_{\text{Treasury}} = 13.50 - 12.00 = 1.50\%.$$

To compute the Z-spread, set the present value of the bond's cash flows equal to today's market price. Discount each cash flow at the appropriate zero-coupon bond spot rate *plus* a fixed spread equals ZS. Solve for ZS in the following equation and you have the Z-spread:

$$89.464 = \frac{9}{(1.04 + ZS)^1} + \frac{9}{(1.08167 + ZS)^2} + \frac{109}{(1.12377 + ZS)^3} \Rightarrow$$

$$ZS = 1.67\% \text{ or } 167 \text{ basis points}$$

Note that this spread is found by trial-and-error. In other words, pick a number "ZS," plug it into the right-hand side of the equation, and see if the result equals 89.464. If the right-hand side equals the left, then you have found the Z-spread. If not, pick another "ZS" and start over.

 Professor's Note: This is not a calculation you are expected to make; this example is to help you understand how a Z-spread differs from a nominal spread.

There are two primary factors that influence the difference between the nominal spread and the Z-spread for a security.

- The steeper the benchmark spot rate curve, the greater the difference between the two spread measures. There is no difference between the nominal and Z-spread when the spot yield curve is flat. If the spot yield curve is upward sloping, the Z-spread is larger than the nominal spread. The Z-spread is less than the nominal spread when the spot yield curve is negatively sloped.
- The earlier bond principal is paid, the greater the difference between the two spread measures. For a given positively sloped yield curve, an amortizing security, such as an MBS, will have a greater difference between its Z-spread and nominal spread than a coupon bond will.

The **option-adjusted spread** (OAS) measure is used when a bond has embedded options. A callable bond, for example, must have a greater yield than an identical option-free bond, and a greater nominal spread or Z-spread. Without accounting for the value of the options, these spread measures will suggest the bond is a great value when, in fact, the additional yield is compensation for call risk. Loosely speaking, the *option-adjusted spread* takes the option yield component out of the Z-spread measure; the option-adjusted spread is the spread to the Treasury spot rate curve that the bond would have if it were option-free. The OAS is the spread for non-option characteristics like credit risk, liquidity risk, and interest rate risk.

 Professor's Note: The actual method of calculation is reserved for Level 2; for our purposes, however, an understanding of what the OAS is will be sufficient.

LOS 65.g: Describe how the option-adjusted spread accounts for the option cost in a bond with an embedded option.

If we calculate an option-adjusted spread for a callable bond, it will be less than the bond's Z-spread. The difference is the extra yield required to compensate for the call option. Calling that extra yield the **option cost**, we can write:

Z-spread – OAS = option cost in percent

> **Example: Cost of an embedded option**
>
> Suppose you learn that a bond is callable and has an OAS of 135bp. You also know that similar bonds have a Z-spread of 167 basis points. Compute the cost of the embedded option.
>
> **Answer:**
>
> The option cost = Z-spread – OAS = 167 – 135 = 32 basis points.

For embedded short calls (e.g., callable bonds): option cost > 0 (you receive compensation for writing the option to the issuer) → OAS < Z-spread. In other words, you *require more yield on the callable bond* than for an option-free bond.

For embedded puts (e.g., putable bonds), option cost < 0 (i.e., you must pay for the option) → OAS > Z-spread. In other words, you *require less yield on the putable bond* than for an option-free bond.

LOS 65.h: Explain a forward rate and compute spot rates from forward rates, forward rates from spot rates, and the value of a bond using forward rates.

A **forward rate** is a borrowing/lending rate for a loan to be made at some future date. The notation used must identify both the length of the lending/borrowing period and when in the future the money will be loaned/borrowed. Thus, $_1f_1$ is the rate for a 1-year loan one year from now and $_1f_2$ is the rate for a 1-year loan to be made two years from

©2009 Kaplan, Inc.

now, and so on. Rather than introduce a separate notation, we can represent the current 1-year rate as $_1f_0$. To get the present values of a bond's expected cash flows, we need to discount each cash flow by the forward rates for each of the periods until it is received. (The present value of $1 to be received in period n, discounted by the forward rates for periods 1 to n, is called the **forward discount factor** for period n.)

The Relationship Between Short-Term Forward Rates and Spot Rates

The idea here is that *borrowing for three years at the 3-year rate or borrowing for 1-year periods, three years in succession, should have the same cost.*

This relation is illustrated as $(1 + S_3)^3 = (1 + {_1f_0})(1 + {_1f_1})(1 + {_1f_2})$ and the reverse as $S_3 = [(1 + {_1f_0})(1 + {_1f_1})(1 + {_1f_2})]^{1/3} - 1$, which is the geometric mean we covered in Quantitative Methods.

Example: Computing spot rates from forward rates

If the current 1-year rate is 2%, the 1-year forward rate $(_1f_1)$ is 3% and the 2-year forward rate $(_1f_2)$ is 4%, what is the 3-year spot rate?

Answer:

$$S_3 = [(1.02)(1.03)(1.04)]^{1/3} - 1 = 2.997\%$$

This can be interpreted to mean that a dollar compounded at 2.997% for three years would produce the same ending value as a dollar that earns compound interest of 2% the first year, 3% the next year, and 4% for the third year.

 Professor's Note: You can get a very good approximation of the 3-year spot rate with the simple average of the forward rates. In the previous example we got 2.997% and the simple average of the three annual rates is $\dfrac{2+3+4}{3} = 3\%$.

Forward Rates Given Spot Rates

We can use the same relationship we used to calculate spot rates from forward rates to calculate forward rates from spot rates.

Our basic relation between forward rates and spot rates (for two periods) is:

$$(1 + S_2)^2 = (1 + {_1f_0})(1 + {_1f_1})$$

Which, again, tells us that an investment has the same expected yield (borrowing has the same expected cost) whether we invest (borrow) for two periods at the 2-period spot rate, S_2, or for one period at the current rate, S_1, and for the next period at the expected forward rate, $_1f_1$. Clearly, given two of these rates, we can solve for the other.

Example: Computing a forward rate from spot rates

The 2-period spot rate, S_2, is 8% and the current 1-period (spot) rate is 4% (this is both S_1 and $_1f_0$). Calculate the forward rate for one period, one period from now, $_1f_1$.

Answer:

The following figure illustrates the problem.

Finding a Forward Rate

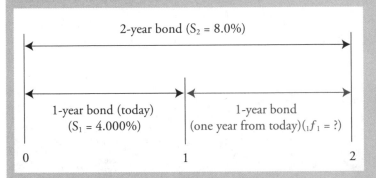

From our original equality, $(1 + S_2)^2 = (1 + S_1)(1 + _1f_1)$, we can get $\dfrac{(1+S_2)^2}{(1+S_1)} - 1 = {_1f_1}$

or, since we know that both choices have the same payoff in two years:

$$(1.08)^2 = (1.04)(1 + {_1f_1})$$

$$(1 + {_1f_1}) = \frac{(1.08)^2}{(1.04)}$$

$$_1f_1 = \frac{(1.08)^2}{(1.04)} - 1 = \frac{1.1664}{1.04} - 1 = 12.154\%$$

In other words, investors are willing to accept 4.0% on the 1-year bond today (when they could get 8.0% on the 2-year bond today) only because they can get 12.154% on a 1-year bond one year from today. This future rate that can be locked in today is a *forward rate*.

Similarly, we can back other forward rates out of the spot rates. We know that:

$$(1 + S_3)^3 = (1 + S_1)(1 + {_1f_1})(1 + {_1f_2})$$

©2009 Kaplan, Inc.

And that:

$$(1 + S_2)^2 = (1 + S_1)(1 + {}_1f_1), \text{ so we can write } (1 + S_3)^3 = (1 + S_2)^2(1 + {}_1f_2)$$

This last equation says that investing for three years at the 3-year spot rate should produce the same ending value as investing for two years at the 2-year spot rate and then for a third year at ${}_1f_2$, the 1-year forward rate, two years from now.

Solving for the forward rate, ${}_1f_2$, we get:

$$\frac{(1+S_3)^3}{(1+S_2)^2} - 1 = {}_1f_2$$

Example: Forward rates from spot rates

Let's extend the previous example to three periods. The current 1-year spot rate is 4.0%, the current 2-year spot rate is 8.0%, and the current 3-year spot rate is 12.0%. Calculate the 1-year forward rates one and two years from now.

Answer:

We know the following relation must hold:

$$(1 + S_2)^2 = (1 + S_1)(1 + {}_1f_1)$$

We can use it to solve for the 1-year forward rate one year from now:

$$(1.08)^2 = (1.04)(1 + {}_1f_1), \text{ so } {}_1f_1 = \frac{(1.08)^2}{(1.04)} - 1 = 12.154\%$$

We also know that the relations:

$$(1 + S_3)^3 = (1 + S_1)(1 + {}_1f_1)(1 + {}_1f_2)$$

and, equivalently $(1 + S_3)^3 = (1 + S_2)^2(1 + {}_1f_2)$ must hold.

Substituting values for S_3 and S_2, we have:

$$(1.12)^3 = (1.08)^2 \times (1 + {}_1f_2)$$

so that the 1-year forward rate two years from now is:

$$_1f_2 = \frac{(1.12)^3}{(1.08)^2} - 1 = 20.45\%$$

To verify these results, we can check our relations by calculating:

$$S_3 = [1(1.04)(1.12154)(1.2045)]^{1/3} - 1 = 12.00\%$$

This may all seem a bit complicated, but the basic relation, that borrowing for successive periods at 1-period rates should have the same cost as borrowing at multiperiod spot rates, can be summed up as:

$$(1 + S_2)^2 = (1 + S_1)(1 + {}_1f_1) \text{ for two periods, and } (1 + S_3)^3 = (1 + S_2)^2(1 + {}_1f_2) \text{ for three periods.}$$

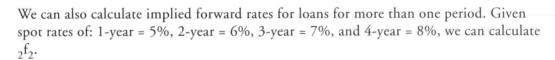

Professor's Note: Simple averages also give decent approximations for calculating forward rates from spot rates. In the above example, we had spot rates of 4% for one year and 8% for two years. Two years at 8% is 16%, so if the first-year rate is 4%, the second-year rate is close to 16 − 4 = 12% (actual is 12.154). Given a 2-year spot rate of 8% and a 3-year spot rate of 12%, we could approximate the 1-year forward rate from time two to time three as (3 × 12) − (2 × 8) = 20. That may be close enough (actual is 20.45) to answer a multiple choice question and, in any case, serves as a good check to make sure the exact rate you calculate is reasonable.

We can also calculate implied forward rates for loans for more than one period. Given spot rates of: 1-year = 5%, 2-year = 6%, 3-year = 7%, and 4-year = 8%, we can calculate $_2f_2$.

The implied forward rate on a 2-year loan two years from now is:

$$\left[\frac{(1+S_4)^4}{(1+S_2)^2}\right]^{1/2} - 1 = \left(\frac{1.08^4}{1.06^2}\right)^{1/2} - 1 = 10.04\%.$$

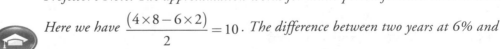

Professor's Note: The approximation works for multi-period forward rates as well. Here we have $\frac{(4\times8 - 6\times2)}{2} = 10$. The difference between two years at 6% and four years at 8% is approximately 20%. Since that is for two years, we divide by two to get an annual rate of approximately 10%.

©2009 Kaplan, Inc.

Valuing a Bond Using Forward Rates

Example: Computing a bond value using forward rates

The current 1-year rate $(_1f_0)$ is 4%, the 1-year forward rate for lending from time = 1 to time = 2 is $_1f_1$ = 5%, and the 1-year forward rate for lending from time = 2 to time = 3 is $_1f_2$ = 6%. Value a 3-year annual-pay bond with a 5% coupon and a par value of $1,000.

Answer:

$$\text{bond value} = \frac{50}{1 + _1f_0} + \frac{50}{(1 + _1f_0)(1 + _1f_1)} + \frac{1{,}050}{(1 + _1f_0)(1 + _1f_1)(1 + _1f_2)} =$$

$$\frac{50}{1.04} + \frac{50}{(1.04)(1.05)} + \frac{1{,}050}{(1.04)(1.05)(1.06)} = \$1{,}000.98$$

 Professor's Note: If you think this looks a little like valuing a bond using spot rates, as we did for arbitrage-free valuation, you are right. The discount factors are equivalent to spot rate discount factors.

KEY CONCEPTS

LOS 65.a
Three sources of return to a coupon bond:
- Coupon interest payments.
- Reinvestment income on the coupon cash flows.
- Capital gain or loss on the principal value.

LOS 65.b
Yield to maturity (YTM) for a semiannual-pay coupon bond is calculated as two times the semiannual discount rate that makes the present value of the bond's promised cash flows equal to its market price plus accrued interest. For an annual-pay coupon bond, the YTM is simply the annual discount rate that makes the present value of the bond's promised cash flows equal to its market price plus accrued interest.

The current yield for a bond is its annual interest payment divided by its market price.

Yield to call (put) is calculated as a YTM but with the number of periods until the call (put) and the call (put) price substituted for the number of periods to maturity and the maturity value.

The cash flow yield is a monthly internal rate of return based on a presumed prepayment rate and the current market price of a mortgage-backed or asset-backed security.

These yield measures are limited by their common assumptions that: (1) all cash flows can be discounted at the same rate; (2) the bond will be held to maturity, with all coupons reinvested to maturity at a rate of return that equals the bond's YTM; and (3) all coupon payments will be made as scheduled.

LOS 65.c
YTM is not the realized yield on an investment unless the reinvestment rate is equal to the YTM.

The amount of reinvestment income required to generate the YTM over a bond's life is the difference between the purchase price of the bond, compounded at the YTM until maturity, and the sum of the bond's interest and principal cash flows.

Reinvestment risk is higher when the coupon rate is greater (maturity held constant) and when the bond has longer maturity (coupon rate held constant).

LOS 65.d
The bond-equivalent yield of an annual-pay bond is:

$$BEY = \left[\sqrt{(1 + \text{annual-pay YTM})} - 1 \right] \times 2$$

©2009 Kaplan, Inc.

The annual-pay yield can be calculated from the YTM of a semiannual-pay bond as:

$$EAY = \left(1 + \frac{\text{semiannual-pay YTM}}{2}\right)^2 - 1$$

LOS 65.e
The theoretical Treasury spot rate curve is derived by calculating the spot rate for each successive period N based on the spot rate for period $N - 1$ and the market price of a bond with N coupon payments.

To compute the value of a bond using spot rates, discount each separate cash flow using the spot rate corresponding to the number of periods until the cash flow is to be received.

LOS 65.f
Three commonly used yield spread measures:
- *Nominal spread*: bond YTM − Treasury YTM.
- *Zero-volatility spread* (Z-spread or static spread): the equal amount of additional yield that must be added to each Treasury spot rate to get spot rates that will produce a present value for a bond equal to its market price.
- *Option-adjusted spread* (OAS): spread to the spot yield curve after adjusting for the effects of embedded options. OAS reflects the spread for credit risk and liquidity risk primarily.

There is no difference between the nominal and Z-spread when the yield curve is flat. The steeper the spot yield curve and the earlier bond principal is paid (amortizing securities), the greater the difference in the two spread measures.

LOS 65.g
The option cost for a bond with an embedded option is Z-spread − OAS.

For callable bonds, Z-spread > OAS and option cost > 0.

For putable bonds, Z-spread < OAS and option cost < 0.

LOS 65.h
Forward rates are current lending/borrowing rates for short-term loans to be made in future periods.

A spot rate for a maturity of N periods is the geometric mean of forward rates over the N periods. The same relation can be used to solve for a forward rate given spot rates for two different periods.

To value a bond using forward rates, discount the cash flows at times 1 through N by the product of one plus each forward rate for periods 1 to N, and sum them.

CONCEPT CHECKERS

Use the following data to answer Questions 1 through 4.

An analyst observes a Widget & Co. 7.125%, 4-year, semiannual-pay bond trading at 102.347% of par (where par = $1,000). The bond is callable at 101 in two years and putable at 100 in two years.

1. What is the bond's current yield?
   A. 6.962%.
   B. 7.328%.
   C. 7.426%.

2. What is the bond's yield to maturity?
   A. 3.225%.
   B. 5.864%.
   C. 6.450%.

3. What is the bond's yield to call?
   A. 3.167%.
   B. 5.664%.
   C. 6.334%.

4. What is the bond's yield to put?
   A. 4.225%.
   B. 5.864%.
   C. 6.450%.

5. Based on semiannual compounding, what would the YTM be on a 15-year, zero-coupon, $1,000 par value bond that's currently trading at $331.40?
   A. 3.750%.
   B. 5.151%.
   C. 7.500%.

6. An analyst observes a bond with an *annual* coupon that's being priced to yield 6.350%. What is this issue's bond equivalent yield?
   A. 3.175%.
   B. 3.126%.
   C. 6.252%.

7. An analyst determines that the cash flow yield of GNMA Pool 3856 is 0.382% *per month*. What is the bond equivalent yield?
   A. 4.628%.
   B. 9.363%.
   C. 9.582%.

©2009 Kaplan, Inc.

8. If the YTM equals the actual compound return an investor realizes on an investment in a coupon bond purchased at a premium to par, it is *least likely* that:
   A. cash flows will be paid as promised.
   B. the bond will not be sold at a capital loss.
   C. cash flows will be reinvested at the YTM rate.

9. The 4-year spot rate is 9.45%, and the 3-year spot rate is 9.85%. What is the 1-year forward rate three years from today?
   A. 8.258%.
   B. 9.850%.
   C. 11.059%.

10. An investor purchases a bond that is putable at the option of the holder. The option has value. He has calculated the *Z*-spread as 223 basis points. The option-adjusted spread will be:
    A. equal to 223 basis points.
    B. less than 223 basis points.
    C. greater than 223 basis points.

Use the following data to answer Questions 11 and 12.

Given:
- Current 1-year rate = 5.5%.
- $_1f_1$ = 7.63%.
- $_1f_2$ = 12.18%.
- $_1f_3$ = 15.5%.

11. The value of a 4-year, 10% annual-pay, $1,000 par value bond would be *closest* to:
    A. $995.89.
    B. $1,009.16.
    C. $1,085.62.

12. Using annual compounding, the value of a 3-year, zero-coupon, $1,000 par value bond would be:
    A. $785.
    B. $852.
    C. $948.

13. A bond's nominal spread, zero-volatility spread, and option-adjusted spread will all be equal for a coupon bond if:
    A. the yield curve is flat.
    B. the bond is option free.
    C. the yield curve is flat and the bond has no embedded options.

14. The zero-volatility spread will be zero:
   A. if the yield curve is flat.
   B. for a zero-coupon bond.
   C. for an on-the-run Treasury bond.

15. Assume the Treasury spot-rate yield curve is upward sloping. Compared to the nominal yield spread between a Treasury bond and an option-free corporate bond of similar maturity, the Z-spread will be:
   A. greater than the nominal spread.
   B. less than the nominal spread.
   C. equal to the nominal spread.

COMPREHENSIVE PROBLEMS

1. An investor buys a 10-year, 7% coupon, semiannual-pay bond for 92.80. He sells it three years later, just after receiving the sixth coupon payment, when its yield to maturity is 6.9%. Coupon interest has been placed in an account that yields 5% (BEY). State the sources of return on this bond and calculate the dollar return from each source based on a $100,000 bond.

2. What is the yield on a bond equivalent basis of an annual-pay 7% coupon bond priced at par?

3. What is the annual-pay yield to maturity of a 7% coupon semi-annual pay bond?

4. The yield to maturity on a bond equivalent basis on 6-month and 1-year T-bills are 2.8% and 3.2%, respectively. A 1.5-year, 4% Treasury note is selling at par.
   A. What is the 18-month Treasury spot rate?
   B. If a 1.5-year corporate bond with a 7% coupon is selling for 102.395, what is the nominal spread for this bond? Is the zero-volatility spread (in basis points) 127, 130, or 133?

5. Assume the following spot rates (as BEYs).

Years to maturity	Spot rates
0.5	4.0%
1.0	4.4%
1.5	5.0%
2.0	5.4%

   A. What is the 6-month forward rate one year from now?
   B. What is the 1-year forward rate one year from now?
   C. What is the value of a 2-year, 4.5% coupon Treasury note?

©2009 Kaplan, Inc.

6. Assume the current 6-month rate is 3.5% and the 6-month forward rates (all as BEYs) are those in the following table.

Periods From Now	Forward Rates
1	3.8%
2	4.0%
3	4.4%
4	4.8%

A. Calculate the corresponding spot rates.
B. What is the value of a 1.5-year, 4% Treasury note?

7. Consider the following three bonds that all have par values of $100,000.
   I. A 10-year zero coupon bond priced at 48.20.
  II. A 5-year 8% semiannual-pay bond priced with a YTM of 8%.
 III. A 5-year 9% semiannual-pay bond priced with a YTM of 8%.

A. What is the dollar amount of reinvestment income that must be earned on each bond if it is held to maturity and the investor is to realize the current YTM?
B. Rank the three bonds in terms of how important reinvestment income is to an investor who wishes to realize the stated YTM of the bond at purchase by holding it to maturity.

ANSWERS – CONCEPT CHECKERS

1. **A**   current yield $= \dfrac{71.25}{1,023.47} = 0.06962$, or 6.962%

2. **C** $1,023.47 = \displaystyle\sum_{t=1}^{8} \dfrac{35.625}{(1+\text{YTM}/2)^t} + \dfrac{1,000}{(1+\text{YTM}/2)^8} \Rightarrow \text{YTM} = 6.450\%$

   N = 8; FV = 1,000; PMT = 35.625; PV = –1,023.47 → CPT I/Y = 3.225 × 2 = 6.45%

3. **C** $1,023.47 = \displaystyle\sum_{t=1}^{4} \dfrac{35.625}{(1+\text{YTC}/2)^t} + \dfrac{1,010}{(1+\text{YTC}/2)^4} \Rightarrow \text{YTC} = 6.334\%$

   N = 4; FV = 1,010; PMT = 35.625; PV = –1,023.47; CPT → I/Y = 3.167 × 2 = 6.334%

4. **B** $1,023.47 = \displaystyle\sum_{t=1}^{4} \dfrac{35.625}{(1+\text{YTP}/2)^t} + \dfrac{1,000}{(1+\text{YTP}/2)^4} \Rightarrow \text{YTP} = 5.864\%$

   N = 4; FV = 1,000; PMT = 35.625; PV = –1,023.47; CPT → I/Y = 2.932 × 2 = 5.864%

5. **C** $\left[\left(\dfrac{1,000}{331.40}\right)^{\frac{1}{30}} - 1\right] \times 2 = 7.5\%$ or,

   Solving with a financial calculator:

   N = 30; FV = 1,000; PMT = 0; PV = –331.40; CPT → I/Y = 3.750 × 2 = 7.500%

6. **C**   bond equivalent yield $= [(1 + \text{EAY})^{1/2} - 1] \times 2 = [(1.0635)^{1/2} - 1] \times 2 = 6.252\%$

7. **A**   bond equivalent yield $= [(1 + \text{CFY})^6 - 1] \times = [(1.00382)^6 - 1] \times 2 = 4.628\%$

8. **B**   For a bond purchased at a premium to par value, a decrease in the premium over time (a capital loss) is already factored into the calculation of YTM.

9. **A** $(1.0945)^4 = (1.0985)^3 \times (1 + {}_1f_3)$

   $\dfrac{(1.0945)^4}{(1.0985)^3} - 1 = {}_1f_3 = 8.258\%$

10. **C**   For embedded puts (e.g., putable bonds): option cost < 0, ⇒ OAS > Z-spread.

©2009 Kaplan, Inc.

11. **B**   Spot rates: $S_1 = 5.5\%$.

$S_2 = [(1.055)(1.0763)]^{1/2} - 1 = 6.56\%$

$S_3 = [(1.055)(1.0763)(1.1218)]^{1/3} - 1 = 8.39\%$

$S_4 = [(1.055)(1.0763)(1.1218)(1.155)]^{1/4} - 1 = 10.13\%$

Bond value:
N = 1; FV = 100; I/Y = 5.5; CPT → PV=   −94.79
N = 2; FV = 100; I/Y = 6.56; CPT → PV=   −88.07
N = 3; FV = 100; I/Y = 8.39; CPT → PV=   −78.53
N = 4; FV = 1,100; I/Y = 10.13; CPT → PV=   −747.77
                                  Total: $1,009.16

12. **A**   Find the spot rate for 3-year lending:

$S_3 = [(1.055)(1.0763)(1.1218)]^{1/3} - 1 = 8.39\%$

Value of the bond: N = 3; FV = 1,000; I/Y = 8.39; CPT→PV = −785.29

or

$$\frac{\$1{,}000}{(1.055)(1.0763)(1.1218)} = \$785.05$$

13. **C**   If the yield curve is flat, the nominal spread and the *Z*-spread are equal. If the bond is option-free, the *Z*-spread and OAS are equal.

14. **C**   A Treasury bond is the best answer. The Treasury spot yield curve will correctly price an on-the-run Treasury bond at its arbitrage-free price, so the *Z*-spread is zero.

15. **A**   The *Z*-spread will be greater than the nominal spread when the spot yield curve is upward sloping.

Answers – Comprehensive Problems

1.   The three sources of return are coupon interest payments, recovery of principal/capital gain or loss, and reinvestment income.

Coupon interest payments: 0.07 / 2 × $100,000 × 6 = $21,000

Recovery of principal/capital gain or loss: Calculate the sale price of the bond:
N = (10 − 3) × 2 = 14; I/Y = 6.9 / 2 = 3.45; PMT = 0.07 / 2 × 100,000 = 3,500; FV = 100,000; CPT → PV = −100,548

Capital gain = 100,548 − 92,800 = $7,748

Reinvestment income: We can solve this by treating the coupon payments as a 6-period annuity, calculating the future value based on the semiannual interest rate, and subtracting the coupon payments. The difference must be the interest earned by reinvesting the coupon payments.

N = 3 × 2 = 6; I/Y = 5 / 2 = 2.5; PV = 0; PMT = −3,500; CPT → FV = $22,357

Reinvestment income = $22{,}357 - (6 \times 3{,}500) = \$1{,}357$

2.   BEY = 2 × semiannual discount rate

semiannual discount rate = $(1.07)^{1/2} - 1 = 0.344 = 3.44\%$

BEY = $2 \times 3.44\% = 6.88\%$

3.   annual-pay YTM = $\left(1 + \dfrac{0.07}{2}\right)^2 - 1 = 0.0712 = 7.12\%$

4.   A.   Since the T-bills are zero coupon instruments, their YTMs are the 6-month and 1-year spot rates. To solve for the 1.5-year spot rate, we set the bond's market price equal to the present value of its (discounted) cash flows:

$$100 = \frac{2}{1 + \dfrac{0.028}{2}} + \frac{2}{\left(1 + \dfrac{0.032}{2}\right)^2} + \frac{102}{\left(1 + \dfrac{S_{1.5}}{2}\right)^3}$$

$$100 = 1.9724 + 1.9375 + \frac{102}{\left(1 + \dfrac{S_{1.5}}{2}\right)^3}$$

$$\left(1 + \frac{S_{1.5}}{2}\right)^3 = \frac{102}{100 - 1.9724 - 1.9375} = 1.0615$$

$$1 + \frac{S_{1.5}}{2} = 1.0615^{1/3} = 1.0201$$

$S_{1.5} = 0.0201 \times 2 = 0.0402 = 4.02\%$

B.   Compute the YTM on the corporate bond:

N = 1.5 × 2 = 3; PV = –102.395; PMT = 7 / 2 = 3.5; FV = 100; CPT → I/Y = 2.6588 × 2 = 5.32%

nominal spread = $\text{YTM}_{\text{Bond}} - \text{YTM}_{\text{Treasury}}$ = 5.32% – 4.0% = 1.32%, or 132 bp

Solve for the zero-volatility spread by setting the present value of the bond's cash flows equal to the bond's price, discounting each cash flow by the Treasury spot rate plus a fixed Z-spread.

$$102.4 = \frac{3.5}{1 + \dfrac{0.028 + \text{ZS}}{2}} + \frac{3.5}{\left(1 + \dfrac{0.032 + \text{ZS}}{2}\right)^2} + \frac{103.5}{\left(1 + \dfrac{0.0402 + \text{ZS}}{2}\right)^3}$$

Substituting each of the choices into this equation gives the following bond values:

Z-spread	Bond value
127 bp	102.4821
130 bp	102.4387
133 bp	102.3953

©2009 Kaplan, Inc.

Since the price of the bond is 102.395, a Z-spread of 133 bp is the correct one.

Note that, assuming one of the three zero-volatility spreads given is correct, you could calculate the bond value using the middle spread (130) basis points, get a bond value (102.4387) that is too high, and know that the higher zero-volatility spread is the only one that could generate a present value equal to the bond's market price.

Also note that according to the LOS, you are not responsible for this calculation. Working through this example, however, should ensure that you understand the concept of a zero-volatility spread well.

5. A. $$\left(1+\frac{S_{1.5}}{2}\right)^3 = \left(1+\frac{S_{1.0}}{2}\right)^2\left(1+\frac{0.5 f_{1.0}}{2}\right)$$

$$\left(1+\frac{0.5 f_{1.0}}{2}\right) = \frac{\left(1+\frac{S_{1.5}}{2}\right)^3}{\left(1+\frac{S_{1.0}}{2}\right)^2} = \frac{1.025^3}{1.022^2} = 1.03103$$

$$_{0.5}f_{1.0} = 0.03103 \times 2 = 0.0621 = 6.21\%$$

B. $_1f_1$ here refers to the 1-year rate, one year from today, expressed as a BEY.

$$\left(1+\frac{S_2}{2}\right)^4 = \left(1+\frac{S_1}{2}\right)^2\left(1+\frac{_1f_1}{2}\right)^2$$

$$\left(1+\frac{_1f_1}{2}\right)^2 = \frac{\left(1+\frac{S_2}{2}\right)^4}{\left(1+\frac{S_1}{2}\right)^2}$$

$$\frac{_1f_1}{2} = \sqrt{\frac{\left(1+\frac{S_2}{2}\right)^4}{\left(1+\frac{S_1}{2}\right)^2}} - 1$$

$$\frac{_1f_1}{2} = \sqrt{\frac{\left(1+\frac{0.054}{2}\right)^4}{\left(1+\frac{0.044}{2}\right)^2}} - 1 = 0.0320$$

$$_1f_1 = 2 \times 0.0320 = 6.40\%$$

Note that the approximation $2 \times 5.4 - 4.4 = 6.4$ works very well here and is quite a bit less work.

C. Discount each of the bond's cash flows (as a percent of par) by the appropriate spot rate:

$$\text{bond value} = \frac{2.25}{1+\dfrac{0.040}{2}} + \frac{2.25}{\left(1+\dfrac{0.044}{2}\right)^2} + \frac{2.25}{\left(1+\dfrac{0.050}{2}\right)^3} + \frac{102.25}{\left(1+\dfrac{0.054}{2}\right)^4}$$

$$= \frac{2.25}{1.02} + \frac{2.25}{1.0445} + \frac{2.25}{1.0769} + \frac{102.25}{1.1125} = 98.36$$

6. A. $$\left(1+\frac{S_{1.0}}{2}\right)^2 = \left(1+\frac{S_{0.5}}{2}\right)\left(1+\frac{_{0.5}f_{0.5}}{2}\right) = \left(1+\frac{0.035}{2}\right)\left(1+\frac{0.038}{2}\right) = 1.0368$$

$$\frac{S_{1.0}}{2} = 1.0368^{1/2} - 1 = 0.0182$$

$S_{1.0} = 0.0182 \times 2 = 0.0364 = 3.64\%$

$$\left(1+\frac{S_{1.5}}{2}\right)^3 = \left(1+\frac{S_{0.5}}{2}\right)\left(1+\frac{_{0.5}f_{0.5}}{2}\right)\left(1+\frac{_{0.5}f_{1.0}}{2}\right)$$

$$= \left(1+\frac{0.035}{2}\right)\left(1+\frac{0.038}{2}\right)\left(1+\frac{0.040}{2}\right) = 1.0576$$

$$\frac{S_{1.5}}{2} = 1.0576^{1/3} - 1 = 0.0188$$

$S_{1.5} = 0.0188 \times 2 = 0.0376 = 3.76\%$

$$\left(1+\frac{S_{2.0}}{2}\right)^4 = \left(1+\frac{S_{0.5}}{2}\right)\left(1+\frac{_{0.5}f_{0.5}}{2}\right)\left(1+\frac{_{0.5}f_{1.0}}{2}\right)\left(1+\frac{_{0.5}f_{1.5}}{2}\right)$$

$$= \left(1+\frac{0.035}{2}\right)\left(1+\frac{0.038}{2}\right)\left(1+\frac{0.040}{2}\right)\left(1+\frac{0.044}{2}\right) = 1.0809$$

$$\frac{S_{2.0}}{2} = 1.0809^{1/4} - 1 = 0.0196$$

$S_{2.0} = 0.0196 \times 2 = 0.0392 = 3.92\%$

B. $$\frac{2}{1+\dfrac{0.035}{2}} + \frac{2}{\left(1+\dfrac{0.0364}{2}\right)^2} + \frac{102}{\left(1+\dfrac{0.0376}{2}\right)^3} = 100.35$$

7. A. Bond (I) has no reinvestment income and will realize its current YTM at maturity unless it defaults. For the coupon bonds to realize their current YTM, their coupon income would have to be reinvested at the YTM.

Bond (II): $(1.04)^{10}$ (100,000) − 100,000 − 10(4,000) = $8,024.43

Bond (III): First, we must calculate the current bond value. N = 5 × 2 = 10; I/Y = 8 / 2 = 4; FV = 100,000; PMT = 4,500; CPT → PV = −104,055.45

$(1.04)^{10}$ (104,055.45) − 100,000 − 10(4,500) = $9,027.49

©2009 Kaplan, Inc.

B. Reinvestment income is most important to the investor with the 9% coupon bond, followed by the 8% coupon bond and the zero-coupon bond. In general, reinvestment risk increases with the coupon rate on a bond.

The following is a review of the Analysis of Fixed Income Investments principles designed to address the learning outcome statements set forth by CFA Institute®. This topic is also covered in:

INTRODUCTION TO THE MEASUREMENT OF INTEREST RATE RISK

Study Session 16

EXAM FOCUS

This topic review is about the relation of yield changes and bond price changes, primarily based on the concepts of duration and convexity. There is really nothing in this study session that can be safely ignored; the calculation of duration, the use of duration, and the limitations of duration as a measure of bond price risk are all important. You should work to understand what convexity is and its relation to the interest rate risk of fixed-income securities. There are two important formulas: the formula for effective duration and the formula for estimating the price effect of a yield change based on both duration and convexity. Finally, you should get comfortable with how and why the convexity of a bond is affected by the presence of embedded options.

LOS 66.a: Distinguish between the full valuation approach (the scenario analysis approach) and the duration/convexity approach for measuring interest rate risk and explain the advantage of using the full valuation approach.

The **full valuation** or **scenario analysis approach** to measuring interest rate risk is based on applying the valuation techniques we have learned for a given change in the yield curve (i.e., for a given *interest rate scenario*). For a single option-free bond, this could be simply, "if the YTM increases by 50 bp or 100 bp, what is the impact on the value of the bond?" More complicated scenarios can be used as well, such as the effect on the bond value of a steepening of the yield curve (long-term rates increase more than short-term rates). If our valuation model is good, the exercise is straightforward: plug in the rates described in the interest rate scenario(s), and see what happens to the values of the bonds. For more complex bonds, such as callable bonds, a pricing model that incorporates yield volatility as well as specific yield curve change scenarios is required to use the full valuation approach. If the valuation models used are sufficiently good, this is the theoretically preferred approach. Applied to a portfolio of bonds, one bond at a time, we can get a very good idea of how different interest rate change scenarios will affect the value of the portfolio. Using this approach with extreme changes in interest rates is called **stress testing** a bond portfolio.

The **duration/convexity approach** provides an approximation of the actual interest rate sensitivity of a bond or bond portfolio. Its main advantage is its simplicity compared to the full valuation approach. The full valuation approach can get quite complex and time consuming for a portfolio of more than a few bonds, especially if some of the bonds have more complex structures, such as call provisions. As we will see shortly, limiting our scenarios to parallel yield curve shifts and "settling" for an estimate of interest rate risk allows us to use the summary measures, duration, and convexity. This greatly simplifies the process of estimating the value impact of overall changes in yield.

©2009 Kaplan, Inc.

Compared to the duration/convexity approach, the full valuation approach is more precise and can be used to evaluate the price effects of more complex interest rate scenarios. Strictly speaking, the duration-convexity approach is appropriate only for estimating the effects of parallel yield curve shifts.

Example: The full valuation approach

Consider two option-free bonds. Bond X is an 8% annual-pay bond with five years to maturity, priced at 108.4247 to yield 6% (N = 5; PMT = 8.00; FV = 100; I/Y = 6.00%; CPT → PV = –108.4247).

Bond Y is a 5% annual-pay bond with 15 years to maturity, priced at 81.7842 to yield 7%.

Assume a $10 million face-value position in each bond and two scenarios. The first scenario is a parallel shift in the yield curve of +50 basis points and the second scenario is a parallel shift of +100 basis points. Note that the bond price of 108.4247 is the price per $100 of par value. With $10 million of par value bonds, the market value will be $10.84247 million.

Answer:

The full valuation approach for the two simple scenarios is illustrated in the following figure.

The Full Valuation Approach

		Market Value of:			
Scenario	Yield Δ	Bond X (in millions)	Bond Y (in millions)	Portfolio	Portfolio Value Δ%
Current	+0 bp	$10.84247	$8.17842	$19.02089	
1	+50 bp	$10.62335	$7.79322	$18.41657	–3.18%
2	+100 bp	$10.41002	$7.43216	$17.84218	–6.20%

N = 5; PMT = 8; FV = 100; I/Y = 6% + 0.5%; CPT → PV = –106.2335

N = 5; PMT = 8; FV = 100; I/Y = 6% + 1%; CPT → PV = –104.1002

N = 15; PMT = 5; FV = 100; I/Y = 7% + 0.5%; CPT → PV = –77.9322

N = 15; PMT = 5; FV = 100; I/Y = 7% + 1%; CPT → PV = –74.3216

Portfolio value change 50 bp: (18.41657 – 19.02089) / 19.02089 = –0.03177 = –3.18%

Study Session 16

Portfolio value change 100 bp: (17.84218 – 19.02089) / 19.02089 = –0.06197 = –6.20%

It's worth noting that, on an individual bond basis, the effect of an increase in yield on the bonds' values is less for Bond X than for Bond Y (i.e., with a 50 bp increase in yields, the value of Bond X falls by 2.02%, while the value of Bond Y falls by 4.71%; and with a 100 bp increase, X falls by 3.99%, while Y drops by 9.12%). This, of course, is totally predictable since Bond Y is a longer-term bond and has a lower coupon—both of which mean more interest rate risk.

Professor's Note: Let's review the effects of bond characteristics on duration (price sensitivity). Holding other characteristics the same, we can state the following:

- *Higher (lower) coupon means lower (higher) duration.*
- *Longer (shorter) maturity means higher (lower) duration.*
- *Higher (lower) market yield means lower (higher) duration.*

Finance professors love to test these relations.

LOS 66.b: Demonstrate the price volatility characteristics for option-free, callable, prepayable, and putable bonds when interest rates change.

LOS 66.c: Describe positive convexity, negative convexity, and their relation to bond price and yield.

We established earlier that the relation between price and yield for a straight coupon bond is negative. An increase in yield (discount rate) leads to a decrease in the value of a bond. The precise nature of this relationship for an option-free, 8%, 20-year bond is illustrated in Figure 1.

Figure 1: Price-Yield Curve for an Option-Free, 8%, 20-Year Bond

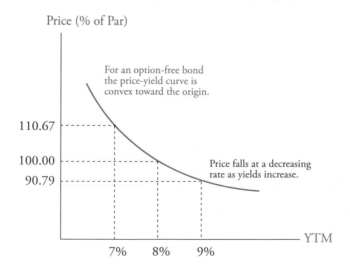

©2009 Kaplan, Inc.

First, note that the price-yield relationship is negatively sloped, so the price falls as the yield rises. Second, note that the relation follows a curve, not a straight line. Since the curve is convex (toward the origin), we say that an option-free bond has **positive convexity**. Because of its positive convexity, the price of an option-free bond *increases more when yields fall than it decreases when yields rise.* In Figure 1 we have illustrated that, for an 8%, 20-year option-free bond, a 1% decrease in the YTM will increase the price to 110.67, a *10.67% increase* in price. A 1% increase in YTM will cause the bond value to decrease to 90.79, a *9.22% decrease* in value.

If the price-yield relation were a straight line, there would be no difference between the price increase and the price decline in response to equal decreases and increases in yields. Convexity is a good thing for a bond owner; for a given volatility of yields, price increases are larger than price decreases. The convexity property is often expressed by saying, "a bond's price falls at a decreasing rate as yields rise." For the price-yield relationship to be convex, the slope (rate of decrease) of the curve must be decreasing as we move from left to right (i.e., towards higher yields).

Note that the duration (interest rate sensitivity) of a bond at any yield is (absolute value of) the slope of the price-yield function at that yield. The convexity of the price-yield relation for an option-free bond can help you remember a result presented earlier, that the duration of a bond is less at higher market yields.

Callable Bonds, Prepayable Securities, and Negative Convexity

With a **callable** or **prepayable debt**, the upside price appreciation in response to decreasing yields is limited (sometimes called price compression). Consider the case of a bond that is currently callable at 102. The fact that the issuer can call the bond at any time for $1,020 per $1,000 of face value puts an effective upper limit on the value of the bond. As Figure 2 illustrates, as yields fall and the price approaches $1,020, the price-yield curve rises more slowly than that of an identical but noncallable bond. When the price begins to *rise at a decreasing rate* in response to further decreases in yield, the price-yield curve "bends over" to the left and exhibits **negative convexity**.

Thus, in Figure 2, so long as yields remain *below level y',* callable bonds will exhibit *negative convexity;* however, at yields *above level y',* those same callable bonds will exhibit *positive convexity.* In other words, at higher yields the value of the call options becomes very small so that a callable bond will act very much like a noncallable bond. It is only at lower yields that the callable bond will exhibit negative convexity.

Figure 2: Price-Yield Function of a Callable vs. an Option-Free Bond

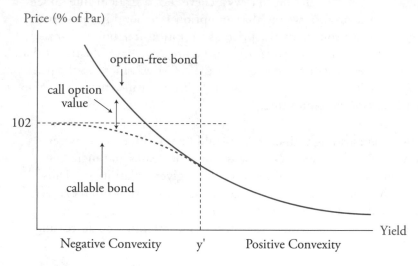

In terms of price sensitivity to interest rate changes, the slope of the price-yield curve at any particular yield tells the story. Note that as yields fall, the slope of the price-yield curve for the callable bond decreases, becoming almost zero (flat) at very low yields. This tells us how a call feature affects price sensitivity to changes in yield. At higher yields, the interest rate risk of a callable bond is very close or identical to that of a similar option-free bond. At lower yields, the price volatility of the callable bond will be much lower than that of an identical but noncallable bond.

The effect of a prepayment option is quite similar to that of a call; at low yields it will lead to negative convexity and reduce the price volatility (interest rate risk) of the security. Note that when yields are low and callable and prepayable securities exhibit less interest rate risk, reinvestment risk rises. At lower yields, the probability of a call and the prepayment rate both rise, increasing the risk of having to reinvest principal repayments at the lower rates.

The Price Volatility Characteristics of Putable Bonds

The value of a put increases at higher yields and decreases at lower yields opposite to the value of a call option. Compared to an option-free bond, a **putable bond** will have *less* price volatility at higher yields. This comparison is illustrated in Figure 3.

©2009 Kaplan, Inc.

Figure 3: Comparing the Price-Yield Curves for Option-Free and Putable Bonds

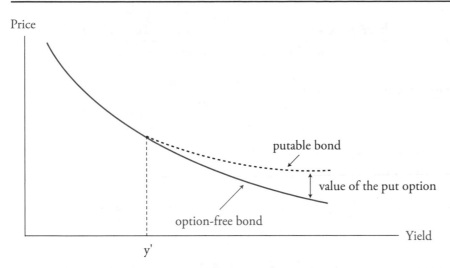

In Figure 3, the price of the putable bond falls more slowly in response to increases in yield above y' because the value of the embedded put rises at higher yields. The slope of the price-yield relation is flatter, indicating less price sensitivity to yield changes (lower duration) for the putable bond at higher yields. At yields below y', the value of the put is quite small, and a putable bond's price acts like that of an option-free bond in response to yield changes.

LOS 66.d: Compute and interpret the effective duration of a bond, given information about how the bond's price will increase and decrease for given changes in interest rates, and compute the approximate percentage price change for a bond, given the bond's effective duration and a specified change in yield.

In our introduction to the concept of duration, we described it as the ratio of the percentage change in price to change in yield. Now that we understand convexity, we know that the price change in response to rising rates is smaller than the price change in response to falling rates for option-free bonds. The formula we will use for calculating the **effective duration** of a bond uses the average of the price changes in response to equal increases and decreases in yield to account for this fact. If we have a callable bond that is trading in the area of negative convexity, the price increase is smaller than the price decrease, but using the average still makes sense.

The formula for calculating the effective duration of a bond is:

$$\text{effective duration} = \frac{(\text{bond price when yields fall} - \text{bond price when yields rise})}{2 \times (\text{initial price}) \times (\text{change in yield in decimal form})}$$

which we will sometimes write as $\text{duration} = \dfrac{V_- - V_+}{2V_0(\Delta y)}$

where:

V_- = bond value if the yield decreases by Δy
V_+ = bond value if the yield increases by Δy
V_0 = initial bond price
Δy = change in yield used to get V_- and V_+, *expressed in decimal form*

Consider the following example of this calculation.

Example: Calculating effective duration

Consider a 20-year, semiannual-pay bond with an 8% coupon that is currently priced at $908.00 to yield 9%. If the yield declines by 50 basis points (to 8.5%), the price will increase to $952.30, and if the yield increases by 50 basis points (to 9.5%), the price will decline to $866.80. Based on these price and yield changes, calculate the effective duration of this bond.

Answer:

Let's approach this intuitively to gain a better understanding of the formula. We begin by computing the average of the percentage change in the bond's price for the yield increase and the percentage change in price for a yield decrease. We can calculate this as:

$$\text{average } percentage \text{ price change} = \frac{(\$952.30 - \$866.80)}{2 \times \$908.00} = 0.0471\%, \text{ or } 4.71\%$$

The 2 in the denominator is to obtain the average price change, and the $908 in the denominator is to obtain this average change as a percentage of the current price.

To get the duration (to scale our result for a 1% change in yield), the final step is to divide this average percentage price change by the change in interest rates that caused it. In the example, the yield change was 0.5%, which we need to write in decimal form as 0.005. Our estimate of the duration is:

$$\frac{0.0471}{0.005} = \frac{4.71\%}{0.50\%} = 9.42 = \text{duration}$$

Using the formula previously given, we have:

$$\text{effective duration} = \frac{(\$952.3 - \$866.8)}{2 \times \$908 \times 0.005} = 9.416$$

©2009 Kaplan, Inc.

The interpretation of this result, as you should be convinced by now, is that a 1% change in yield produces an approximate change in the price of this bond of 9.42%. Note, however, that this estimate of duration was based on a change in yield of 0.5% and will perform best for yield changes close to this magnitude. Had we used a yield change of 0.25% or 1%, we would have obtained a slightly different estimate of effective duration.

This is an important concept, and you are required to learn the formula for the calculation. To further help you understand this formula and remember it, consider the following.

The price increase in response to a 0.5% decrease in rates was $\frac{\$44.30}{\$908} = 4.879\%$.

The price decrease in response to a 0.5% increase in rates was $\frac{\$41.20}{\$908} = 4.537\%$.

The average of the percentage price increase and the percentage price decrease is 4.71%. Since we used a 0.5% change in yield to get the price changes, we need to double this and get a 9.42% change in price for a 1% change in yield. The duration is 9.42.

For bonds with no embedded options, modified duration and effective duration will be equal or very nearly equal. In order to calculate effective duration for a bond with an embedded option, we need a pricing model that takes account of how the cash flows change when interest rates change.

Approximate Percentage Price Change for a Bond Based on Effective Duration

Multiply effective duration by the change in yield to get the magnitude of the price change and then change the sign to get the direction of the price change right (yield up, price down).

percentage change in bond price = –effective duration × change in yield in percent

Example: Using effective duration

What is the expected percentage price change for a bond with an effective duration of nine in response to an increase in yield of 30 basis points?

Answer:

–9 × 0.3% = –2.7%

We expect the bond's price to decrease by 2.7% in response to the yield change. If the bond were priced at $980, the new price is 980 × (1 − 0.027) = $953.54.

LOS 66.e: Distinguish among the alternative definitions of duration and explain why effective duration is the most appropriate measure of interest rate risk for bonds with embedded options.

The formula we used to calculate duration based on price changes in response to equal increases and decreases in YTM, $\text{duration} = \dfrac{V_- - V_+}{2V_0(\Delta y)}$, is the formula for effective (option-adjusted) duration. This is the preferred measure because it gives a good approximation of interest rate sensitivity for both option-free bonds and *bonds with embedded options*.

Macaulay duration is an estimate of a bond's interest rate sensitivity based on the time, in years, until promised cash flows will arrive. Since a 5-year zero-coupon bond has only one cash flow five years from today, its Macaulay duration is five. The change in value in response to a 1% change in yield for a 5-year zero-coupon bond is approximately 5%. A 5-year coupon bond has some cash flows that arrive earlier than five years from today (the coupons), so its Macaulay duration is less than five. This is consistent with what we learned earlier: the higher the coupon, the less the price sensitivity (duration) of a bond.

Macaulay duration is the earliest measure of duration, and because it was based on the time, duration is often stated as years. Because Macaulay duration is based on the expected cash flows for an option-free bond, it is not an appropriate estimate of the price sensitivity of bonds with embedded options.

Modified duration is derived from Macaulay duration and offers a slight improvement over Macaulay duration in that it takes the current YTM into account. Like Macaulay duration, and for the same reasons, modified duration is not an appropriate measure of interest rate sensitivity for bonds with embedded options. For option-free bonds, however, effective duration (based on small changes in YTM) and modified duration will be very similar.

Professor's Note: The LOS here do not require that you calculate either Macaulay duration or modified duration, only effective duration. For your own understanding, however, note that the relation is

$\text{modified duration} = \dfrac{Macaulay\ duration}{1 + periodic\ market\ yield}$. *This accounts for the fact we*

learned earlier that duration decreases as YTM increases. Graphically, the slope of the price-yield curve is less steep at higher yields.

Effective Duration for Bonds With Embedded Options

As noted earlier, in comparing the various duration measures, both Macaulay and modified duration are calculated directly from the promised cash flows for a bond with no adjustment for the effect of any embedded options on cash flows. Effective duration is calculated from expected price changes in response to changes in yield that explicitly take into account a bond's option provisions (i.e., they are in the price-yield function used).

©2009 Kaplan, Inc.

Interpreting Duration

We can interpret duration in three different ways.

First, duration is the slope of the price-yield curve at the bond's current YTM. Mathematically, the slope of the price-yield curve is the first derivative of the price-yield curve with respect to yield.

A second interpretation of duration, as originally developed by Macaulay, is a weighted average of the time (in years) until each cash flow will be received. The weights are the proportions of the total bond value that each cash flow represents. The answer, again, comes in years.

A third interpretation of duration is the approximate percentage change in price for a 1% change in yield. This interpretation, price sensitivity in response to a change in yield, is the preferred, and most intuitive, interpretation of duration.

> *Professor's Note: The fact that duration was originally calculated and expressed in years has been a source of confusion for many candidates and finance students. Practitioners regularly speak of "longer duration securities." This confusion is the reason for this part of the LOS. The most straightforward interpretation of duration is the one that we have used up to this point: "It is the approximate percentage change in a bond's price for a 1% change in YTM." I have seen duration expressed in years in CFA exam questions; just ignore the years and use the number. I have also seen questions asking whether duration becomes longer or shorter in response to a change; longer means higher or more interest rate sensitivity. A duration of 6.82 years means that for a 1% change in YTM, a bond's value will change approximately 6.82%. This is the best way to "interpret" duration.*

LOS 66.f: Compute the duration of a portfolio, given the duration of the bonds comprising the portfolio, and explain the limitations of portfolio duration.

The concept of duration can also be applied to portfolios. In fact, one of the benefits of duration as a measure of interest rate risk is that the **duration of a portfolio** is simply the weighted average of the durations of the individual securities in the portfolio. Mathematically, the duration of a portfolio is:

portfolio duration = $w_1 D_1 + w_2 D_2 + \ldots + w_N D_N$

where:
w_i = market value of bond i divided by the market value of the portfolio
D_i = the duration of bond i
N = the number of bonds in the portfolio

Example: Calculating portfolio duration

Suppose you have a two-security portfolio containing Bonds A and B. The market value of Bond A is $6,000, and the market value of Bond B is $4,000. The duration of Bond A is 8.5, and the duration of Bond B is 4.0. Calculate the duration of the portfolio.

Answer:

First, find the weights of each bond. Since the market value of the portfolio is $10,000 = $6,000 + $4,000, the weight of each security is as follows:

$$\text{weight in Bond A} = \frac{\$6,000}{\$10,000} = 60\%$$

$$\text{weight in Bond B} = \frac{\$4,000}{\$10,000} = 40\%$$

Using the formula for the duration of a portfolio, we get:

$$\text{portfolio duration} = (0.6 \times 8.5) + (0.4 \times 4.0) = 6.7$$

Limitations of Portfolio Duration

The limitations of portfolio duration as a measure of interest rate sensitivity stem from the fact that yields may not change equally on all the bonds in the portfolio. With a portfolio that includes bonds with different maturities, credit risks, and embedded options, there is no reason to suspect that the yields on individual bonds will change by equal amounts when the yield curve changes. As an example, a steepening of the yield curve can increase yields on long-term bonds and leave the yield on short-term bonds unchanged. It is for this reason that we say that duration is a good measure of the sensitivity of portfolio value to *parallel* changes in the yield curve.

LOS 66.g: Describe the convexity measure of a bond and estimate a bond's percentage price change, given the bond's duration and convexity and a specified change in interest rates.

Convexity is a measure of the curvature of the price-yield curve. The more curved the price-yield relation is, the greater the convexity. A straight line has a convexity of zero. If the price-yield "curve" were, in fact, a straight line, the convexity would be zero. The reason we care about convexity is that the more curved the price-yield relation is, the worse our duration-based estimates of bond price changes in response to changes in yield are.

As an example, consider again an 8%, 20-year Treasury bond priced at $908 so that it has a yield to maturity of 9%. We previously calculated the effective duration of this bond as 9.42. Figure 4 illustrates the differences between actual bond price changes and duration-based estimates of price changes at different yield levels.

Figure 4: Duration-Based Price Estimates vs. Actual Bond Prices

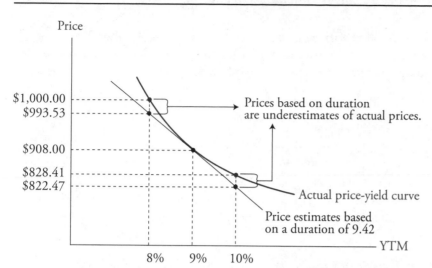

Based on a value of 9.42 for duration, we would estimate the new prices after 1% changes in yield (to 8% and to 10%) as $1.0942 \times 908 = \$993.53$ and $(1 - 0.0942) \times 908 = \$822.47$, respectively. These price estimates are shown in Figure 4 along the straight line tangent to the actual price-yield curve.

The actual price of the 8% bond at a YTM of 8% is, of course, par value ($1,000). Based on a YTM of 10%, the actual price of the bond is $828.41, about $6 higher than our duration based estimate of $822.47. Note that price estimates based on duration are less than the actual prices for both a 1% increase and a 1% decrease in yield.

Figure 4 illustrates why convexity is important and why estimates of price changes based solely on duration are inaccurate. If the price-yield relation were a straight line (i.e., if convexity were zero), duration alone would provide good estimates of bond price changes for changes in yield of any magnitude. The greater the convexity, the greater the error in price estimates based solely on duration.

A Bond's Approximate Percentage Price Change Based on Duration and Convexity

By combining duration and convexity, we can obtain a more accurate estimate of the percentage change in price of a bond, especially for relatively large changes in yield. The formula for estimating a bond's percentage price change based on its convexity and duration is:

$$\text{percentage change in price} = \text{duration effect} + \text{convexity effect}$$

$$= \left\{ \left[-\text{duration} \times (\Delta y) \right] + \left[\text{convexity} \times (\Delta y)^2 \right] \right\} \times 100$$

With Δy entered as a decimal, the "$\times 100$" is necessary to get an answer in percent.

Example: Estimating price changes with duration and convexity

Consider an 8% Treasury bond with a current price of $908 and a YTM of 9%. Calculate the percentage change in price of both a 1% increase and a 1% decrease in YTM based on a duration of 9.42 and a convexity of 68.33.

Answer:

The duration effect, as we calculated earlier, is $9.42 \times 0.01 = 0.0942 = 9.42\%$. The convexity effect is $68.33 \times 0.01^2 \times 100 = 0.00683 \times 100 = 0.683\%$. The total effect for a *decrease in yield of 1%* (from 9% to 8%) is $9.42\% + 0.683\% = +10.103\%$, and the estimate of the new price of the bond is $1.10103 \times 908 = 999.74$. This is much closer to the actual price of $1,000 than our estimate using only duration.

The total effect for an *increase in yield of 1%* (from 9% to 10%) is $-9.42\% + 0.683\% = -8.737\%$, and the estimate of the bond price is $(1 - 0.08737)(908) = \$828.67$. Again, this is much closer to the actual price ($828.40) than the estimate based solely on duration.

There are a few points worth noting here. First, the convexity adjustment is always positive when convexity is positive because $(\Delta y)^2$ is always positive. This goes along with the illustration in Figure 4, which shows that the duration-only based estimate of a bond's price change suffered from being an underestimate of the percentage increase in the bond price when yields fell, and an overestimate of the percentage decrease in the bond price when yields rose. Recall, that for a callable bond, convexity can be negative at low yields. When convexity is negative, the convexity adjustment to the duration-only based estimate of the percentage price change will be negative for both yield increases and yield decreases.

Professor's Note: Different dealers may calculate the convexity measure differently. Often the measure is calculated in a way that requires us to divide the measure by two in order to get the correct convexity adjustment. For exam purposes, the formula we've shown here is the one you need to know. However, you should also know that there can be some variation in how different dealers calculate convexity.

LOS 66.h: Differentiate between modified convexity and effective convexity.

Effective convexity takes into account changes in cash flows due to embedded options, while modified convexity does not. The difference between modified convexity and effective convexity mirrors the difference between modified duration and effective duration. Recall that modified duration is calculated without any adjustment to a bond's cash flows for embedded options. Also recall that effective duration was appropriate for bonds with embedded options because the inputs (prices) were calculated under the assumption that the cash flows could vary at different yields because of the embedded options in the securities. Clearly, effective convexity is the appropriate measure to use for bonds with embedded options, since it is based on bond values that incorporate the effect of embedded options on the bond's cash flows.

LOS 66.i: Compute the price value of a basis point (PVBP), and explain its relationship to duration.

The **price value of a basis point** (PVBP) is the dollar change in the price/value of a bond or a portfolio when the yield changes by one basis point, or 0.01%. We can calculate the PVBP directly for a bond by changing the YTM by one basis point and computing the change in value. As a practical matter, we can use duration to calculate the price value of a basis point as:

price value of a basis point = duration × 0.0001 × bond value

The following example demonstrates this calculation.

> **Example: Calculating the price value of a basis point**
>
> A bond has a market value of $100,000 and a duration of 9.42. What is the price value of a basis point?
>
> **Answer:**
>
> Using the duration formula, the percentage change in the bond's price for a change in yield of 0.01% is 0.01% × 9.42 = 0.0942%. We can calculate 0.0942% of the original $100,000 portfolio value as 0.000942 × 100,000 = $94.20. If the bond's yield increases (decreases) by one basis point, the portfolio value will fall (rise) by $94.20. $94.20 is the (duration-based) price value of a basis point for this bond.
>
> We could also directly calculate the price value of a basis point for this bond by increasing the YTM by 0.01% (0.0001) and calculating the change in bond value. This would give us the PVBP for an increase in yield. This would be very close to our duration-based estimate because duration is a very good estimate of interest rate risk for small changes in yield. We can ignore the convexity adjustment here because it is of very small magnitude: $(\Delta y)^2 = (0.0001)^2 = 0.00000001$, which is very small indeed!

KEY CONCEPTS

LOS 66.a

The full valuation approach to measuring interest rate risk involves using a pricing model to value individual bonds and can be used to find the price impact of any scenario of interest rate/yield curve changes. Its advantages are its flexibility and precision.

The duration/convexity approach is based on summary measures of interest rate risk and, while simpler to use for a portfolio of bonds than the full valuation approach, is theoretically correct only for parallel shifts in the yield curve.

LOS 66.b

Callable bonds and prepayable securities will have less price volatility (lower duration) at low yields, compared to option-free bonds.

Putable bonds will have less price volatility at high yields, compared to option-free bonds.

LOS 66.c

Option-free bonds have a price-yield relationship that is curved (convex toward the origin) and are said to exhibit positive convexity. In this case, bond prices fall less in response to an increase in yield than they rise in response to an equal-sized decrease in yield.

Callable bonds exhibit negative convexity at low yield levels. In this case, bond prices rise less in response to a decrease in yield than they fall in response to an equal-sized increase in yield.

LOS 66.d

Effective duration is calculated as the ratio of the average percentage price change for an equal-sized increase and decrease in yield, to the change in yield.

$$\text{effective duration} = \frac{V_- - V_+}{2V_0(\Delta y)}$$

Approximate percentage change in bond price = −duration × change in yield in percent.

LOS 66.e

The most intuitive interpretation of duration is as the percentage change in a bond's price for a 1% change in yield to maturity.

Macaulay duration and modified duration are based on a bond's promised cash flows.

Effective duration is appropriate for estimating price changes in bonds with embedded options because it takes into account the effect of embedded options on a bond's cash flows.

©2009 Kaplan, Inc.

LOS 66.f

The duration of a bond portfolio is equal to a weighted average of the individual bond durations, where the weights are the proportions of total portfolio value in each bond position.

Portfolio duration is limited because it gives the sensitivity of portfolio value only to yield changes that are equal for all bonds in the portfolio, an unlikely scenario for most portfolios.

LOS 66.g

Because of convexity, the duration measure is a poor approximation of price sensitivity for yield changes that are not absolutely small. The convexity adjustment accounts for the curvature of the price-yield relationship.

Incorporating both duration and convexity, we can estimate the percentage change in price in response to a change in yield of (Δy) as:

$$\left\{\left[(-\text{duration})(\Delta y)\right] + \left[(\text{convexity})(\Delta y)^2\right]\right\} \times 100$$

LOS 66.h

Effective convexity considers expected changes in cash flows that may occur for bonds with embedded options, while modified convexity does not.

LOS 66.i

Price value of a basis point (PVBP) is an estimate of the change in a bond's or a bond portfolio's value for a one basis point change in yield.

$$\text{PVBP} = \text{duration} \times 0.0001 \times \text{bond (or portfolio) value}$$

CONCEPT CHECKERS

1. Why is the price/yield profile of a callable bond less convex than that of an otherwise identical option-free bond? The price:
   A. increase is capped from above, at or near the call price as the required yield decreases.
   B. increase is capped from above, at or near the call price as the required yield increases.
   C. decrease is limited from below, at or near the call price as the required yield increases.

2. The 4.65% semiannual-pay Portage Health Authority bonds have exactly 17 years to maturity and are currently priced to yield 4.39%. Using the full valuation approach, the interest rate exposure (in percent of value) for these bonds, given a 75 basis point increase in required yield, is *closest* to:
   A. −9.104%.
   B. −9.031%.
   C. −8.344%.

3. A 14% semiannual-pay coupon bond has six years to maturity. The bond is currently trading at par. Using a 25 basis point change in yield, the effective duration of the bond is *closest* to:
   A. 0.389.
   B. 3.889.
   C. 3.970.

4. Suppose that the bond in Question 3 is callable at par today. Using a 25 basis point change in yield, the bond's effective duration assuming that its price cannot exceed 100 is *closest* to:
   A. 1.972.
   B. 1.998.
   C. 19.72.

5. The modified duration of a bond is 7.87. The percentage change in price using duration for a yield decrease of 110 basis points is *closest* to:
   A. −8.657%.
   B. +7.155%.
   C. +8.657%.

6. A bond has a convexity of 57.3. The convexity effect if the yield decreases by 110 basis points is *closest* to:
   A. −1.673%.
   B. +0.693%.
   C. +1.673%.

7. Assume a bond has an effective duration of 10.5 and a convexity of 97.3. Using both of these measures, the estimated percentage change in price for this bond, in response to a decline in yield of 200 basis points, is *closest* to:
   A. 19.05%.
   B. 22.95%.
   C. 24.89%.

©2009 Kaplan, Inc.

8. An analyst has determined that if market yields rise by 100 basis points, a certain high-grade corporate bond will have a convexity effect of 1.75%. Further, she's found that the total estimated percentage change in price for this bond should be −13.35%. Given this information, it follows that the bond's percentage change in price due to duration is:
    A. −15.10%.
    B. −11.60%.
    C. +16.85%.

9. The total price volatility of a typical noncallable bond can be found by:
    A. adding the bond's convexity effect to its effective duration.
    B. adding the bond's negative convexity to its modified duration.
    C. subtracting the bond's negative convexity from its positive convexity.

10. The current price of a $1,000, 7-year, 5.5% semiannual coupon bond is $1,029.23. The bond's PVBP is *closest* to:
    A. $0.05.
    B. $0.60.
    C. $5.74.

11. The effect on a bond portfolio's value of a decrease in yield would be *most accurately* estimated by using:
    A. the full valuation approach.
    B. the price value of a basis point.
    C. both the portfolio's duration and convexity.

12. An analyst has noticed lately that the price of a particular bond has risen less when the yield falls by 0.1% than the price falls when rates increase by 0.1%. She could conclude that the bond:
    A. is an option-free bond.
    B. has an embedded put option.
    C. has negative convexity.

13. Which of the following measures is *lowest* for a currently callable bond?
    A. Macaulay duration.
    B. Effective duration.
    C. Modified duration.

COMPREHENSIVE PROBLEMS

Use the following information to answer Questions 1 through 6.

A bond dealer provides the following selected information on a portfolio of fixed-income securities.

Par Value	Mkt. Price	Coupon	Modified Duration	Effective Duration	Effective Convexity
$2 million	100	6.5%	8	8	154
$3 million	93	5.5%	6	1	50
$1 million	95	7%	8.5	8.5	130
$4 million	103	8%	9	5	–70

1.   What is the effective duration for the portfolio?

2.   Calculate the price value of a basis point for this portfolio.

3.   Which bond(s) likely has (have) no embedded options? (identify bonds by coupon)

4.   Which bond(s) is (are) likely callable?

5.   Which bond(s) is (are) likely putable?

6.   What is the approximate price change for the 7% bond if its yield to maturity increases by 25 basis points?

7.   Why might two bond dealers differ in their estimates of a portfolio's effective duration?

8.   Why might portfolio effective duration be an inadequate measure of interest rate risk for a bond portfolio even if we assume the bond effective durations are correct?

©2009 Kaplan, Inc.

ANSWERS – CONCEPT CHECKERS

1. **A**   As the required yield decreases on a callable bond, the rate of increase in the price of the bond begins to slow down and eventually level off as it approaches the call price, a characteristic known as "negative convexity."

2. **C**   We need to compare the value of the bond today to the value if the YTM increases by 0.75%.

    Price today = 103.092

    $$N = 34;\ PMT = \frac{4.65}{2} = 2.325;\ FV = 100;$$

    $$I/Y = \frac{4.39}{2} = 2.195\%;\ CPT \to PV = -103.092$$

    Price after a 75 basis point increase in the YTM is 94.490

    $$N = 34;\ PMT = \frac{4.65}{2} = 2.325;\ FV = 100;$$

    $$I/Y = \frac{5.14}{2} = 2.57\%;\ CPT \to PV = -94.490$$

    $$\text{Interest rate exposure} = \frac{94.490 - 103.092}{103.092} = -8.344\%$$

3. **C** $V_- = 100.999$

    $$N = 12;\ PMT = \frac{14.00}{2} = 7.00;\ FV = 100;$$

    $$I/Y = \frac{13.75}{2} = 6.875\%;\ CPT \to PV = -100.999$$

    $V_+ = 99.014$

    $$N = 12;\ PMT = \frac{14.00}{2} = 7.00;\ FV = 100;$$

    $$I/Y = \frac{14.25}{2} = 7.125\%;\ CPT \to PV = -99.014$$

    $V_0 = 100.000$

    $\Delta y = 0.0025$

    $$\text{duration} = \frac{V_- - V_+}{2V_0(\Delta y)} = \frac{100.999 - 99.014}{2(100)0.0025} = 3.970$$

4. **A** $V_- = 100$

    $V_+ = 99.014$

    $V_0 = 100$

    $\Delta y = 0.0025$

    $$\text{duration} = \frac{V_- - V_+}{2V_0(\Delta y)} = \frac{100 - 99.014}{2(100)0.0025} = 1.972$$

5. **C** $\text{Est.}[\Delta V_-\%] = -7.87 \times (-1.10\%) = 8.657\%$

6. **B**   convexity effect = convexity × $(\Delta y)^2 = \left[57.3(0.011)^2\right] \times 100 = 0.693\%$

7. **C**   Total estimated price change = (duration effect + convexity effect)

    $$\left\{\left[-10.5 \times (-0.02)\right] + \left[97.3 \times (-0.02)^2\right]\right\} \times 100 = 21.0\% + 3.89\% = 24.89\%$$

8. **A**   Total percentage change in price = duration effect + convexity effect. Thus:

    $$-13.35 = \text{duration effect} + 1.75 \Rightarrow \text{duration effect} = -15.10\%\cdot$$

    (Note: the duration effect must be negative because yields are rising.)

9. **A**   Total percentage change in price = duration effect + convexity effect. Thus:

    Total percentage change in price = effective duration + convexity effect.

    (Note: since this is a noncallable bond, you can use either effective or modified duration in the above equation.)

10. **B**   PVBP = initial price − price if yield is changed by 1 bp. First, we need to calculate the yield so that we can calculate the price of the bond with a 1 basis point change in yield. Using a financial calculator: PV = −1,029.23; FV = 1,000; PMT = 27.5 = (0.055 × 1,000) / 2; N =14 = 2 × 7 years; CPT → I/Y = 2.49998, multiplied by 2 = 4.99995, or 5.00%. Next, compute the price of the bond at a yield of 5.00% + 0.01%, or 5.01%. Using the calculator: FV = 1,000; PMT = 27.5; N = 14; I/Y = 2.505 (5.01 / 2); CPT → PV = $1,028.63. Finally, PVBP = $1,029.23 − $1,028.63 = $0.60.

11. **A**   The full valuation approach is the most complex method, but also the most accurate.

12. **C**   A bond with negative convexity will rise less in price in response to a decrease in yield than it will fall in response to an equal-sized increase in rates.

13. **B**   The interest rate sensitivity of a bond with an embedded call option will be less than that of an option-free bond. Effective duration takes the effect of the call option into account and will, therefore, be less than Macaulay or modified duration.

©2009 Kaplan, Inc.

ANSWERS – COMPREHENSIVE PROBLEMS

1. Portfolio effective duration is the weighted average of the effective durations of the portfolio bonds.

   Numerators in weights are market values (par value × price as percent of par). Denominator is total market value of the portfolio.

   $$\frac{2}{9.86}(8)+\frac{2.79}{9.86}(1)+\frac{0.95}{9.86}(8.5)+\frac{4.12}{9.86}(5)=4.81 \text{ (weights are in millions)}$$

2. Price value of a basis point can be calculated using effective duration for the portfolio and the portfolio's market value, together with a yield change of 0.01%. Convexity can be ignored for such a small change in yield.

   4.81 × 0.0001 × 9,860,000 = $4,742.66

3. The 6.5% and 7% coupon bonds likely have no embedded options. For both of these bonds, modified duration and effective duration are identical, which would be the case if they had no embedded options. (It is possible that these bonds have options that are so far out of the money that the bond prices act as if there is no embedded option. One example might be a conversion option to common stock at $40 per share when the market value of the shares is $2.)

4. The 8% bond is likely callable. It is trading at a premium, its effective duration is less than modified duration, and it exhibits negative convexity. Remember, call price can be above par.

5. The 5.5% bond is likely putable. It is trading at a significant discount, its effective duration is much lower than its modified duration (close to zero in fact), and its convexity is positive but low. Note that a putable bond may trade below par when the put price is below par (also if there is risk that the issuer cannot honor the put). If it were callable, we would expect its modified and effective durations to be closer in value because the market price is significantly below likely call prices.

6. Based on the effective duration and effective convexity of the 7% bond, the approximate price change is:

   [−8.5 × 0.0025] + [130 × 0.0025^2] × 950,000 = −$19,415.63

7. In order to estimate effective duration, the dealers must use a pricing model for the bonds and choose a specific yield change. Differences in models or the yield change used can lead to differences in their estimates of effective duration.

8. Effective duration is based on small changes in yield and is appropriate for parallel changes in the yield curve (or equal changes in the yields to maturity for all portfolio bonds). Other types of yield changes will make portfolio duration an inadequate measure of portfolio interest rate risk.

14 questions, 21 minutes

1. An estimate of the price change for an option-free bond caused by a 1% decline in its yield to maturity based only on its modified duration will result in an answer that:
    A. is too small.
    B. is too large.
    C. may be too small or too large.

2. Alfred LeBon purchased a semiannual pay, 7%, U.S. Treasury bond with 19 years to maturity for 91.16 the day after it had made a coupon payment. Two years later, the YTM was unchanged when he sold the bond. LeBon's gain when he sold the bond is *closest* to:
    A. 0.483%.
    B. 0.733%.
    C. 0.931%.

3. Which statement about the theories of the term structure of interest rates is *most accurate*?
    A. Under the liquidity preference theory, the yield curve will be positively sloped.
    B. A yield curve that slopes up and then down (humped) is consistent with the market segmentation theory but not with the pure expectations theory.
    C. Evidence that life insurance companies have a strong preference for 30-year bonds supports the market segmentation theory.

4. Which of the following is *least likely* a common form of external credit enhancement?
    A. Portfolio insurance.
    B. A corporate guarantee.
    C. A letter of credit from a bank.

5. A bond with an embedded put option has a modified duration of 7, an effective duration of 6 and a convexity of 62.5. If interest rates rise 25 basis points, the bond's price will change by *approximately*:
    A. 1.46%.
    B. 1.50%.
    C. 1.54%.

6. Which of the following bonds would be the best one to own if the yield curve shifts down by 50 basis points at all maturities?
    A. 4-year 8%, 8% YTM.
    B. 5-year 8%, 7.5% YTM.
    C. 5-year 8.5%, 8% YTM.

©2009 Kaplan, Inc.

7. Which of the following provisions would *most likely* decrease the yield to maturity on a debt security?
   A. Call option.
   B. Conversion option.
   C. Cap on a floating-rate security.

8. The price of a 10-year zero coupon bond with a current YTM of 9.4% is 39.91. If the YTM increases to 9.9%, the price will decrease to 38.05. If the YTM decreases to 8.9%, the price will increase to 41.86. The effective duration is *closest* to:
   A. 9.38.
   B. 9.48.
   C. 9.55.

9. The effects of a decrease in interest rate (yield) volatility on the market yield of a debt security with a prepayment option and on a debt security with a put option are *most likely* a(n):

	Prepayment option	Put option
A.	Increase	Decrease
B.	Decrease	Increase
C.	Decrease	Decrease

10. Bond A has an embedded option, a nominal yield spread to Treasuries of 1.6%, a zero-volatility spread of 1.4%, and an option-adjusted spread of 1.2%. Bond B is identical to Bond A except that it does not have the embedded option, has a nominal yield spread to Treasuries of 1.4%, a zero-volatility spread of 1.3%, and an option-adjusted spread of 1.3%. The *most likely* option embedded in Bond A, and the bond that is the better value, are:

	Embedded option	Better value
A.	Put	Bond A
B.	Call	Bond A
C.	Call	Bond B

11. A bank loan department is trying to determine the correct rate for a 2-year loan to be made two years from now. If current implied Treasury effective annual spot rates are: 1-year = 2%, 2-year = 3%, 3-year = 3.5%, 4-year = 4.5%, the base (risk-free) forward rate for the loan before adding a risk premium is *closest* to:
    A. 4.5%.
    B. 6.0%.
    C. 9.0%.

12. Compared to mortgage passthrough securities, CMOs created from them *most likely* have:
    A. less prepayment risk.
    B. greater average yields.
    C. a different claim to the mortgage cash flows.

13. The arbitrage-free approach to bond valuation *most likely*:
    A. can only be applied to Treasury securities.
    B. requires each cash flow to be discounted at a rate specific to its time period.
    C. shows that discounting each cash flow at the yield to maturity must result in the correct value for a bond.

14. Which of the following statements *least accurately* describes a form of risk associated with investing in fixed income securities?
   A. Credit risk has only two components, default risk and downgrade risk.
   B. Other things equal, a bond is more valuable to an investor when it has less liquidity risk.
   C. Bonds that are callable, prepayable, or amortizing have more reinvestment risk than otherwise equivalent bonds without these features.

©2009 Kaplan, Inc.

SELF-TEST ANSWERS: FIXED INCOME INVESTMENTS

1. **A** Duration is a linear measure, but the relationship between bond price and yield for an option-free bond is convex. For a given decrease in yield, the estimated price increase using duration alone will be smaller than the actual price increase.

2. **A** First, determine the semiannual yield to maturity:

   N=38, PMT=3.5, PV= −91.16, FV=100 CPT→I/Y = 3.9534.

   Second, retain TVM info and enter:

   N = 34 CPT→PV = 91.60 for a gain of (91.60 − 91.16)/91.16 = 0.4827%.

3. **C** The market segmentation theory is based on the idea that different market participants (both borrowers and lenders) have strong preferences for different segments of the yield curve. If expectations are that future short-term interest rates will be falling enough, then the yield curve could be downward sloping even given that there is an increasing premium for lack of liquidity at longer maturities. A humped yield curve is consistent with expectations that short-term rates will rise over the near term and then decline.

4. **A** External credit enhancements are financial guarantees from third parties that generally support the performance of the bond. Portfolio insurance is not a third party guarantee.

5. **A** Effective duration must be used with bonds that have embedded options.

   $\Delta P = (-)(ED)(\Delta y) + (C)(\Delta y)^2$

   $\Delta P = (-)(6)(0.0025) + (62.5)(0.0025)^2 = -0.015 + 0.00039 = -0.014610\%$ or -1.461%

6. **B** The bond with the highest duration will benefit the most from a decrease in rates. The lower the coupon, lower the yield to maturity, and longer the time to maturity, the higher will be the duration.

7. **B** A conversion provision is an embedded option that favors the buyer, not the issuer, so buyers will accept a lower YTM with a conversion option. Call options and caps favor the issuer and increase the YTM that buyers will require.

8. **C** Effective duration = (41.86 − 38.05)/(39.91 × 2 × 0.005) = 9.546. Note that the price changes are based on a 50 basis points change in yield, so $\Delta y = 0.005$.

9. **B** A decrease in yield volatility will decrease the values of embedded options. The security holder is short the prepayment option. The decrease in the value of the prepayment option increases the value of the security, and the required yield will decrease. The security holder is long the put option so the value of a putable bond will decrease with a decrease in yield volatility and the required yield will increase.

10. **C** Since the OAS is less than the Z-spread for Bond A, the effect of the embedded option is to decrease the required yield, so it must be a call option and not a put option. The OAS is the spread after taking out the effect of the embedded option. Since the OAS is higher for Bond B, it represents the better value after adjusting for the value of the call in Bond A.

11. **B** The forward rate is $[1.045^4/1.03^2]^{1/2} - 1 = 6.02\%$, or use the approximation $[4.5(4) - 3(2)]/2 = 6$.

12. **C** CMOs are created to have different claims to the cash flows (principal, scheduled repayments, prepayments) than those of the underlying mortgage passthrough securities. On average, the yield will likely be lower on the CMO, since the reason to create them is to lower overall funding costs. They can have more or less prepayment risk, but on average will have the same prepayment risk as the underlying MBS.

13. **B** The arbitrage-free valuation approach discounts each cash flow at a discount rate specific to its maturity. For Treasury securities these discount rates are theoretical Treasury spot rates. For non-Treasury securities, these discount rates are Treasury spot rates plus a spread to account for liquidity risk, credit risk, and any other relevant risks that differ from those of a Treasury bond of similar maturity.

14. **A** Even if a bond does not default and is not downgraded, it still faces credit spread risk as the premium in the market for the bond's credit risk may increase. Lower liquidity risk (i.e., higher liquidity) is preferred by investors, reduces a bond's required rate of return, and increases its value, other things equal. Reinvestment risk is higher for callable, prepayable, or amortizing bonds as all these features lead to a greater probability of receiving principal repayment earlier, which means there are more funds to be reinvested over the life of the bond.

©2009 Kaplan, Inc.

The following is a review of the Derivative Investments principles designed to address the learning outcome statements set forth by CFA Institute®. This topic is also covered in:

DERIVATIVE MARKETS AND INSTRUMENTS

Study Session 17

EXAM FOCUS

This topic review contains introductory material for the upcoming reviews of specific types of derivatives. Derivatives-specific definitions and terminology are presented along with information about derivatives markets. Upon completion of this review, candidates should be familiar with the basic concepts that underlie derivatives and the general arbitrage framework. There is little contained in this review that will not be elaborated upon in the five reviews that follow.

LOS 67.a: Define a derivative and differentiate between exchange-traded and over-the-counter derivatives.

A **derivative** is a security that *derives* its value from the value or return of another asset or security.

A physical exchange exists for many options contracts and futures contracts. **Exchange-traded derivatives** are standardized and backed by a clearinghouse.

Forwards and *swaps* are custom instruments and are traded/created by dealers in a market with no central location. A dealer market with no central location is referred to as an **over-the-counter** market. They are largely unregulated markets and each contract is with a counterparty, which may expose the owner of a derivative to default risk (when the counterparty does not honor their commitment).

Some *options* trade in the over-the-counter market, notably bond options.

LOS 67.b: Define a forward commitment and a contingent claim.

A **forward commitment** is a legally binding promise to perform some action in the future. Forward commitments include forward contracts, futures contracts, and swaps. Forward contracts and futures contracts can be written on equities, indexes, bonds, physical assets, or interest rates.

A **contingent claim** is a claim (to a payoff) that depends on a particular event. **Options** are contingent claims that depend on a stock price at some future date. While forwards, futures, and swaps have payments that are made based on a price or rate outcome whether the movement is up or down, contingent claims only require a payment if a certain threshold price is broken (e.g., if the price is above X or the rate is below Y). It takes two options to replicate a future or forward.

LOS 67.c: Differentiate the basic characteristics of forward contracts, futures contracts, options (calls and puts), and swaps.

In a **forward contract**, one party agrees to buy, and the counterparty to sell, a physical asset or a security at a specific price on a specific date in the future. If the future price of the asset increases, the buyer (at the older, lower price) has a gain, and the seller a loss.

A **futures contract** is a forward contract that is standardized and exchange-traded. The main differences with forwards are that futures are traded in an active secondary market, are regulated, backed by the clearinghouse, and require a daily settlement of gains and losses.

A **swap** is a series of forward contracts. In the simplest swap, one party agrees to pay the short-term (floating) rate of interest on some principal amount, and the counterparty agrees to pay a certain (fixed) rate of interest in return. Swaps of different currencies and equity returns are also common.

An option to buy an asset at a particular price is termed a **call option**. The seller of the option has an *obligation* to sell the asset at the agreed-upon price, if the call buyer chooses to exercise the right to buy the asset.

An option to sell an asset at a particular price is termed a **put option**. The seller of the option has an *obligation* to purchase the asset at the agreed-upon price, if the put buyer chooses to exercise the right to sell the asset.

 Professor's Note: To remember these terms, note that the owner of a call can "call the asset in" (i.e., buy it); the owner of a put has the right to "put the asset to" the writer of the put.

LOS 67.d: Discuss the purposes and criticisms of derivative markets.

The *criticism of derivatives* is that they are "too risky," especially to investors with limited knowledge of sometimes complex instruments. Because of the high leverage involved in derivatives payoffs, they are sometimes likened to gambling.

The *benefits of derivatives* markets are that they:

- Provide price information.
- Allow risk to be managed and shifted among market participants.
- Reduce transactions costs.

©2009 Kaplan, Inc.

LOS 67.e: Explain arbitrage and the role it plays in determining prices and promoting market efficiency.

Arbitrage is an important concept in valuing (pricing) derivative securities. In its purest sense, arbitrage is riskless. If a return greater than the risk-free rate can be earned by holding a portfolio of assets that produces a certain (riskless) return, then an arbitrage opportunity exists.

Arbitrage opportunities arise when assets are mispriced. Trading by arbitrageurs will continue until they affect supply and demand enough to bring asset prices to efficient (no-arbitrage) levels.

There are two arbitrage arguments that are particularly useful in the study and use of derivatives.

The first is based on the "law of one price." Two securities or portfolios that have identical cash flows in the future, regardless of future events, should have the same price. If A and B have the identical future payoffs, and A is priced lower than B, buy A and sell B. You have an immediate profit, and the payoff on A will satisfy the (future) liability of being short on B.

The second type of arbitrage is used where two securities with uncertain returns can be combined in a portfolio that will have a certain payoff. If a portfolio consisting of A and B has a certain payoff, the portfolio should yield the risk-free rate. If this no-arbitrage condition is violated in that the certain return of A and B together is higher than the risk-free rate, an arbitrage opportunity exists. An arbitrageur could borrow at the risk-free rate, buy the A + B portfolio, and earn arbitrage profits when the certain payoff occurs. The payoff will be more than is required to pay back the loan at the risk-free rate.

 Professor's Note: We will discuss arbitrage further in our review of options.

KEY CONCEPTS

LOS 67.a

A derivative has a value that is "derived" from the value of another asset or interest rate.

Exchange-traded derivatives, notably futures and some options, are traded in centralized locations and are standardized, regulated, and default risk free.

Forwards and swaps are customized contracts (over-the-counter derivatives) created by dealers and by financial institutions. There is very limited trading of these contracts in secondary markets and default (counterparty) risk must be considered.

LOS 67.b

A forward commitment is a binding promise to buy or sell an asset or make a payment in the future. Forward contracts, futures contracts, and swaps are all forward commitments.

A contingent claim is an asset that has value only if some future event takes place (e.g., asset price is greater than a specified price). Options are contingent claims.

LOS 67.c

Forward contracts obligate one party to buy, and another to sell, a specific asset at a predetermined price at a specific time in the future.

Swaps contracts are equivalent to a series of forward contracts on interest rates, currencies, or equity returns.

Futures contracts are much like forward contracts, but are exchange-traded, quite liquid, and require daily settlement of any gains or losses.

A call option gives the holder the right, but not the obligation, to buy an asset at a predetermined price at some time in the future.

A put option gives the holder the right, but not the obligation, to sell an asset at a predetermined price at some time in the future.

LOS 67.d

Derivative markets are criticized for their risky nature. However, many market participants use derivatives to manage and reduce existing risk exposures.

Derivative securities play an important role in promoting efficient market prices and reducing transaction costs.

LOS 67.e

Riskless arbitrage refers to earning more than the risk-free rate of return with no risk, or earning an immediate gain with no possible future liability.

Arbitrage can be expected to force the prices of two securities or portfolios of securities to be equal if they have the same future cash flows regardless of future events.

©2009 Kaplan, Inc.

CONCEPT CHECKERS

1. Which of the following *most accurately* describes a derivative security?
    A derivative:
    A. always increases risk.
    B. has no expiration date.
    C. has a payoff based on another asset.

2. Which of the following statements about exchange-traded derivatives is *least accurate*?
    A. They are liquid.
    B. They are standardized contracts.
    C. They carry significant default risk.

3. A customized agreement to purchase a certain T-bond next Thursday for $1,000 is:
    A. an option.
    B. a futures contract.
    C. a forward commitment.

4. A futures contract is *least likely*:
    A. exchange-traded.
    B. a contingent claim.
    C. adjusted for profits and losses daily.

5. A swap is:
    A. highly regulated.
    B. a series of forward contracts.
    C. the exchange of one asset for another.

6. A call option gives the holder:
    A. the right to sell at a specific price.
    B. the right to buy at a specific price.
    C. an obligation to sell at a certain price.

7. Arbitrage prevents:
    A. market efficiency.
    B. profit higher than the risk-free rate of return.
    C. two assets with identical payoffs from selling at different prices.

8. Derivatives are *least likely* to provide or improve:
    A. liquidity.
    B. price information.
    C. inflation reduction.

ANSWERS – CONCEPT CHECKERS

1. **C** A derivative's value is "derived" from another asset.

2. **C** Exchange-traded derivatives have relatively low default risk because the clearinghouse stands between the counterparties involved in most contracts.

3. **C** This non-standardized type of contract is a forward commitment.

4. **B** A contingent claim has payoffs that depend on some future event (e.g., an option).

5. **B** A swap is an agreement to buy or sell an underlying asset periodically over the life of the swap contract. It is equivalent to a series of forward contracts.

6. **B** A call gives the owner the right to call an asset away (buy it) from the seller.

7. **C** Arbitrage forces two assets with the same expected future value to sell for the same current price. If this were not the case, you could simultaneously buy the cheaper asset and sell the more expensive one for a guaranteed riskless profit.

8. **C** Inflation is a monetary phenomenon, unaffected by derivatives.

©2009 Kaplan, Inc.

The following is a review of the Derivative Investments principles designed to address the learning outcome statements set forth by CFA Institute®. This topic is also covered in:

FORWARD MARKETS AND CONTRACTS

Study Session 17

EXAM FOCUS

This topic review introduces forward contracts in general and covers the characteristics of forward contracts on various financial securities, as well as interest rates. It is not easy material, and you should take the time to learn it well. This material on forward contracts provides a good basis for futures contracts and many of the characteristics of both types of contracts are the same. Take the time to understand the intuition behind the valuation of forward rate agreements.

FORWARD CONTRACTS

A **forward contract** is a bilateral contract that obligates one party to buy and the other to sell a specific quantity of an asset, at a set price, on a specific date in the future. Typically, neither party to the contract pays anything to get into the contract. If the expected future price of the asset increases over the life of the contract, the right to buy at the contract price will have positive value, and the obligation to sell will have an equal negative value. If the future price of the asset falls below the contract price, the result is opposite and the right to sell (at an above-market price) will have the positive value. The parties may enter into the contract as a speculation on the future price. More often, a party seeks to enter into a forward contract to hedge a risk it already has. The forward contract is used to eliminate uncertainty about the future price of an asset it plans to buy or sell at a later date. Forward contracts on physical assets, such as agricultural products, have existed for centuries. The Level 1 CFA curriculum, however, focuses on their (more recent) use for financial assets, such as T-bills, bonds, equities, and foreign currencies.

LOS 68.a: Explain delivery/settlement and default risk for both long and short positions in a forward contract.

The party to the forward contract that agrees to buy the financial or physical asset has a **long forward position** and is called the *long*. The party to the forward contract that agrees to sell or deliver the asset has a **short forward position** and is called the *short*.

We will illustrate the mechanics of the basic forward contract through an example based on the purchase and sale of a Treasury bill. Note that while forward and futures contracts on T-bills are usually quoted in terms of a discount percentage from face value, we will use dollar prices to make the example easy to follow. Actual pricing conventions and calculations are among the contract characteristics covered later in this review.

Consider a contract under which Party A agrees to buy a $1,000 face value, 90-day Treasury bill from Party B 30 days from now at a price of $990. Party A is the long and Party B is the short. Both parties have removed uncertainty about the price they will pay/receive for the T-bill at the future date. If 30 days from now T-bills are trading at $992, the short must deliver the T-bill to the long in exchange for a $990 payment. If T-bills are trading at $988 on the future date, the long must purchase the T-bill from the short for $990, the contract price.

Each party to a forward contract is exposed to **default risk** (or **counterparty risk**), the probability that the other party (the counterparty) will not perform as promised. It is unusual for any cash to actually be exchanged at the inception of a forward contract, unlike futures contracts in which each party posts an initial deposit (margin) as a guarantee of performance.

At any point in time, including the settlement date, only one party to the forward contract will "owe" money, meaning that side of the contract has a negative value. The other side of the contract will have a positive value of an equal amount. Following the example, if the T-bill price is $992 at the (future) settlement date and the short does not deliver the T-bill for $990 as promised, the short has defaulted.

LOS 68.b: Describe the procedures for settling a forward contract at expiration and discuss how termination alternatives prior to expiration can affect credit risk.

The previous example was for a **deliverable forward contract**. The short contracted to deliver the actual instrument, in this case a $1,000 face value, 90-day T-bill.

This is one procedure for settling a forward contract at the *settlement date* or expiration date specified in the contract.

An alternative settlement method is **cash settlement**. Under this method, the party that has a position with negative value is obligated to pay that amount to the other party. In the previous example, if the price of the T-bill were $992 on the expiration date, the short would satisfy the contract by paying $2 to the long. Ignoring transactions costs, this method yields the same result as asset delivery. If the short had the T-bill, it could be sold in the market for $992. The short's net proceeds, however, would be $990 after subtracting the $2 payment to the long. If the T-bill price at the settlement date were $988, the long would make a $2 payment to the short. Purchasing a T-bill at the market price of $988, together with this $2 payment, would make the total cost $990, just as it would be if it were a deliverable contract.

On the expiration (or settlement) date of the contract, the long receives a payment if the price of the asset is above the agreed-upon (forward) price; the short receives a payment if the price of the asset is below the contract price.

Terminating a Position Prior to Expiration

A party to a forward contract can **terminate the position** prior to expiration by entering into an opposite forward contract with an expiration date equal to the time remaining on the original contract.

©2009 Kaplan, Inc.

Study Session 17

Recall our example and assume that ten days after inception (it was originally a 30-day contract), the 20-day forward price of a $1,000 face value, 90-day T-bill is $992. The short, expecting the price to be even higher by the delivery date, wishes to terminate the contract. Since the short is obligated to sell the T-bill 20 days in the future, he can effectively exit the contract by entering into a new (20-day) forward contract to buy an identical T-bill (a long position) at the current forward price of $992.

The position of the original short now is two-fold, an obligation to sell a T-bill in 20 days for $990 (under the original contract) and an obligation to purchase an identical T-bill in 20 days for $992. He has "locked in" a $2 loss, but has effectively exited the contract since the amount owed at settlement is $2, regardless of the market price of the T-bill at the settlement date. No matter what the price of a 90-day T-bill is 20 days from now, he has the contractual right and obligation to buy one at $992 and to sell one at $990.

However, if the short's new forward contract is with a different party than the first forward contract, some **credit risk** remains. If the price of the T-bill at the expiration date is above $992, and the counterparty to the second forward contract fails to perform, the short's losses could exceed $2.

An alternative is to enter into the second (offsetting) contract with the same party as the original contract. This would avoid credit risk since the short could make a $2 payment to the counterparty at contract expiration, the amount of his net exposure. In fact, if the original counterparty were willing to take the short position in the second (20-day) contract at the $992 price, a payment of the present value of the $2 (discounted for the 20 days until the settlement date) would be an equivalent transaction. The original counterparty would be willing to allow termination of the original contract for an immediate payment of that amount.

If the original counterparty requires a payment larger than the present value of $2 to exit the contract, the short must weight this additional cost to exit the contract against the default risk he bears by entering into the offsetting contract with a different counterparty at a forward price of $992.

LOS 68.c: Differentiate between a dealer and an end user of a forward contract.

The **end user of a forward contract** is typically a corporation, government unit, or nonprofit institution that has existing risk they wish to avoid by locking in the future price of an asset. A U.S. corporation that has an obligation to make a payment in Euros 60 days from now can eliminate its exchange rate risk by entering into a forward contract to purchase the required amount of Euros for a certain dollar-denominated payment with a settlement date 60 days in the future.

Dealers are often banks, but can also be nonbank financial institutions such as securities brokers. Ideally, dealers will balance their overall long positions with their overall short positions by entering forward contracts with end users who have opposite existing risk exposures. A dealer's quote desk will quote a buying price (at which they will assume a long position) and a slightly higher selling price (at which they will assume a short position). The bid/ask spread between the two is the dealer's compensation for administrative costs as well as bearing default risk and any asset price risk from unbalanced (unhedged) positions. Dealers will also enter into contracts with other dealers to hedge a net long or net short position.

LOS 68.d: Describe the characteristics of equity forward contracts and forward contracts on zero-coupon and coupon bonds.

Equity forward contracts where the underlying asset is a single stock, a portfolio of stocks, or a stock index, work in much the same manner as other forward contracts. An investor who wishes to sell 10,000 shares of IBM stock 90 days from now and wishes to avoid the uncertainty about the stock price on that date, could do so by taking a short position in a forward contract covering 10,000 IBM shares. (We will leave the motivation for this and the pricing of such a contract aside for now.)

A dealer might quote a price of $100 per share, agreeing to pay $1 million for the 10,000 shares 90 days from now. The contract may be deliverable or settled in cash as described above. The stock seller has locked in the selling price of the shares and will get no more if the price (in 90 days) is actually higher, and will get no less if the price actually lower.

A portfolio manager who wishes to sell a portfolio of several stocks 60 days from now can similarly request a quote, giving the dealer the company names and the number of shares of each stock in the portfolio. The only difference between this type of forward contract and several forward contracts each covering a single stock, is that the pricing would be better (a higher total price) for the portfolio because overall administration/origination costs would be less for the portfolio forward contract.

A forward contract on a stock index is similar except that the contract will be based on a notional amount and will very likely be a cash-settlement contract.

> **Example: Equity index forward contracts**
>
> A portfolio manager desires to generate $10 million 100 days from now from a portfolio that is quite similar in composition to the S&P 100 index. She requests a quote on a short position in a 100-day forward contract based on the index with a notional amount of $10 million and gets a quote of 525.2. If the index level at the settlement date is 535.7, calculate the amount the manager will pay or receive to settle the contract.
>
> **Answer:**
>
> The actual index level is 2% *above* the contract price, or:
>
> $$535.7 \,/\, 525.2 - 1 = 0.02 = 2\%$$

©2009 Kaplan, Inc.

As the short party, the portfolio manager must pay 2% of the $10 million notional amount, $200,000, to the long.

Alternatively, if the index were 1% below the contract level, the portfolio manager would receive a payment from the long of $100,000, which would approximately offset any decrease in the portfolio value.

Dividends are usually not included in equity forward contracts, as the uncertainty about dividend amounts and payment dates is small compared to the uncertainty about future equity prices. Since forward contracts are custom instruments, the parties could specify a total return value (including dividends) rather than simply the index value. This would effectively remove dividend uncertainty as well.

Forward Contracts on Zero-Coupon and Coupon Bonds

Forward contracts on short-term, zero-coupon bonds (T-bills in the United States) and coupon interest-paying bonds are quite similar to those on equities. However, while equities do not have a maturity date, bonds do, and the forward contract must settle before the bond matures.

As we noted earlier, T-bill prices are often quoted as a percentage discount from face value. The percentage discount for T-bills is annualized so that a 90-day T-bill quoted at a 4% discount will be priced at a (90 / 360) × 4% = 1% discount from face value. This is equivalent to a price quote of (1 − 0.01) × $1,000 = $990 per $1,000 of face value.

Example: Bond forwards

A forward contract covering a $10 million face value of T-bills that will have 100 days to maturity at contract settlement is priced at 1.96 on a discount yield basis. Compute the dollar amount the long must pay at settlement for the T-bills.

Answer

The 1.96% annualized discount must be "unannualized" based on the 100 days to maturity.

0.0196 × (100 / 360) = 0.005444 is the actual discount.

The dollar settlement price is (1 − 0.005444) × $10 million = $9,945,560.

Please note that when market interest rates increase, discounts increase, and T-bill prices fall. A long, who is obligated to purchase the bonds, will have losses on the forward contract when interest rates rise, and gains on the contract when interest rates fall. The outcomes for the short will be opposite.

The price specified in forward contracts on coupon-bearing bonds is typically stated as a yield to maturity as of the settlement date, exclusive of accrued interest. If the contract is on bonds with the possibility of default, there must be provisions in the contract to define default and specify the obligations of the parties in the event of default. Special provisions must also be included if the bonds have embedded options such as call features or conversion features. Forward contracts can be constructed covering individual bonds or portfolios of bonds.

LOS 68.e: Describe the characteristics of the Eurodollar time deposit market and define LIBOR and Euribor.

Eurodollar deposit is the term for deposits in large banks outside the United States denominated in U.S. dollars. The lending rate on dollar-denominated loans between banks is called the London Interbank Offered Rate (LIBOR). It is quoted as an annualized rate based on a 360-day year. In contrast to T-bill discount yields, LIBOR is an add-on rate, like a yield quote on a short-term certificate of deposit. LIBOR is used as a reference rate for floating rate U.S. dollar-denominated loans worldwide.

> **Example: LIBOR-based loans**
>
> Compute the amount that must be repaid on a $1 million loan for 30 days if 30-day LIBOR is quoted at 6%.
>
> **Answer:**
>
> The add-on interest is calculated as $1 million × 0.06 × (30 / 360) = $5,000. The borrower would repay $1,000,000 + $5,000 = $1,005,000 at the end of 30 days.

LIBOR is published daily by the British Banker's Association and is compiled from quotes from a number of large banks; some are large multinational banks based in other countries that have London offices.

There is also an equivalent Euro lending rate called **Euribor**, or Europe Interbank Offered Rate. Euribor, established in Frankfurt, is published by the European Central Bank.

The floating rates are for various periods and are quoted as such. For example, the terminology is 30-day LIBOR (or Euribor), 90-day LIBOR, and 180-day LIBOR, depending on the term of the loan. For longer-term floating-rate loans, the interest rate is reset periodically based on the then-current LIBOR for the relevant period.

©2009 Kaplan, Inc.

LOS 68.f: Describe the characteristics and calculate the gain/loss of forward rate agreements (FRAs).

LOS 68.g: Calculate and interpret the payoff of an FRA, and explain each of the component terms.

A **forward rate agreement** (FRA) can be viewed as a forward contract to borrow/lend money at a certain rate at some future date. In practice, these contracts settle in cash, but no actual loan is made at the settlement date. This means that the creditworthiness of the parties to the contract need not be considered in the forward interest rate, so an essentially riskless rate, such as LIBOR, can be specified in the contract. (The parties to the contract may still be exposed to default risk on the amount owed at settlement.)

The long position in an FRA is the party that would borrow the money (long the loan with the contract price being the interest rate on the loan). If the floating rate at contract expiration (LIBOR or Euribor) is above the rate specified in the forward agreement, the long position in the contract can be viewed as the right to borrow at below market rates and the long will receive a payment. If the reference rate at the expiration date is below the contract rate, the short will receive a cash payment from the long. (The right to lend at rates *higher than* market rates would have a positive value.)

To calculate the cash payment at settlement for a forward rate agreement, we need to calculate the value as of the settlement date of making a loan at a rate that is either above or below the market rate. Since the interest savings would come at the end of the "loan" period, the cash payment at settlement of the forward is the present value of the interest "savings." We need to calculate the discounted value at the settlement date of the interest savings or excess interest at the end of the loan period. An example will illustrate the calculation of the payment at expiration and some terminology of FRAs.

> **Example: FRAs**
>
> Consider an FRA that:
>
> - Expires/settles in 30 days.
> - Is based on a notional principal amount of $1 million.
> - Is based on 90-day LIBOR.
> - Specifies a forward rate of 5%.
>
> Assume that the actual 90-day LIBOR 30-days from now (at expiration) is 6%. Compute the cash settlement payment at expiration, and identify which party makes the payment.

Answer:

If the long could borrow at the contract rate of 5%, rather than the market rate of 6%, the interest saved on a 90-day $1 million loan would be:

$$(0.06 - 0.05)(90 / 360) \times 1 \text{ million} = 0.0025 \times 1 \text{ million} = \$2,500$$

The $2,500 in interest savings would not come until the end of the 90-day loan period. The value at settlement is the present value of these savings. The correct discount rate to use is the actual rate at settlement, 6%, not the contract rate of 5%.

The payment at settlement from the short to the long is:

$$\frac{2,500}{1 + \left[(0.06) \times (90 / 360)\right]} = \$2,463.05$$

In doing the calculation of the settlement payment, remember that the term of the FRA and the term of the underlying "loan" need not be the same and are *not* interchangeable. While the settlement date can be any future date, in practice it is usually some multiple of 30 days. The specific market rate on which we calculate the value of the contract will typically be similar, 30-day, 60-day, 90-day, or 180-day LIBOR. If we describe an FRA as a 60-day FRA on 90-day LIBOR, settlement or expiration is 60 days from now and the payment at settlement is based on 90-day LIBOR 60 days from now. Such an FRA could be quoted in (30-day) months, and would be described as a 2-by-5 FRA (or 2 × 5 FRA). The 2 refers to the number of months until contract expiration and the 5 refers to the total time until the end of the interest rate period (2 + 3 = 5).

The general formula for the payment to the long at settlement is:

$$(\text{notional principal}) \frac{(\text{floating} - \text{forward})\left(\dfrac{\text{days}}{360}\right)}{1 + (\text{floating})\left(\dfrac{\text{days}}{360}\right)}$$

where:
days = number of days in the loan term

The numerator is the "interest savings" in percent, and the denominator is the discount factor.

Note that if the *floating* rate underlying the agreement turns out to be below the *forward* rate specified in the contract, the numerator in the formula is negative and the short receives a payment from the long.

FRAs for non-standard periods (e.g., a 45-day FRA on 132-day LIBOR) are termed off-the-run FRAs.

©2009 Kaplan, Inc.

LOS 68.h: Describe the characteristics of currency forward contracts.

Under the terms of a **currency forward contract**, one party agrees to exchange a certain amount of one currency for a certain amount of another currency at a future date. This type of forward contract in practice will specify an exchange rate at which one party can buy a fixed amount of the currency underlying the contract. If we need to exchange 10 million Euros for U.S. dollars 60 days in the future, we might receive a quote of USD0.95. The forward contract specifies that we (the long) will purchase USD9.5 million for EUR10 million at settlement. Currency forward contracts can be deliverable or settled in cash. As with other forward contracts, the cash settlement amount is the amount necessary to compensate the party who would be disadvantaged by the actual change in market rates as of the settlement date. An example will illustrate this.

Example: Currency forwards

Gemco expects to receive EUR50 million three months from now and enters into a cash settlement currency forward to exchange these euros for U.S. dollars at USD1.23 per euro. If the market exchange rate is USD1.25 per euro at settlement, what is the amount of the payment to be received or paid by Gemco?

Answer:

Under the terms of the contract Gemco would receive:

$$\text{EUR50 million} \times \frac{\text{USD}}{\text{EUR}} 1.23 = \text{USD61.5 million}$$

Without the forward contract, Gemco would receive:

$$\text{EUR50 million} \times \frac{\text{USD}}{\text{EUR}} 1.25 = \text{USD62.5 million}$$

The counterparty would be disadvantaged by the difference between the contract rate and the market rate in an amount equal to the advantage that would have accrued to Gemco had they not entered into the currency forward.

Gemco must make a payment of USD1.0 million to the counterparty.

A direct calculation of the value of the long (USD) position at settlement is:

$$\left(\frac{\text{USD}}{\text{EUR}} 1.23 - \frac{\text{USD}}{\text{EUR}} 1.25 \right) \times \text{EUR50 million} = -\text{USD1.0 million}$$

KEY CONCEPTS

LOS 68.a

A deliverable forward contract on an asset specifies that the long (the buyer) will pay a certain amount at a future date to the short, who will deliver a certain amount of an asset.

Default risk in a forward contract is the risk that the other party to the contract will not perform at settlement, since typically no money changes hands at the initiation of the contract.

LOS 68.b

A forward contract with cash settlement does not require delivery of the underlying asset, but a cash payment at the settlement date from one counterparty to the other, based on the contract price and the market price of the asset at settlement.

Early termination of a forward contract can be accomplished by entering into a new forward contract with the opposite position, at the then-current expected forward price. This early termination will fix the amount of the gain or loss at the settlement date. If this new forward is with a different counterparty than the original, there is credit or default risk to consider since one of the two counterparties may fail to honor its obligation under the forward contract.

LOS 68.c

An end user of a forward contract is most often a corporation hedging an existing risk.

Forward dealers, large banks, or brokerages originate forward contracts and take the long side in some contracts and the short side in others, with a spread in pricing to compensate them for actual costs, bearing default risk, and any unhedged price risk they must bear.

LOS 68.d

An equity forward contract may be on a single stock, a customized portfolio, or an equity index, and is used to hedge the risk of equity prices at some future date.
- Equity forward contracts can be written on a total return basis (including dividends), but are typically based solely on an index value.
- Index forwards settle in cash based on the notional amount and the percentage difference between the index value in the forward contract and the actual index level at settlement.

Forward contracts in which bonds are the underlying asset may be quoted in terms of the discount on zero-coupon bonds (e.g., T-bills) or in terms of the yield to maturity on coupon bonds. Forwards on corporate bonds must contain special provisions to deal with the possibility of default as well as with any call or conversion features. Forward contracts may also be written on portfolios of fixed income securities or on bond indexes.

©2009 Kaplan, Inc.

LOS 68.e

Eurodollar time deposits are USD-denominated short-term unsecured loans to large money-center banks outside the United States.

The London Interbank Offered Rate (LIBOR) is an international reference rate for Eurodollar deposits and is quoted for 30-day, 60-day, 90-day, 180-day, or 360-day (1-year) terms.

Euribor is the equivalent for short-term Euro-denominated bank deposits (loans to banks).

For both LIBOR and Euribor, rates are expressed as annual rates and actual interest is based on the loan term as a proportion of a 360-day year.

LOS 68.f

Forward rate agreements (FRAs) serve to hedge the uncertainty about short-term rates (e.g. 30 or 90-day LIBOR) that will prevail in the future. If rates rise, the long receives a payment at settlement. The short receives a payment if the specified rate falls to a level below the contract rate.

LOS 68.g

The payment to the long at settlement on an FRA is:

$$\text{notional principal amount} \left\{ \frac{\left(\text{reference rate at settlement} - \text{FRA rate}\right)\left[\dfrac{\text{days in loan term}}{360}\right]}{1 + \text{reference rate at settlement} \times \left[\dfrac{\text{days in loan term}}{360}\right]} \right\}$$

The numerator is the difference between the rate on a loan for the specified period at the forward contract rate and the rate at settlement, and the denominator is to discount this interest differential back to the settlement date at the market rate at settlement.

LOS 68.h

Currency forward contracts specify that one party will deliver a certain amount of one currency at the settlement date in exchange for a certain amount of another currency.

Under cash settlement, a single cash payment is made at settlement based on the difference between the exchange rate fixed in the contract and the market exchange rate at the settlement date.

CONCEPT CHECKERS

1. The short in a deliverable forward contract:
   A. has no default risk.
   B. is obligated to deliver the specified asset.
   C. makes a cash payment to the long at settlement.

2. On the settlement date of a forward contract:
   A. the short may be required to sell the asset.
   B. the long must sell the asset or make a cash payment.
   C. at least one party must make a cash payment to the other.

3. Which of the following statements regarding early termination of a forward contract is *most accurate*?
   A. A party who enters into an offsetting contract to terminate has no risk.
   B. A party who terminates a forward contract early must make a cash payment.
   C. Early termination through an offsetting transaction with the original counterparty eliminates default risk.

4. A dealer in the forward contract market:
   A. cannot be a bank.
   B. may enter into a contract with another dealer.
   C. gets a small payment for each contract at initiation.

5. Which of the following statements regarding equity forward contracts is *least accurate*?
   A. Equity forwards may be settled in cash.
   B. Dividends are never included in index forwards.
   C. A short position in an equity forward could not hedge the risk of a purchase of that equity in the future.

6. Which of the following statements regarding forward contracts on 90-day T-bills is *most accurate*?
   A. The face value must be paid by the long at settlement.
   B. There is no default risk on these forwards because T-bills are government-backed.
   C. If short-term yields increase unexpectedly after contract initiation, the short will profit on the contract.

7. A Eurodollar time deposit:
   A. is priced on a discount basis.
   B. may be issued by a Japanese bank.
   C. is a certificate of deposit denominated in Euros.

8. One difference between LIBOR and Euribor is that:
   A. LIBOR is for London deposits.
   B. they are for different currencies.
   C. LIBOR is slightly higher due to default risk.

©2009 Kaplan, Inc.

9. Which of the following statements regarding a LIBOR-based FRA is *most accurate*?
   A. The short will settle the contract by making a loan.
   B. FRAs can be based on interest rates for 30-, 60-, or 90-day periods.
   C. If LIBOR increases unexpectedly over the contract term, the long will be required to make a cash payment at settlement.

10. Consider a $2 million FRA with a contract rate of 5% on 60-day LIBOR. If 60-day LIBOR is 6% at settlement, the long will:
   A. pay $3,333.
   B. receive $3,300.
   C. receive $3,333.

11. Party A has entered a currency forward contract to purchase €10 million at an exchange rate of $0.98 per euro. At settlement, the exchange rate is $0.97 per euro. If the contract is settled in cash, Party A will:
   A. make a payment of $100,000.
   B. receive a payment of $100,000.
   C. receive a payment of $103,090.

12. If the quoted discount yield on a 128-day, $1 million T-bill decreases from 3.15% to 3.07%, how much has the holder of the T-bill gained or lost?
   A. Lost $284.
   B. Gained $284.
   C. Gained $800.

13. 90-day LIBOR is quoted as 3.58%. How much interest would be owed at maturity for a 90-day loan of $1.5 million at LIBOR + 1.3%?
   A. $17,612.
   B. $18,300.
   C. $32,925.

14. A company treasurer needs to borrow 10 million euros for 180 days, 60 days from now. The type of FRA and the position he should take to hedge the interest rate risk of this transaction are:

FRA	Position
A. 2 × 6	Short
B. 2 × 8	Long
C. 2 × 8	Short

ANSWERS – CONCEPT CHECKERS

1. **B** The short in a forward contract is obligated to deliver the specified asset at the contract price on the settlement date. Either party may have default risk if there is any probability that the counterparty may not perform under the terms of the contract.

2. **A** A forward contract may call for settlement in cash or for delivery of the asset. Under a deliverable contract, the short is required to deliver the asset at settlement, not to make a cash payment.

3. **C** Terminating a forward contract early by entering into an offsetting forward contract with a different counterparty exposes a party to default risk. If the offsetting transaction is with the original counterparty, default risk is eliminated. No cash payment is required if an offsetting contract is used for early termination.

4. **B** Forward contracts dealers are commonly banks and large brokerage houses. They frequently enter into forward contracts with other dealers to offset long or short exposure. No payment is typically made at contract initiation.

5. **B** Index forward contracts may be written as total return contracts, which include dividends. Contracts may be written to settle in cash, or to be deliverable. A *long* position is used to reduce the price risk of an expected future purchase.

6. **C** When short-term rates increase, T-bill prices fall and the short position will profit. The price of a T-bill prior to maturity is always less than its face value. The deliverable security is a T-bill with 90 days to maturity. There is default risk on the *forward*, even though the underlying asset is considered risk free.

7. **B** Eurodollar time deposits are U.S. dollar-denominated accounts with banks outside the United States and are quoted as an add-on yield rather than on a discount basis.

8. **B** LIBOR is for U.S. dollar-denominated accounts while Euribor is for euro-denominated accounts. Neither is location-specific. Differences in these rates are due to the different currencies involved, not differences in default risk.

9. **B** A LIBOR-based contract can be based on LIBOR for various terms. They are settled in cash. The long will receive a payment when LIBOR is higher than the contract rate at settlement.

10. **B** $(0.06 - 0.05) \times (60 / 360) \times \$2 \text{ million} \times 1 / (1 + 0.06 / 6) = \$3,300.33$.

11. **A** $(\$0.98 - \$0.97) \times 10 \text{ million} = \$100,000$ loss. The long, Party A, is obligated to buy euros at \$0.98 when they are only worth \$0.97 and must pay $\$0.01 \times 10 \text{ million} = \$100,000$.

12. **B** The actual discount has decreased by:

$$(0.0315 - 0.0307) \times \frac{128}{360} = 0.0284\% \text{ of } \$1,000,000 \text{ or } \$284.$$

A decrease in the discount is an increase in value.

©2009 Kaplan, Inc.

13. **B** $(0.0358 + 0.013)\left(\dfrac{90}{360}\right)1.5$ million $= \$18,300$. Both LIBOR and any premium to LIBOR

are quoted as annualized rates.

14. **B** This requires a long position in a 2 × 8 FRA.

FUTURES MARKETS AND CONTRACTS

EXAM FOCUS

Candidates should focus on the terminology of futures markets, how futures differ from forwards, the mechanics of margin deposits, and the process of marking to market. Limit price moves, delivery options, and the characteristics of the basic types of financial futures contracts are also likely exam topics. Learn the ways a futures position can be terminated prior to contract expiration and understand how cash settlement is accomplished by the final mark to market at contract expiration.

LOS 69.a: Describe the characteristics of futures contracts.

LOS 69.b: Distinguish between futures contracts and forward contracts.

Futures contracts are very much like the forward contracts we learned about in the previous topic review. They are *similar* in that both:

- Can be either deliverable or cash settlement contracts.
- Are priced to have zero value at the time an investor enters into the contract.

Futures contracts *differ* from forward contracts in the following ways:

- Futures contracts trade on organized exchanges. Forwards are private contracts and do not trade.
- Futures contracts are highly standardized. Forwards are customized contracts satisfying the needs of the parties involved.
- A single clearinghouse is the counterparty to all futures contracts. Forwards are contracts with the originating counterparty.
- The government regulates futures markets. Forward contracts are usually not regulated.

Characteristics of Futures Contracts

Standardization. A major difference between forwards and futures is that futures contracts have standardized contract terms. Futures contracts specify the quality and quantity of goods that can be delivered, the delivery time, and the manner of delivery. The exchange also sets the minimum price fluctuation (which is called the tick size). For example, the basic price movement, or tick, for a 5,000-bushel grain contract is a quarter of a point (1 point = $0.01) per bushel, or $12.50 per contract. Contracts also have a daily price limit, which sets the maximum price movement allowed in a single day. For example, wheat cannot move more than $0.20 from its close the preceding day. The maximum price limits expand during periods of high volatility and are not in effect during the delivery month. The exchange also sets the trading times for each contract.

©2009 Kaplan, Inc.

It would appear that these rules would restrict trading activity, but in fact, they stimulate trading. Why? Standardization tells traders exactly what is being traded and the conditions of the transaction. *Uniformity promotes market liquidity.*

The purchaser of a futures contract is said to have gone long or taken a *long position*, while the seller of a futures contract is said to have gone short or taken a *short position*. For each contract traded, there is a buyer and a seller. The long has contracted to buy the asset at the contract price at contract expiration, and the short has an obligation to sell at that price. Futures contracts are used by *speculators* to gain exposure to changes in the price of the asset underlying a futures contract. A *hedger*, in contrast, will use futures contracts to reduce exposure to price changes in the asset (hedge their asset price risk). An example is a wheat farmer who sells wheat futures to reduce the uncertainty about the price of wheat at harvest time.

Clearinghouse. Each exchange has a *clearinghouse*. The clearinghouse guarantees that traders in the futures market will honor their obligations. The clearinghouse does this by splitting each trade once it is made and acting as the opposite side of each position. The clearinghouse acts as the buyer to every seller and the seller to every buyer. By doing this, the clearinghouse allows either side of the trade to reverse positions at a future date without having to contact the other side of the initial trade. This allows traders to enter the market knowing that they will be able to reverse their position. Traders are also freed from having to worry about the counterparty defaulting since the counterparty is now the clearinghouse. In the history of U.S. futures trading, the clearinghouse has never defaulted on a trade.

Professor's Note: The terminology is that you "bought" bond futures if you entered into the contract with the long position. In my experience, this terminology has caused confusion for many candidates. You don't purchase the contract, you enter into it. You are contracting to buy an asset on the long side. "Buy" means take the long side, and "sell" means take the short side in futures.

LOS 69.c: Differentiate between margin in the securities markets and margin in the futures markets, and explain the role of initial margin, maintenance margin, variation margin, and settlement in futures trading.

In securities markets, margin on a stock or bond purchase is a percentage of the market value of the asset. Initially, 50% of the stock purchase amount may be borrowed, and the remaining amount, the equity in the account, must be paid in cash. There is interest charged on the borrowed amount, the margin loan. The margin percentage, the percent of the security value that is "owned," will vary over time and must be maintained at some minimum percentage of market value.

In the futures markets, margin is a performance guarantee. It is money deposited by both the long and the short. There is no *loan* involved and, consequently, no interest charges.

Each futures exchange has a clearinghouse. To safeguard the clearinghouse, the exchange requires traders to post margin and settle their accounts on a daily basis. Before trading, the trader must deposit funds (called margin) with a broker (who, in turn, will post margin with the clearinghouse).

In securities markets, the cash deposited is paid to the seller of the security, with the balance of the purchase price provided by the broker. This is why the unpaid balance is a loan, with interest charged to the buyer who purchased on margin.

Initial margin is the money that must be deposited in a futures account before any trading takes place. It is set for each type of underlying asset. Initial margin per contract is relatively low and equals about one day's maximum price fluctuation on the total value of the contract's underlying asset.

Maintenance margin is the amount of margin that must be maintained in a futures account. If the margin balance in the account falls below the maintenance margin due to a change in the contract price for the underlying asset, additional funds must be deposited to bring the margin balance back up to the initial margin requirement.

This is in contrast to equity account margins, which require investors only to bring the margin percentage up to the maintenance margin, not back to the initial margin level.

Variation margin is the funds that must be deposited into the account to bring it back to the initial margin amount. If account margin exceeds the initial margin requirement, funds can be withdrawn or used as initial margin for additional positions.

The **settlement price** is analogous to the closing price for a stock but is not simply the price of the last trade. It is an average of the prices of the trades during the last period of trading, called the closing period, which is set by the exchange. This feature of the settlement price prevents manipulation by traders. The settlement price is used to make margin calculations at the end of each trading day.

Initial and minimum margins in securities accounts are set by the Federal Reserve, although brokerage houses can require more. Initial and maintenance margins in the futures market are set by the clearinghouse and are based on historical daily price volatility of the underlying asset since margin is resettled daily in futures accounts. Margin in futures accounts is typically *much lower* as a percentage of the value of the assets covered by the futures contract. This means that the leverage, based on the actual cash required, is much higher for futures accounts.

How a Futures Trade Takes Place

In contrast to forward contracts in which a bank or brokerage is usually the counterparty to the contract, there is a buyer and a seller on each side of a futures trade. The futures exchange selects the contracts that will trade. The asset, the amount of the asset, and the settlement/delivery date are standardized in this manner (e.g., a June futures contract on 90-day T-bills with a face amount of $1 million). Each time there is a trade, the delivery price for that contract is the equilibrium price at that point in time, which depends on supply (by those wishing to be short) and demand (by those wishing to be long).

©2009 Kaplan, Inc.

The mechanism by which supply and demand determine this equilibrium is open outcry at a particular location on the exchange floor called a "pit." Each trade is reported to the exchange so that the equilibrium price, at any point in time, is known to all traders.

LOS 69.d: Describe price limits and the process of marking to market and compute and interpret the margin balance, given the previous day's balance and the change in the futures price.

Many futures contracts have **price limits**, which are exchange-imposed limits on how much the contract price can change from the previous day's settlement price. Exchange members are prohibited from executing trades at prices outside these limits. If the (equilibrium) price at which traders would willingly trade is above the upper limit or below the lower limit, trades cannot take place.

Consider a futures contract that has daily price limits of two cents and settled the previous day at $1.04. If, on the following trading day, traders wish to trade at $1.07 because of changes in market conditions or expectations, no trades will take place. The settlement price will be reported as $1.06 (for the purposes of marking-to-market). The contract will be said to have made a **limit move**, and the price is said to be **limit up** (from the previous day). If market conditions had changed such that the price at which traders are willing to trade is below $1.02, $1.02 will be the settlement price, and the price is said to be **limit down**. If trades cannot take place because of a limit move, either up or down, the price is said to be **locked limit** since no trades can take place and traders are "locked" into their existing positions.

Marking to market is the process of adjusting the margin balance in a futures account each day for the change in the value of the contract assets from the previous trading day, based on the new settlement price.

The futures exchanges can require a mark-to-market more frequently (than daily) under extraordinary circumstances.

Computing the Margin Balance

> **Example: Margin balance**
>
> Consider a long position of five July wheat contracts, each of which covers 5,000 bushels. Assume that the contract price is $2.00 and that each contract requires an initial margin deposit of $150 and a maintenance margin of $100. The total initial margin required for the 5-contract trade is $750. The maintenance margin for the account is $500. Compute the margin balance for this position after a 2-cent decrease in price on Day 1, a 1-cent increase in price on Day 2, and a 1-cent decrease in price on Day 3.

Answer:

Each contract is for 5,000 bushels so that a price change of $0.01 per bushel changes the contract value by $50, or $250 for the five contracts: $(0.01)(5)(5,000) = \$250.00$.

The following figure illustrates the change in the margin balance as the price of this contract changes each day. Note that the initial balance is the initial margin requirement of $750 and that the required deposit is based on the previous day's price change.

Margin Balances

Day	Required Deposit	Price/Bushel	Daily Change	Gain/Loss	Balance
0 (Purchase)	$750	$2.00	0	0	$750
1	0	$1.98	−$0.02	−$500	$250
2	$500	$1.99	+$0.01	+$250	$1,000
3	0	$1.98	−$0.01	−$250	$750

At the close on Day 1, the margin balance has gone below the minimum or maintenance margin level of $500. Therefore, a deposit of $500 is required to bring the margin back to the initial margin level of $750. We can interpret the margin balance at any point as the amount the investor would realize if the position were closed out by a reversing trade at the most recent settlement price used to calculate the margin balance.

LOS 69.e: Describe how a futures contract can be terminated at or prior to expiration.

There are **four ways to terminate a futures contract:**

1. A short can terminate the contract by delivering the goods, and a long can terminate the contract by accepting delivery and paying the contract price to the short. This is called **delivery.** The location for delivery (for physical assets), terms of delivery, and details of exactly what is to be delivered are all specified in the contract. Deliveries represent less than 1% of all contract terminations.

2. In a **cash-settlement contract**, delivery is not an option. The futures account is marked-to-market based on the settlement price on the last day of trading.

3. You may make a **reverse**, or **offsetting**, trade in the futures market. This is similar to the way we described exiting a forward contract prior to expiration. With futures, however, the other side of your position is held by the clearinghouse—if you make an exact opposite trade (maturity, quantity, and good) to your current position, the clearinghouse will net your positions out, leaving you with a zero balance. This is how most futures positions are settled. The contract price can differ between the

two contracts. If you initially are long one contract at $370 per ounce of gold and subsequently sell (take the short position in) an identical gold contract when the price is $350/oz., $20 times the number of ounces of gold specified in the contract will be deducted from the margin deposit(s) in your account. The sale of the futures contract ends the exposure to future price fluctuations on the first contract. Your position has been *reversed*, or **closed out**, by a *closing* trade.

4. A position may also be settled through an **exchange for physicals**. Here, you find a trader with an opposite position to your own and deliver the goods and settle up between yourselves, off the floor of the exchange (called an ex-pit transaction). This is the sole exception to the federal law that requires that all trades take place on the floor of the exchange. You must then contact the clearinghouse and tell them what happened. An exchange for physicals differs from a delivery in that the traders actually exchange the goods, the contract is not closed on the floor of the exchange, and the two traders privately negotiate the terms of the transaction. Regular delivery involves only one trader and the clearinghouse.

Delivery Options in Futures Contracts

Some futures contracts grant **delivery options** to the short; options on what, where, and when to deliver. Some Treasury bond contracts give the short a choice of several bonds that are acceptable to deliver and options as to when to deliver during the expiration month. Physical assets, such as gold or corn, may offer a choice of delivery locations to the short. These options can be of significant value to the holder of the short position in a futures contract.

LOS 69.f: Describe the characteristics of the following types of futures contracts: Eurodollar, Treasury bond, stock index, and currency.

Let's introduce financial futures by first examining the mechanics of a T-bill futures contract. **Treasury bill futures contracts** are based on a $1 million face value 90-day (13-week) T-bill and settle in cash. The price quotes are 100 minus the annualized discount in percent on the T-bills.

A price quote of 98.52 represents an annualized discount of 1.48%, an actual discount from face of $0.0148 \times (90 / 360) = 0.0037$, and a "delivery" price of $(1 - 0.0037) \times 1$ million = $996,300.

T-bill futures contracts are not as important as they once were. Their prices are heavily influenced by U.S. Federal Reserve operations and overall monetary policy. T-bill futures have lost importance in favor of Eurodollar futures contracts, which represent a more free-market and more global measure of short-term interest rates to top quality borrowers for U.S. dollar-denominated loans.

Eurodollar futures are based on 90-day LIBOR, which is an add-on yield, rather than a discount yield. By convention, however, the price quotes follow the same convention as T-bills and are calculated as (100 – annualized LIBOR in percent). These contracts settle in cash, and the minimum price change is one "tick," which is a price change of 0.0001 = 0.01%, representing $25 per $1 million contract. A quote of 97.60 corresponds to an annualized LIBOR of (100 – 97.6) = 2.4% and an effective 90-day yield of 2.4 / 4 = 0.6%.

Professor's Note: One of the first things a new T-bill futures trader learns is that each change in price of 0.01 in the price of a T-bill futures contract is worth $25. If you took a long position at 98.52 and the price fell to 98.50, your loss is $50 per contract. Since Eurodollar contracts on 90-day LIBOR are the same size and priced in a similar fashion, a price change of 0.01 represents a $25 change in value for these as well.

Treasury bond futures contracts:

• Are traded for Treasury bonds with maturities greater than 15 years.
• Are a deliverable contract.
• Have a face value of $100,000.
• Are quoted as a percent and fractions of 1% (measured in 1/32nds) of face value.

The short in a Treasury bond futures contract has the option to deliver any of several bonds that will satisfy the delivery terms of the contract. This is called a delivery option and is valuable to the short because at expiration, one particular Treasury bond will be the **cheapest-to-deliver** bond.

Each bond is given a *conversion factor*, which is used to adjust the long's payment at delivery so that the more valuable bonds receive a higher payment. These factors are multipliers for the futures price at settlement. The long pays the futures price at expiration times the conversion factor.

Stock index futures. The most popular stock index future is the S&P 500 Index Future that trades in Chicago. Settlement is in cash and is based on a multiplier of 250.

The value of a contract is 250 times the level of the index stated in the contract. With an index level of 1,000, the value of each contract is $250,000. Each index point in the futures price represents a gain or loss of $250 per contract. A long stock index futures position on S&P 500 index futures at 1,051 would show a gain of $1,750 in the trader's account if the index were 1,058 at the settlement date ($250 × 7 = $1,750). A smaller contract is traded on the same index and has a multiplier of 50.

Futures contracts covering several other popular indices are traded, and the pricing and contract valuation are the same, although the multiplier can vary from contract to contract.

Currency futures. The currency futures market is smaller in volume than the forward currency market we described in the previous topic review. In the United States, currency contracts trade on the euro (EUR), Mexican peso (MXP), and yen (JPY), among others. Contracts are set in units of the foreign currency, and the price is stated in USD/unit. The size of the peso contract is MXP500,000, and the euro contract is on EUR125,000. A change in the price of the currency unit of USD0.0001 translates into a gain or loss of USD50 on a MXP500,000 unit contract and USD12.50 on a EUR125,000 unit contract.

©2009 Kaplan, Inc.

KEY CONCEPTS

LOS 69.a

Like forward contracts, futures contracts are most commonly for delivery of commodities and financial assets at a future date and can require delivery or settlement in cash.

LOS 69.b

Compared to forward contracts, futures contracts:
- Are more liquid, trade on exchanges, and can be closed out by an offsetting trade.
- Do not have counterparty risk; the clearinghouse acts as counterparty to each side of the contract.
- Have lower transactions costs.
- Require margin deposits and are marked to market daily.
- Are standardized contracts as to asset quantity, quality, settlement dates, and delivery requirements.

LOS 69.c

Futures margin deposits are not loans, but deposits to ensure performance under the terms of the contract.

Initial margin is the deposit required to initiate a futures position.

Maintenance margin is the minimum margin amount. When margin falls below this amount, it must be brought back up to its initial level by depositing variation margin.

Margin calculations are based on the daily settlement price, the average of the prices for trades during a closing period set by the exchange.

LOS 69.d

Trades cannot take place at prices that differ from the previous day's settlement prices by more than the price limit and are said to be limit down (up) when the new equilibrium price is below (above) the minimum (maximum) price for the day.

Marking-to-market is the process of adding gains to or subtracting losses from the margin account daily, based on the change in settlement prices from one day to the next.

The mark-to-market adjustment either adds the day's gains in contract value to the long's margin balance and subtracts them from the short's margin balance, or subtracts the day's loss in contract value from the long's margin balance and adds them to the short's margin balance.

LOS 69.e

A futures position can be terminated by:
- An offsetting trade, entering into an opposite position in the same contract.
- Cash payment at expiration (cash-settlement contract).
- Delivery of the asset specified in the contract.
- An exchange for physicals (asset delivery off the exchange).

LOS 69.f

Eurodollar futures contracts are for a face value of $1,000,000, are quoted as 100 minus annualized 90-day LIBOR in percent, and settle in cash.

Treasury bond contracts are for a face value of $100,000, give the short a choice of bonds to deliver, and use conversion factors to adjust the contract price for the bond that is delivered.

Stock index futures have a multiplier that is multiplied by the index to calculate the contract value, and settle in cash.

Currency futures are for delivery of standardized amounts of foreign currency.

©2009 Kaplan, Inc.

CONCEPT CHECKERS

1. Which of the following statements about futures markets is *least accurate*?
   A. Hedgers trade to reduce some preexisting risk exposure.
   B. The clearinghouse guarantees that traders in the futures market will honor their obligations.
   C. If an account rises to or exceeds the maintenance margin, the trader must deposit variation margin.

2. The daily process of adjusting the margin in a futures account is called:
   A. variation margin.
   B. marking-to-market.
   C. maintenance margin.

3. A trader buys (takes a long position in) a Eurodollar futures contract ($1 million face value) at 98.14 and closes it out at a price of 98.27. On this contract the trader has:
   A. lost $325.
   B. gained $325.
   C. gained $1,300.

4. In the futures market, a contract does not trade for two days because trades are not permitted at the equilibrium price. The market for this contract is:
   A. limit up.
   B. limit down.
   C. locked limit.

5. The existence of a delivery option with respect to Treasury bond futures means that the:
   A. short can choose which bond to deliver.
   B. short has the option to settle in cash or by delivery.
   C. long chooses which of a number of bonds will be delivered.

6. Assume the holder of a long futures position negotiates privately with the holder of a short futures position to accept delivery to close out both the long and short positions. Which of the following statements about the transaction is *most accurate*? The transaction is:
   A. also known as delivery.
   B. also known as an exchange for physicals.
   C. the most common way to close a futures position.

7. A conversion factor in a Treasury bond contract is:
   A. used to adjust the number of bonds to be delivered.
   B. multiplied by the face value to determine the delivery price.
   C. multiplied by the futures price to determine the delivery price.

8.   Three 125,000 euro futures contracts are sold at a price of $1.0234. The next day the price settles at $1.0180. The mark-to-market for this account changes the previous day's margin by:
    A.   +$675.
    B.   −$675.
    C.   +$2,025.

9.   In the futures market, the clearinghouse is *least likely* to:
    A.   decide which contracts will trade.
    B.   set initial and maintenance margins.
    C.   act as the counterparty to every trade.

10.   Funds deposited to meet a margin call are termed:
    A.   daily margin.
    B.   settlement costs.
    C.   variation margin.

11.   Compared to forward contracts, futures contracts are *least likely* to be:
    A.   standardized.
    B.   larger in size.
    C.   less subject to default risk.

©2009 Kaplan, Inc.

ANSWERS – CONCEPT CHECKERS

1. **C** If an account rises to or exceeds the maintenance margin, no payment needs to be made, and the trader has the option to remove the excess funds from the account. Only if an account falls below the maintenance margin does variation margin need to be paid to bring the level of the account back up to the level of the initial margin.

2. **B** The *process* is called marking-to-market. Variation margin is the funds that must be deposited when marking-to-market draws the margin balance below the maintenance margin.

3. **B** The price is quoted as 100 minus the annualized discount in percent. Remember that the gains and losses on T-bill and Eurodollar futures are $25 per basis point of the price quote. The price is up 13 ticks, and 13 × $25 is a gain of $325 for a long position.

4. **C** This describes the situation when the equilibrium price is either above or below the prior day's settle price by more than the permitted (limit) daily price move. We do not know whether it is limit up or limit down.

5. **A** The short has the option to deliver any of a number of permitted bonds. The delivery price is adjusted by a conversion factor that is calculated for each permitted bond.

6. **B** When the holder of a long position negotiates directly with the holder of the short position to accept delivery of the underlying commodity to close out both positions, this is called an *exchange for physicals*. (This is a private transaction that occurs *ex-pit* and is one exception to the federal law that all trades take place on the exchange floor.) Note that the exchange for physicals differs from an offsetting trade in which no delivery takes place and also differs from delivery in which the commodity is simply delivered as a result of the futures expiration with no secondary agreement. Most futures positions are settled by an *offsetting trade*.

7. **C** It adjusts the delivery price based on the futures price at contract expiration.

8. **C** (1.0234 – 1.0180) × 125,000 × 3 = $2,025. The contracts were sold and the price declined, so the adjustment is an addition to the account margin.

9. **A** The exchange determines which contracts will trade.

10. **C** When insufficient funds exist to satisfy margin requirements, a variation margin must be posted.

11. **B** Size is not one of the things that distinguishes forwards and futures, although the contract size of futures is standardized, whereas forwards are customized for each party.

The following is a review of the Derivative Investments principles designed to address the learning outcome statements set forth by CFA Institute®. This topic is also covered in:

OPTION MARKETS AND CONTRACTS

EXAM FOCUS

This derivatives review introduces options, describes their terms and trading, and provides derivations of several options valuation results. Candidates should spend some time understanding how the payoffs on several types of options are determined. This includes options on stocks, bonds, stock indices, interest rates, currencies, and futures. The assigned material on establishing upper and lower bounds is extensive, so it should not be ignored. Candidates must learn at least one of the put-call parity relations and how to construct an arbitrage strategy. The notation, formulas, and relations may seem daunting, but if you put in the time to understand what the notation is saying (and why), you can master the important points.

OPTIONS CHARACTERISTICS

An **option contract** gives its owner the right, but not the legal obligation, to conduct a transaction involving an underlying asset at a predetermined future date (the exercise date) and at a predetermined price (the exercise or strike price). Options give the option buyer the right to decide whether or not the trade will eventually take place. The seller of the option has the obligation to perform if the buyer exercises the option.

- The owner of a *call option* has the right to purchase the underlying asset at a specific price for a specified time period.
- The owner of a *put option* has the right to sell the underlying asset at a specific price for a specified time period.

For every owner of an option, there must be a seller. The seller of the option is also called the *option writer*. There are four possible options positions:

1. Long call: the buyer of a call option—has the right to buy an underlying asset.

2. Short call: the writer (seller) of a call option—has the obligation to sell the underlying asset.

3. Long put: the buyer of a put option—has the right to sell the underlying asset.

4. Short put: the writer (seller) of a put option—has the obligation to buy the underlying asset.

To acquire these rights, owners of options must buy them by paying a price called the *option premium* to the seller of the option.

Listed stock option contracts trade on exchanges and are normally for 100 shares of stock. After issuance, stock option contracts are adjusted for stock splits but not cash dividends.

©2009 Kaplan, Inc.

To see how an option contract works, consider the stock of ABC Company. It sells for $55 and has a call option available on it that sells for a premium of $10. This call option has an exercise price of $50 and has an expiration date in five months. The *exercise price* of $50 is often called the option's *strike price*.

 Professor's Note: The option premium is simply the price of the option. Please do not confuse this with the exercise price of the option, which is the price at which the underlying asset will be bought/sold if the option is exercised.

If the ABC call option is purchased for $10, the buyer can purchase ABC stock from the option seller over the next five months for $50. The seller, or writer, of the option gets to keep the $10 premium no matter what the stock does during this time period. If the option buyer exercises the option, the seller will receive the $50 strike price and must deliver to the buyer a share of ABC stock. If the price of ABC stock falls to $50 or below, the buyer is not obligated to exercise the option. Note that option holders will only exercise their right to act if it is profitable to do so. The option writer, however, has an obligation to act at the request of the option holder.

A put option on ABC stock is the same as a call option except the buyer of the put (long position) has the right to sell a share of ABC for $50 at any time during the next five months. The put writer (short position) has the obligation to buy ABC stock at the exercise price in the event that the option is exercised.

The owner of the option is the one who decides whether to exercise the option or not. If the option has value, the buyer may either exercise the option or sell the option to another buyer in the secondary options market.

LOS 70.a: Define European option, American option, and the concept of moneyness of an option.

American options may be exercised at any time up to and including the contract's expiration date.

European options can be exercised only on the contract's expiration date.

 Professor's Note: The name of the option does not imply where the option trades— they are just names.

At expiration, an American option and a European option on the same asset with the same strike price are identical. They may either be exercised or allowed to expire. Before expiration, however, they are different and may have different values, so you must distinguish between the two.

If two options are identical (maturity, underlying stock, strike price, etc.) in all ways, except that one is a European option and the other is an American option, the value of the American option will equal or exceed the value of the European option. Why? The

Study Session 17

early exercise feature of the American option gives it more flexibility, so it should be worth at least as much and possibly more.

Moneyness refers to whether an option is *in the money* or *out of the money*. If immediate exercise of the option would generate a positive payoff, it is in the money. If immediate exercise would result in a loss (negative payoff), it is out of the money. When the current asset price equals the exercise price, exercise will generate neither a gain nor loss, and the option is *at the money*.

The following describe the conditions for a **call option** to be in, out of, or at the money.

- *In-the-money call options.* If $S - X > 0$, a call option is in the money. $S - X$ is the amount of the payoff a call holder would receive from immediate exercise, buying a share for X and selling it in the market for a greater price S.
- *Out-of-the-money call options.* If $S - X < 0$, a call option is out of the money.
- *At-the-money call options.* If $S = X$, a call option is said to be at the money.

The following describe the conditions for a **put option** to be in, out of, or at the money.

- *In-the-money put options.* If $X - S > 0$, a put option is in the money. $X - S$ is the amount of the payoff from immediate exercise, buying a share for S and exercising the put to receive X for the share.
- *Out-of-the-money put options.* When the stock's price is greater than the strike price, a put option is said to be out of the money. If $X - S < 0$, a put option is out of the money.
- *At-the-money put options.* If $S = X$, a put option is said to be at the money.

Example: Moneyness

Consider a July 40 call and a July 40 put, both on a stock that is currently selling for $37/share. Calculate how much these options are in or out of the money.

 Professor's Note: A July 40 call is a call option with an exercise price of $40 and an expiration date in July.

Answer:

The call is $3 out of the money because $S - X = -\$3.00$. The put is $3 in the money because $X - S = \$3.00$.

LOS 70.b: Differentiate between exchange-traded options and over-the-counter options.

Exchange-traded or **listed options** are regulated, standardized, liquid, and backed by the Options Clearing Corporation for Chicago Board Options Exchange transactions. Most exchange-listed options have expiration dates within two to four months of the current date. Exchanges also list **long-term equity anticipatory securities** (LEAPS), which are equity options with expiration dates longer than one year.

©2009 Kaplan, Inc.

Over-the-counter (OTC) options on stocks for the retail trade all but disappeared with the growth of the organized exchanges in the 1970s. There is now, however, an active market in OTC options on currencies, swaps, and equities, primarily for institutional buyers. Like the forward market, the OTC options market is largely unregulated, consists of custom options, involves counterparty risk, and is facilitated by dealers in much the same way forwards markets are.

LOS 70.c: Identify the types of options in terms of the underlying instruments.

The three types of options we consider are (1) financial options, (2) options on futures, and (3) commodity options.

Financial options include equity options and other options based on stock indices, Treasury bonds, interest rates, and currencies. The strike price for financial options can be in terms of yield-to-maturity on bonds, an index level, or an exchange rate for *foreign currency options*. LIBOR-based *interest rate options* have payoffs based on the difference between LIBOR at expiration and the strike rate in the option.

Bond options are most often based on Treasury bonds because of their active trading. There are relatively few listed options on bonds—most are over-the-counter options. Bond options can be deliverable or settle in cash. The mechanics of bond options are like those of equity options, but are based on bond prices and a specific face value of the bond. The buyer of a call option on a bond will gain if interest rates fall and bond prices rise. A put buyer will gain when rates rise and bond prices fall.

Index options settle in cash, nothing is delivered, and the payoff is made directly to the option holder's account. The payoff on an index call (long) is the amount (if any) by which the index level at expiration exceeds the index level specified in the option (the strike price), multiplied by the *contract multiplier*. An equal amount will be deducted from the account of the index call option writer.

> **Example: Index options**
>
> Assume that you own a call option on the S&P 500 Index with an exercise price equal to 950. The multiplier for this contract is 250. Compute the payoff on this option assuming that the index is 962 at expiration.
>
> **Answer:**
>
> This is a call, so the expiration date payoff is $(962 - 950) \times \$250 = \$3,000$.

Options on futures, sometimes called futures options, give the holder the right to buy or sell a specified futures contract on or before a given date at a given futures price, the strike price.

- *Call options* on futures contracts give the holder the right to enter into the long side of a futures contract at a given futures price. Assume that you hold a call option on a bond future at 98 (percent of face) and at expiration the futures price on the bond contract is 99. By exercising the call, you take on a long position in the futures contract, and the account is immediately marked to market based on the settlement price. Your account would be credited with cash in an amount equal to 1% (99 – 98) of the face value of the bonds covered by the contract. The seller of the exercised call will take on the short position in the futures contract and the mark to market value of this position will generate the cash deposited to your account.

- *Put options* on futures contracts give the holder the option to take on a short futures position at a futures price equal to the strike price. The writer has the obligation to take on the opposite (long) position if the option is exercised.

Commodity options give the holder the right to either buy or sell a fixed quantity of some physical asset at a fixed (strike) price.

Some capital investment projects have provisions that give the company flexibility to adjust the project's cash flows while it is in progress (for example, an option to abandon the project before completion). Such **real options** have values that should be considered when evaluating a project's NPV.

 Professor's Note: Evaluating projects with real options is covered in the Study Session on corporate finance at Level 2.

LOS 70.d: Compare and contrast interest rate options with forward rate agreements (FRAs).

Interest rate options are similar to the stock options except that the exercise price is an interest rate and the underlying asset is a reference rate such as LIBOR. Interest rate options are also similar to FRAs because there is no deliverable asset. Instead they are settled in cash, in an amount that is based on a notional amount and the spread between the strike rate and the reference rate. Most interest rate options are European options.

To see how interest rate options work, consider a long position in a 1-year LIBOR-based interest rate call option with a notional amount of $1,000,000 and a strike rate of 5%. For our example, let's assume that this option is costless for simplicity. If at expiration, LIBOR is greater than 5%, the option can be exercised and the owner will receive $1,000,000 × (LIBOR – 5%). If LIBOR is less than 5%, the option expires worthless and the owner receives nothing.

Now, let's consider a short position in a LIBOR-based interest rate put option with the same features as the call that we just discussed. Again, the option is assumed to be costless, with a strike rate of 5% and notional amount of $1,000,000. If at expiration, LIBOR falls below 5%, the option writer (short) must pay the put holder an amount equal to $1,000,000 × (5% – LIBOR). If at expiration, LIBOR is greater than 5%, the option expires worthless and the put writer makes no payments. If the rate is for less than one year, the payoff is adjusted. For example, if the reference rate for the option is 60-day LIBOR, the payoff would be $1,000,000 × (5% – LIBOR)(60/360) since the actual LIBOR rate and the strike rate are annualized rates.

©2009 Kaplan, Inc.

Notice the one-sided payoff on these interest rate options. The long call receives a payoff when LIBOR exceeds the strike rate and receives nothing if LIBOR is below the strike rate. On the other hand, the short put position makes payments if LIBOR is below the strike rate, and makes no payments when LIBOR exceeds the strike rate.

The combination of the long interest rate call option plus a short interest rate put option has the same payoff as a forward rate agreement (FRA). To see this, consider the fixed-rate payer in a 5% fixed-rate, $1,000,000 notional, LIBOR-based FRA. Like our long call position, the fixed-rate payer will receive $1,000,000 × (LIBOR − 5%). And, like our short put position, the fixed rate payer will pay $1,000,000 × (5% − LIBOR).

 Professor's Note: For the exam, you need to know that a long interest rate call combined with a short interest rate put can have the same payoff as a long position in an FRA.

LOS 70.e: Define interest rate caps, floors, and collars.

An **interest rate cap** is a series of interest rate call options, having expiration dates that correspond to the reset dates on a floating-rate loan. Caps are often used to protect a floating-rate borrower from an increase in interest rates. Caps place a maximum (upper limit) on the interest payments on a floating-rate loan.

Caps pay when rates rise above the cap rate. In this regard, a cap can be viewed as a series of interest rate call options with strike rates equal to the cap rate. Each option in a cap is called a *caplet*.

An **interest rate floor** is a series of interest rate put options, having expiration dates that correspond to the reset dates on a floating-rate loan. Floors are often used to protect a floating-rate lender from a decline in interest rates. Floors place a minimum (lower limit) on the interest payments that are received from a floating-rate loan.

An interest rate floor on a loan operates just the opposite of a cap. The floor rate is a minimum rate on the payments on a floating-rate loan.

Floors pay when rates fall below the floor rate. In this regard, a floor can be viewed as a series of interest rate put options with strike rates equal to the floor rate. Each option in a floor is called a *floorlet*.

An **interest rate collar** combines a cap and a floor. A borrower with a floating-rate loan may *buy* a cap for protection against rates above the cap and *sell* a floor in order to defray some of the cost of the cap.

Let's review the information in Figure 1, which illustrates the payments from a cap and a floor. On each reset date of a floating-rate loan, the interest for the next period (e.g., 90 days) is determined on the basis of some reference rate. Here, we assume that LIBOR is the reference rate and that we have quarterly payment dates on the loan.

The figure shows the effect of a cap that is set at 10%. In the event that LIBOR rises above 10%, the cap will make a payment to the cap buyer to offset any interest expense in excess of an annual rate of 10%. A cap may be structured to cover a certain number of periods or for the entire life of a loan. The cap will make a payment at any future interest payment due date whenever the reference rate (LIBOR in our example) exceeds the cap rate. As indicated in the figure, the cap's payment is based on the difference between the reference rate and the cap rate. The amount of the payment will equal the notional amount specified in the cap contract times the difference between the cap rate and the reference rate. When used to hedge a loan, the notional amount is usually equal to the loan amount.

Figure 1 also illustrates a floor of 5% for our LIBOR-based loan. For any payment where the reference rate on the loan falls below 5%, there is an additional payment required by the floor to bring the total payment to 5% (1.25% quarterly on a 90-day LIBOR-based loan). Note that the issuer of a floating-rate note with both a cap and a floor (a collar) is long a cap and *short* (has "sold") a floor. The note issuer receives a payment when rates are above the cap, and makes an additional payment when rates are below the floor (compared to just paying the reference rate).

Figure 1: Interest Rate Caps and Floors

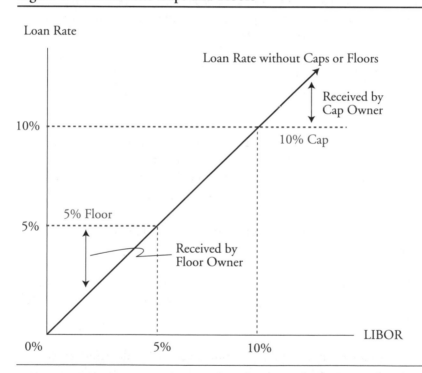

LOS 70.f: Compute and interpret option payoffs, and explain how interest rate option payoffs differ from the payoffs of other types of options.

Calculating the payoff for a stock option, or other type of option with a monetary-based exercise price, is straightforward. At expiration, a call owner receives any amount by which the asset price exceeds the strike price, and zero otherwise. The holder of a put will receive any amount that the asset price is below the strike price at expiration, and zero otherwise.

©2009 Kaplan, Inc.

While bonds are quoted in terms of yield-to-maturity, T-bills in discount yield, indices in index points, and currencies as an exchange rate, the same principle applies. That is, in each case, to get the payoff per unit of the relevant asset, we need to translate the asset value to a dollar value and the strike price (or rate, or yield) to a dollar strike price. We can then multiply this payoff times however many units of the asset are covered by the options contract.

- For a stock index option, we saw that these dollar values were obtained from multiplying the index level and the strike level by the multiplier specified in the contract. The resulting dollar payoffs are per contract.
- The payoff on options on futures is the cash the option holder receives when he exercises the option and the resulting futures position is marked to market.

The **payoffs on interest rate options** are different. For example, a call option based on 90-day LIBOR makes a payment based on a stated notional amount and the difference between 90-day LIBOR and the option's strike rate, times 90/360 to adjust for the interest rate period. The payment is made, not at option expiration, but at a future date corresponding to the term of the reference rate. For example, an option based on 90-day LIBOR will make a payment 90 days after the expiration date of the option. This payment date often corresponds to the date on which a LIBOR-based borrower would make the next interest payment on a loan.

Example: Computing the payoff for an interest rate option

Assume you bought a 60-day call option on 90-day LIBOR with a notional principal of $1 million and a strike rate of 5%. Compute the payment that you will receive if 90-day LIBOR is 6% at contract expiration, and determine when the payment will be received.

Answer:

The interest savings on a $1 million 90-day loan at 5% versus 6% is:

$$1 \text{ million} \times (0.06 - 0.05)(90 / 360) = \$2,500$$

This is the amount that will be paid by the call writer 90 days after expiration.

LOS 70.g: Define intrinsic value and time value and explain their relationship.

An option's **intrinsic value** is the amount by which the option is in-the-money. It is the amount that the option owner would receive if the option were exercised. An option has zero intrinsic value if it is at the money or out of the money, regardless of whether it is a call or a put option.

Let's look at the value of a call option *at expiration*. If the expiration date price of the stock exceeds the strike price of the option, the call owner will exercise the option and receive S – X. If the price of the stock is less than or equal to the strike price, the call holder will let the option expire and get nothing.

The *intrinsic value of a call* option is the greater of (S – X) or 0. That is:

$$C = \max[0, S - X]$$

Similarly, the *intrinsic value of a put* option is (X – S) or 0, whichever is greater. That is:

$$P = \max[0, X - S]$$

Example: Intrinsic value

Consider a call option with a strike price of $50. Compute the intrinsic value of this option for stock prices of $55, $50, and $45.

Answer:

stock price = $55: $C = \max[0, S - X] = \max[0, (55 - 50)] = \$5$

stock price = $50: $C = \max[0, S - X] = \max[0, (50 - 50)] = \$0$

stock price = $45: $C = \max[0, S - X] = \max[0, (45 - 50)] = \$0$

Notice that at expiration, if the stock is worth $50 or below, the call option is worth $0. Why? Because a rational option holder will not exercise the call option and take the loss. This "one-sided" feature of call options is illustrated in the option payoff diagram presented in Figure 2 for the call option we have used in this example.

 Professor's Note: Option payoff diagrams are commonly used tools to illustrate the value of an option at expiration.

Figure 2: Call Option Payoff Diagram

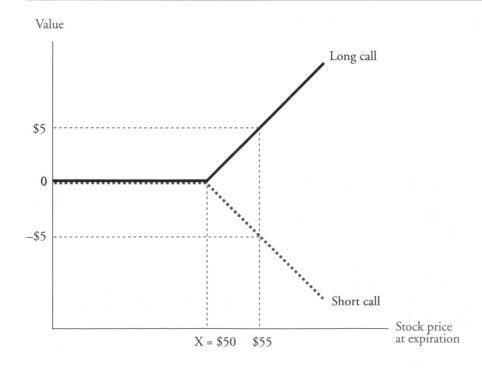

©2009 Kaplan, Inc.

As indicated in Figure 2, the expiration date payoff to the owner is either zero or the amount that the option is in the money. For a call option writer (seller), the payoff is either zero or minus the amount it is in the money. There are no positive payoffs for an option writer. The option writer receives the premium and takes on the obligation to pay whatever the call owner gains.

With reference to Figure 2, you should make the following observations:

- The payoff to a long call position (the solid line) is a flat line which angles upward to the right at a 45 degree angle from the strike price, X.
- The payoff to the writer of a call (dotted line), is a flat line which angles downward to the right at a 45 degree angle from the strike price, X.
- Options are a zero-sum game. If you add the long call option's payoff to the short option's payoff, you will get a net payoff of zero.
- At a stock price of $55, the payoff to the long is $5, which is a $5 loss to the short.

Similar to our payoff diagram for a call option, Figure 3 illustrates the at-expiration payoff values for a put option. As indicated here, if the price of the stock is less than the strike price, the put owner will exercise the option and receive $(X - S)$. If the price of the stock is greater than or equal to the strike price, the put holder will let the put option expire and get nothing (0). At a stock price of $40, the payoff on a long put is $10; the seller of the put (the short) would have a negative payoff since he must buy the stock at $50 and receive stock worth $40.

Figure 3: Put Option Payoff Diagram

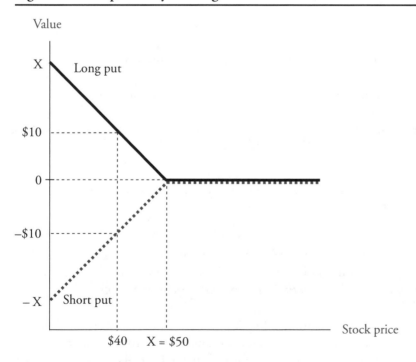

The **time value** of an option is the amount by which the option premium exceeds the intrinsic value and is sometimes called the speculative value of the option. This relationship can be written as:

    option value = intrinsic value + time value

As we discussed earlier, the intrinsic value of an option is the amount by which the option is in the money. At any point during the life of an options contract, its value will typically be greater than its intrinsic value. This is because there is some probability that the stock price will change in an amount that gives the option a positive payoff at expiration greater than the (current) intrinsic value. Recall that an option's intrinsic value (to a buyer) is the amount of the payoff at expiration and is bounded by zero. When an option reaches expiration there is no "time" remaining and the time value is zero. For American options and in most cases for European options, the longer the time to expiration, the greater the time value and, other things equal, the greater the option's premium (price).

LOS 70.h: Determine the minimum and maximum values of European options and American options.

LOS 70.i: Calculate and interpret the lowest prices of European and American calls and puts based on the rules for minimum values and lower bounds.

The following is some option terminology that we will use when addressing these LOS:

S_t = the price of the underlying stock at time t

X = the exercise price of the option

T = the time to expiration

c_t = the price of a European call at any time t prior to expiration at time = T

C_t = the price of an American call at any time t prior to expiration at time = T

P_t = the price of a European put at any time t prior to expiration at time = T

P_t = the price of an American put at any time t prior to expiration at time = T

RFR = the risk-free rate

 Professor's Note: Please notice that lowercase letters are used to represent European-style options.

Lower bound. Theoretically, no option will sell for less than its intrinsic value and no option can take on a negative value. This means that the lower bound for any option is zero. *The lower bound of zero applies to both American and European options.*

Upper bound for call options. The maximum value of either an American or a European *call* option at any time t is the time-t share price of the underlying stock. This makes sense because no one would pay a price for the right to buy an asset that exceeded the asset's value. It would be cheaper to simply buy the underlying asset. At time $t = 0$, the upper boundary condition can be expressed respectively for American and European call options as:

$$C_0 \leq S_0 \text{ and } c_0 \leq S_0$$

Upper bound for put options. The price for an American put option cannot be more than its strike price. This is the exercise value in the event the underlying stock price goes to zero. However, since European puts cannot be exercised prior to expiration, the maximum value is the present value of the exercise price discounted at the risk-free rate. Even if the stock price goes to zero, and is expected to stay at zero, the intrinsic value, X, will not be received until the expiration date. At time t = 0, the upper boundary condition can be expressed for American and European put options, respectively, as:

$$P_0 \leq X \text{ and } p_0 \leq \frac{X}{(1+RFR)^T}$$

The minimum and maximum boundary conditions for the various types of options at any time *t* are summarized in Figure 4.

Figure 4: Option Value Limits

Option	Minimum Value	Maximum Value
European call	$c_t \geq 0$	$c_t \leq S_t$
American call	$C_t \geq 0$	$C_t \leq S_t$
European put	$p_t \geq 0$	$p_t \leq X/(1 + RFR)^{(T-t)}$
American put	$P_t \geq 0$	$P_t \leq X$

Professor's Note: The values in the table are the theoretical limits on the value of options. In the next section, we will establish more restrictive limits for option prices.

Calculating an Option's Lower Bound

Professor's Note: The option boundary conditions that we discuss below will be important when you study option pricing models. For now, if you follow the logic leading up to the results presented in Figure 5, you will be prepared to deal with these LOS. Knowing and understanding the results in Figure 5 satisfy the requirements of these LOS; the following derivation of those results need not be memorized.

At this point, we know that for **American-style options**, which can be immediately exercised, the minimum price has to be the option's intrinsic value. For at-the-money and out-of-the money options, this minimum is zero, since options cannot have negative values. For in-the-money American options, the minima are simply the intrinsic values S – X for calls, and X – S for puts. If this were not the case, you could buy the option for less than its intrinsic value and immediately exercise it for a guaranteed profit. So, for American options, we can express the *lower bound on the option price* at any time *t* prior to expiration as:

$C_t = \max[0, S_t - X]$
$P_t = \max[0, X - S_t]$

For European options, however, the minima are not so obvious because these options are not exercisable immediately. To determine the **lower bounds for European options**, we can examine the value of a portfolio in which the option is combined with a long or short position in the stock and a pure discount bond.

For a *European call option,* construct the following portfolio:

- A long at-the-money European call option with exercise price X, expiring at time $t = T$.
- A long discount bond priced to yield the risk-free rate that pays X at option expiration.
- A short position in one share of the underlying stock priced at $S_0 = X$.

The current value of this portfolio is $c_0 - S_0 + X / (1 + RFR)^T$.

At expiration time, $t = T$, this portfolio will pay $c_T - S_T + X$. That is, we will collect $c_T = \max[0, S_T - X]$ on the call option, pay S_T to cover our short stock position, and collect X from the maturing bond.

- If $S_T \geq X$, the call is in-the-money, and the portfolio will have a zero payoff because the call pays $S_T - X$, the bond pays $+X$, and we pay $-S_T$ to cover our short position. That is, the time $t = T$ payoff is: $S_T - X + X - S_T = 0$.
- If $X > S_T$ the call is out-of-the-money, and the portfolio has a positive payoff equal to $X - S_T$ because the call value, c_T, is zero, we collect X on the bond, and pay $-S_T$ to cover the short position. So, the time $t = T$ payoff is: $0 + X - S_T = X - S_T$.

Note that no matter whether the option expires in-the-money, at-the-money, or out-of-the-money, the portfolio value will be equal to or greater than zero. We will never have to make a payment.

To prevent arbitrage, any portfolio that has no possibility of a negative payoff cannot have a negative value. Thus, we can state the value of the portfolio *at time t = 0* as:

$$c_0 - S_0 + X / (1 + RFR)^T \geq 0$$

which allows us to conclude that:

$$c_0 \geq S_0 - X / (1 + RFR)^T$$

Combining this result with the earlier minimum on the call value of zero, we can write:

$$c_0 \geq \max[0, S_0 - X / (1 + RFR)^T]$$

Note that $X / (1 + RFR)^T$ is the present value of a pure discount bond with a face value of X.

Based on these results, we can now state the **lower bound for the price of an American call** as:

$$C_0 \geq \max[0, S_0 - X / (1 + RFR)^T]$$

©2009 Kaplan, Inc.

How can we say this? This conclusion follows from the following two facts:

1. The early exercise feature on an American call makes it worth at least as much as an equivalent European call (i.e., $C_t \geq c_t$).

2. The lower bound for the value of a European call is equal to or greater than the theoretical lower bound for an American call. For example, $\max[0, S_0 - X/(1 + RFR)^T] \geq \max[0, S_0 - X]\}$.

 Professor's Note: Don't get bogged down here. We just use the fact that an American call is worth at least as much as a European call to claim that the lower bound on an American call is at least as much as the lower bound on a European call.

Derive the **minimum value of a European put option** by forming the following portfolio at time t = 0:

- A long at-the-money European put option with exercise price X, expiring at t = T.
- A short position on a risk-free bond priced at $X/(1 + RFR)^T$. This is the same as borrowing an amount equal to $X/(1 + RFR)^T$.
- A long position in a share of the underlying stock priced at S_0.

At expiration time t = T, this portfolio will pay $p_T + S_T - X$. That is, we will collect $p_T = \max[0, X - S_T]$ on the put option, receive S_T from the stock, and pay $-X$ on the bond issue (loan).

- If $S_T > X$, the payoff will equal: $p_T + S_T - X = S_T - X$.
- If $S_T \leq X$, the payoff will be zero.

Again, a no-arbitrage argument can be made that the portfolio value must be zero or greater, since there are no negative payoffs to the portfolio.

At time t = 0, this condition can be written as:

$$p_0 + S_0 - X/(1 + RFR)^T \geq 0$$

and rearranged to state the minimum value for a European put option at time t = 0 as:

$$p_0 \geq X/(1 + RFR)^T - S_0$$

We have now established the **minimum bound on the price of a European put option** as:

$$p_0 \geq \max[0, X/(1 + RFR)^T - S_0]$$

Professor's Note: Notice that the lower bound on a European put is below that of an American put option (i.e., max[0, X − S₀]). This is because when it's in the money, the American put option can be exercised immediately for a payoff of X − S₀.

Figure 5 summarizes what we now know regarding the boundary prices for American and European options at any time *t* prior to expiration at time t = T.

Figure 5: Lower and Upper Bounds for Options

Option	*Minimum Value*	*Maximum Value*
European call	$c_t \geq \max[0, S_t - X / (1 + RFR)^{T-t}]$	S_t
American call	$C_T \geq \max[0, S_t - X / (1 + RFR)^{T-t}]]$	S_t
European put	$p_t \geq \max[0, X / (1 + RFR)^{T-t} - S_t]$	$X / (1 + RFR)^{T-t}$
American put	$P_t \geq \max[0, X - S_t]$	X

Professor's Note: For the exam, know the price limits in Figure 5. You will not be asked to derive them, but you may be expected to use them.

Example: Minimum prices for American vs. European puts

Compute the lowest possible price for 4-month American and European 65 puts on a stock that is trading at 63 when the risk-free rate is 5%.

Answer:

American put: $P_0 \geq \max[0, X - S_0] = \max[0,2] = \$2$

European put: $p_0 \geq \max[0, X / (1 + RFR)^T - S_0] = \max[0, 65 / 1.05^{0.333} - 63] = \$0.95$

Example: Minimum prices for American vs. European calls

Compute the lowest possible price for 3-month American and European 65 calls on a stock that is trading at 68 when the risk-free rate is 5%.

Answer:

$C_0 \geq \max[0, S_0 - X / (1 + RFR)^T] = \max[0, 68 - 65 / 1.05^{0.25}] = \$3.79$

$c_0 \geq \max[0, S_0 - X / (1 + RFR)^T] = \max[0, 68 - 65 / 1.05^{0.25}] = \$3.79$

©2009 Kaplan, Inc.

LOS 70.j: Explain how option prices are affected by the exercise price and the time to expiration.

The result we are after here is a simple and somewhat intuitive one. That is, given two puts that are identical in all respects except exercise price, the one with the higher exercise price will have at least as much value as the one with the lower exercise price. This is because the underlying stock can be sold at a higher price. Similarly, given two calls that are identical in every respect except exercise price, the one with the lower exercise price will have at least as much value as the one with the higher exercise price. This is because the underlying stock can be purchased at a lower price.

 Professor's Note: The derivation of this result is included here although it is not explicitly required by the LOS.

The method here, for both puts and calls, is to combine two options with different exercise prices into a portfolio and examine the portfolio payoffs at expiration for the three possible stock price ranges. We use the fact that a portfolio with no possibility of a negative payoff cannot have a negative value to establish the pricing relations for options with differing times to expiration.

For $X_1 < X_2$, consider a portfolio at time t that holds the following positions:

$c_t(X_1)$ = a long call with an exercise price of X_1

$c_t(X_2)$ = a short call with an exercise price of X_2

The three expiration date (t = T) conditions and payoffs that need to be considered here are summarized in Figure 6.

Figure 6: Exercise Price vs. Call Price

Expiration Date Condition	Option Value	Portfolio Payoff
$S_T \leq X_1$	$c_T(X_1) = c_T(X_2) = 0$	0
$X_1 < S_T < X_2$	$c_T(X_1) = S_T - X_1$ $c_T(X_2) = 0$	$S_T - X_1 > 0$
$X_2 \leq S_T$	$c_T(X_1) = S_T - X_1$ $c_T(X_2) = S_T - X_2$	$(S_T - X_1) - (S_T - X_2)$ $= X_2 - X_1 > 0$

With no negative payoffs at expiration, the current portfolio of $c_0(X_1) - c_0(X_2)$ must have a value greater than or equal to zero, and we have proven that $c_0(X_1) \geq c_0(X_2)$.

Similarly, consider a portfolio short a put with exercise price X_1 and long a put with exercise price X_2, where $X_1 < X_2$. The expiration date payoffs that we need to consider are summarized in Figure 7.

Figure 7: Exercise Price vs. Put Price

Expiration Date Condition	Option Value	Portfolio Payoff
$S_T \geq X_2$	$p_T(X_1) = p_T(X_2) = 0$	0
$X_2 > S_T > X_1$	$p_T(X_1) = 0$ $p_T(X_2) = X_2 - S_T$	$X_2 - S_T > 0$
$X_1 \geq S_T$	$p_T(X_1) = X_1 - S_T$ $p_T(X_2) = X_2 - S_T$	$(X_2 - S_T) - (X_1 - S_T)$ $= X_2 - X_1 > 0$

Here again, with no negative payoffs at expiration, the current portfolio of $p_0(X_2) - p_0(X_1)$ must have a value greater than or equal to zero, which proves that $p_0(X_2) \geq p_0(X_1)$.

In summary, we have shown that, all else being equal:

- Call prices are inversely related to exercise prices.
- Put prices are directly related to exercise price.

In general, a **longer time to expiration** will increase an option's value. For far out-of-the-money options, the extra time may have no effect, but we can say the longer-term option will be no less valuable that the shorter-term option.

The case that doesn't fit this pattern is the European put. Recall that the minimum value of an in-the-money European put at any time t prior to expiration is $X / (1 + RFR)^{T-t} - S_t$. While longer time to expiration increases option value through increased volatility, it decreases the present value of any option payoff at expiration. For this reason, we cannot state positively that the value of a longer European put will be greater than the value of a shorter-term put.

If volatility is high and the discount rate low, the extra time value will be the dominant factor and the longer-term put will be more valuable. Low volatility and high interest rates have the opposite effect and the value of a longer-term in-the-money put option can be less than the value of a shorter-term put option.

LOS 70.k: Explain put-call parity for European options, and relate put-call parity to arbitrage and the construction of synthetic options.

Our derivation of **put-call parity** is based on the payoffs of two portfolio combinations, a fiduciary call and a protective put.

©2009 Kaplan, Inc.

A *fiduciary call* is a combination of a pure-discount, riskless bond that pays X at maturity and a call with exercise price X. The payoff for a fiduciary call at expiration is X when the call is out of the money, and $X + (S - X) = S$ when the call is in the money.

A *protective put* is a share of stock together with a put option on the stock. The expiration date payoff for a protective put is $(X - S) + S = X$ when the put is in the money, and S when the put is out of the money.

 Professor's Note: When working with put-call parity, it is important to note that the exercise prices on the put and the call and the face value of the riskless bond are all equal to X.

When the put is in the money, the call is out of the money, and both portfolios pay X at expiration.

Similarly, when the put is out of the money and the call is in the money, both portfolios pay S at expiration.

Put-call parity holds that portfolios with identical payoffs must sell for the same price to prevent arbitrage. We can express the put-call parity relationship as:

$$c + X / (1 + RFR)^T = S + p$$

Equivalencies for each of the individual securities in the put-call parity relationship can be expressed as:

$$S = c - p + X / (1 + RFR)^T$$
$$p = c - S + X / (1 + RFR)^T$$
$$c = S + p - X / (1 + RFR)^T$$
$$X / (1 + RFR)^T = S + p - c$$

The single securities on the left-hand side of the equations all have exactly the same payoffs as the portfolios on the right-hand side. The portfolios on the right-hand side are the "synthetic" equivalents of the securities on the left. Note that the options must be European-style and the puts and calls must have the same exercise price for these relations to hold.

For example, to synthetically produce the payoff for a long position in a share of stock, you use the relationship:

$$S = c - p + X / (1 + RFR)^T$$

This means that the payoff on a long stock can be synthetically created with a long call, a short put, and a long position in a risk-free discount bond.

The other securities in the put-call parity relationship can be constructed in a similar manner.

Professor's Note: After expressing the put-call parity relationship in terms of the security you want to synthetically create, the sign on the individual securities will indicate whether you need a long position (+ sign) or a short position (– sign) in the respective securities.

Example: Call option valuation using put-call parity

Suppose that the current stock price is $52 and the risk-free rate is 5%. You have found a quote for a 3-month put option with an exercise price of $50. The put price is $1.50, but due to light trading in the call options, there was not a listed quote for the 3-month, $50 call. Estimate the price of the 3-month call option.

Answer:

Rearranging put-call parity, we find that the call price is:

$$call = put + stock - present\ value(X)$$

$$call = \$1.50 + \$52 - \frac{\$50}{1.05^{0.25}} = \$4.11$$

This means that if a 3-month, $50 call is available, it should be priced at $4.11 per share.

LOS 70.l: Contrast American options with European options in terms of the lower bounds on option prices and the possibility of early exercise.

Earlier we established that American calls on non-dividend-paying stocks are worth at least as much as European calls, which means that the lower bound on the price of both types of options is $\max[0, S_t - X / (1 + RFR)^{T-t}]$. If exercised, an American call will pay $S_t - X$, which is less than its minimum value of $S_t - X / (1 + RFR)^{T-t}$. Thus, *there is no reason for early exercise of an American call option* on stocks with no dividends.

For American call options on dividend-paying stocks, the argument presented above against early exercise does not necessarily apply. Keeping in mind that options are not typically adjusted for dividends, it may be advantageous to exercise an American call prior to the stock's ex-dividend date, particularly if the dividend is expected to significantly decrease the price of the stock.

For American put options, early exercise may be warranted if the company that issued the underlying stock is in bankruptcy so that its stock price is zero. It is better to get X now than at expiration. Similarly, a very low stock price might also make an American put "worth more dead than alive."

©2009 Kaplan, Inc.

LOS 70.m: Explain how cash flows on the underlying asset affect put-call parity and the lower bounds of option prices.

If the asset has positive cash flows over the period of the option, the cost of the asset is less by the present value of the cash flows. You can think of buying a stock for S and simultaneously borrowing the present value of the cash flows, PV_{CF}. The cash flow(s) will provide the payoff of the loan(s), and the loan(s) will reduce the net cost of the asset to $S - PV_{CF}$. Therefore, for assets with positive cash flows over the term of the option, we can **substitute this (lower) net cost, $S - PV_{CF}$,** for S in the lower bound conditions and in all the parity relations.

The lower bounds for European options at time t = 0 can be expressed as:

$$c_0 \geq \max[0, S_0 - PV_{CF} - X / (1 + RFR)^T], \text{ and}$$
$$p_0 \geq \max[0, X / (1 + RFR)^T - (S_0 - PV_{CF})]$$

The put-call parity relations can be adjusted to account for asset cash flows in the same manner. That is:

$$(S_0 - PV_{CF}) = C - P + X / (1 + RFR)^T, \text{ and}$$
$$C + X / (1 + RFR)^T = (S_0 - PV_{CF}) + P$$

LOS 70.n: Indicate the directional effect of an interest rate change or volatility change on an option's price.

When interest rates increase, the value of a call option increases and the value of a put option decreases (holding the price of the underlying security constant). This general result may not apply to interest rate options or to bond or T-bill options, where a change in the risk-free rate may affect the value of the underlying asset.

The no-arbitrage relations for puts and calls make these statements obvious:

$$C = S + P - X / (1 + RFR)^T$$
$$P = C - S + X / (1 + RFR)^T$$

Here we can see that an increase in RFR decreases $X / (1 + RFR)^T$. This will have the effect of increasing the value of the call, and decreasing the value of the put. A decrease in interest rates will decrease the value of a call option and increase the value of a put option.

 Professor's Note: Admittedly, this is a partial analysis of these equations, but it does give the right directions for the effects of interest rate changes and will help you remember them if this relation is tested on the exam.

Greater volatility in the value of an asset or interest rate underlying an option contract increases the values of both puts and calls (and caps and floors). The reason is that options are "one-sided." Since an option's value falls no lower than zero when it expires out of the money, the increased upside potential (with no greater downside risk) from increased volatility, increases the option's value.

KEY CONCEPTS

LOS 70.a

American options can be exercised at any time up to the option's expiration date.

European options can be exercised only at the option's expiration date.

Moneyness for puts and calls is determined by the difference between the strike price (X) and the market price of the underlying stock (S):

Moneyness	Call Option	Put Option
In the money	S > X	S < X
At the money	S = X	S = X
Out of the money	S < X	S > X

LOS 70.b

Exchange-traded options are standardized, regulated, and backed by a clearinghouse. Over-the-counter options are largely unregulated custom options that have counterparty risk.

LOS 70.c

Options are available on financial securities, futures contracts, interest rates, and commodities.

LOS 70.d

Interest rate option payoffs are the difference between the market and strike rates, adjusted for the loan period, multiplied by the principal amount.

At expiration, an interest rate call receives a payment when the reference rate is above the strike rate, and an interest rate put receives a payment when the reference rate is below the strike rate.

An FRA can be replicated with two interest rate options: a long call and a short put.

LOS 70.e

Interest rate caps put a maximum (upper limit) on the payments on a floating-rate loan and are equivalent (from the borrower's perspective) to a series of long interest rate calls at the cap rate.

Interest rate floors put a minimum (lower limit) on the payments on a floating-rate loan and are equivalent (from the borrower's perspective) to a series of short interest rate puts at the floor rate.

An interest rate collar combines a cap and a floor. A borrower can create a collar on a floating-rate loan by buying a cap and selling a floor.

©2009 Kaplan, Inc.

LOS 70.f

The payoff to the holder of a call or put option on a stock is the option's intrinsic value. Payment occurs at expiration of the option.

Payoffs on interest rate options are paid after expiration, at the end of the interest rate (loan) period specified in the contract.

LOS 70.g

The intrinsic value of an option is the payoff from immediate exercise if the option is in the money, and zero otherwise.

The time (speculative) value of an option is the difference between its premium (market price) and its intrinsic value. At expiration, time value is zero.

LOS 70.h,i

Minimum and maximum option values:

Option	Minimum value	Maximum value
European call	$c_t \geq \max[0, S_t - X / (1 + RFR)^{T-t}]$	S_t
American call	$C_t \geq \max[0, S_t - X / (1 + RFR)^{T-t}]$	S_t
European put	$p_t \geq \max[0, X / (1 + RFR)^{T-t} - S_t]$	$X / (1 + RFR)^{T-t}$
American put	$P_t \geq \max[0, X - S_t]$	X

LOS 70.j

Calls with lower exercise prices are worth at least as much as otherwise identical calls with higher exercise prices (and typically more).

Puts with higher exercise prices are worth at least as much as otherwise identical puts with lower exercise prices (and typically more).

Otherwise identical options are worth more when there is more time to expiration, with two exceptions:
- Far out-of-the-money options with different expiration dates may be equal in value.
- With European puts, longer time to expiration may decrease an option's value when they are deep in the money.

LOS 70.k

A fiduciary call (a call option and a risk-free zero-coupon bond that pays the strike price X at expiration) and a protective put (a share of stock and a put at X) have the same payoffs at expiration, so arbitrage will force these positions to have equal prices: $c + X / (1 + RFR)^T = S + p$. This establishes put-call parity for European options.

Based on the put-call parity relation, a synthetic security (stock, bond, call or put) can be created by combining long and short positions in the other three securities.
- $c = S + p - X / (1 + RFR)^T$
- $p = c - S + X / (1 + RFR)^T$
- $S = c - p + X / (1 + RFR)^T$
- $X / (1 + RFR)^T = S + p - c$

LOS 70.l

An American call on a non-dividend-paying stock will not be exercised early because the payoff if exercised early is less than its minimum value.

For American puts, and for American calls on dividend-paying stocks, early exercise is sometimes advantageous.

LOS 70.m

When the underlying asset has positive cash flows, the minima, maxima, and put-call parity relations are adjusted by subtracting the present value of the expected cash flows from the assets over the life of the option. That is, S can be replaced by (S – PV of expected cash flows).

LOS 70.n

An increase in the risk-free rate will increase call values and decrease put values (for options that do not explicitly depend on interest rates or bond values).

Increased volatility of the underlying asset or interest rate increases both put values and call values.

©2009 Kaplan, Inc.

CONCEPT CHECKERS

1. Which of the following statements about moneyness is *least accurate*? When:
   A. $S - X$ is > 0, a call option is in the money.
   B. $S - X = 0$, a call option is at the money.
   C. $S > X$, a put option is in the money.

2. Which of the following statements about American and European options is *most accurate*?
   A. There will always be some price difference between American and European options because of exchange-rate risk.
   B. European options allow for exercise on or before the option expiration date.
   C. Prior to expiration, an American option may have a higher value than an equivalent European option.

3. Which of the following statements about put and call options is *least accurate*?
   A. The price of the option is less volatile than the price of the underlying stock.
   B. Option prices are generally higher the longer the time until the option expires.
   C. For put options, the higher the strike price relative to the stock's underlying price, the more the put is worth.

4. Which of the following statements about options is *most accurate*?
   A. The writer of a put option has the obligation to sell the asset to the holder of the put option.
   B. The holder of a call option has the obligation to sell to the option writer should the stock's price rise above the strike price.
   C. The holder of a put option has the right to sell to the writer of the option.

5. A *decrease* in the risk-free rate of interest will:
   A. increase put and call prices.
   B. decrease put prices and increase call prices.
   C. increase put prices and decrease call prices.

6. A $40 call on a stock trading at $43 is priced at $5. The time value of the option is:
   A. $2.
   B. $5.
   C. $8.

7. Prior to expiration, an American put option on a stock:
   A. is bounded by $S - X / (1 + RFR)^T$.
   B. will never sell for less than its intrinsic value.
   C. can never sell for more than its intrinsic value.

8. The owner of a call option on oil futures with a strike price of $68.70:
   A. can exercise the option and take delivery of the oil.
   B. can exercise the option and take a long position in oil futures.
   C. would never exercise the option when the spot price of oil is less than the strike price.

9. The lower bound for a European put option is:
   A. $\max(0, S - X)$.
   B. $\max[0, X / (1 + RFR)^T - S]$.
   C. $\max[0, S - X / (1 + RFR)^T]$.

10. The lower bound for an American call option is:
    A. $\max(0, S - X)$.
    B. $\max[0, X /(1 + RFR)^T - S]$.
    C. $\max[0, S - X / (1 + RFR)^T]$.

11. To account for positive cash flows from the underlying asset, we need to adjust the put-call parity formula by:
    A. adding the future value of the cash flows to S.
    B. adding the future value of the cash flows to X.
    C. subtracting the present value of the cash flows from S.

12. A forward rate agreement is equivalent to the following interest rate options:
    A. long a call and a put.
    B. short a call and long a put.
    C. long a call and short a put.

13. The payoff on an interest rate option:
    A. comes only at exercise.
    B. is greater the higher the "strike" rate.
    C. comes some period after option expiration.

14. An interest rate floor on a floating-rate note (from the issuer's perspective) is equivalent to a series of:
    A. long interest rate puts.
    B. short interest rate puts.
    C. short interest rate calls.

15. Which of the following relations is *least likely* accurate?
    A. $P = C - S + X / (1 + RFR)^T$.
    B. $C = S - P + X / (1 + RFR)^T$.
    C. $X / (1 + RFR)^T - P = S - C$.

16. A stock is selling at $40, a 3-month put at $50 is selling for $11, a 3-month call at $50 is selling for $1, and the risk-free rate is 6%. How much, if anything, can be made on an arbitrage?
    A. $0 (no arbitrage).
    B. $0.28.
    C. $0.72.

17. Which of the following will *increase* the value of a put option?
    A. An increase in volatility.
    B. A decrease in the exercise price.
    C. A decrease in time to expiration.

©2009 Kaplan, Inc.

ANSWERS – CONCEPT CHECKERS

1. **C** A put option is out of the money when S > X and in the money when S < X. The other statements are true.

2. **C** American and European options both give the holder the right to exercise the option at expiration. An American option also gives the holder the right of early exercise, so American options will be worth more than European options when the right to early exercise is valuable, and they will have equal value when it is not, $C_t \geq c_t$ and $P_t \geq p_t$.

3. **A** Option prices are *more* volatile than the price of the underlying stock. The other statements are true. Options have time value, which means prices are higher the longer the time until the option expires, and a higher strike price increases the value of a put option.

4. **C** The holder of a put option has the right to sell to the writer of the option. The writer of the put option has the obligation to buy, and the holder of the call option has the right, but not the obligation to buy.

5. **C** Interest rates are inversely related to put prices and directly related to call prices.

6. **A** The intrinsic value is S – X = $43 – $40 = $3. So, the time value is $5 – $3 = $2.

7. **B** At any time t, an American put will never sell below intrinsic value, but may sell for more than that. The lower bound is, max[0, X – S_t].

8. **B** A call on a futures contract gives the holder the right to buy (go long) a futures contract at the exercise price of the call. It is not the current spot price of the asset underlying the futures contract that determines whether a futures option is in the money, it is the futures contract price (which may be higher).

9. **B** The lower bound for a European put ranges from zero to the present value of the exercise price less the prevailing stock price, where the exercise price is discounted at the risk-free rate.

10. **C** The lower bound for an American call ranges from zero to the prevailing stock price less the present value of the exercise price discounted at the risk-free rate.

11. **C** If the underlying asset used to establish the put-call parity relationship generates a cash flow prior to expiration, the asset's value must be reduced by the present value of the cash flow discounted at the risk-free rate.

12. **C** The payoff to a FRA is equivalent to that of a long interest rate call option and a short interest rate put option.

13. **C** The payment on a long put increases as the strike rate increases, but not for calls. There is only one payment and it comes after option expiration by the term of the underlying rate.

14. **B** Short interest rate puts require a payment when the market rate at expiration is below the strike rate, just as lower rates can require a payment from a floor.

15. **B**   The put-call parity relationship is $S + P = C + X / (1 + RFR)^T$. All individual securities can be expressed as rearrangements of this basic relationship.

16. **C**   A synthetic stock is: $S = C - P + X / (1 + RFR)^T = \$1 - \$11 + 50 / (1.06)^{0.25} = \$39.28$. Since the stock is selling for $40, you can short a share of stock for $40 and buy the synthetic for an immediate arbitrage profit of $0.72.

17. **A**   Increased volatility of the underlying asset increases both put values and call values.

©2009 Kaplan, Inc.

Swap Markets and Contracts

Exam Focus

This topic review introduces swaps. The first thing you must learn is the mechanics of swaps so that you can calculate the payments on any of the types of swaps covered. Beyond that, you should be able to recognize that the cash flows of a swap can be duplicated with capital markets transactions (make a loan, issue a bond) or with other derivatives (a series of forward rate agreements or interest rate options). Common mistakes include forgetting that the current-period floating rate determines the next payment, forgetting to adjust the interest rates for the payment period, forgetting to add any margin above the floating rate specified in the swap, and forgetting that currency swaps involve an exchange of currencies at the initiation and termination of the swap. Don't do these things.

Swap Characteristics

Before we get into the details of swaps, a simple introduction may help as you go through the different types of swaps. You can view interest rate swaps as the exchange of one loan for another. If you lend me $10,000 at a floating rate, and I lend you $10,000 at a fixed rate, we have created a swap. There is no reason for the $10,000 to actually change hands. The two equal loans make this pointless. At each payment date I will make a payment to you based on the floating rate, and you will make one to me based on the fixed rate. Again, it makes no sense to exchange the full amounts; the one with the larger payment liability will make a payment of the difference to the other. This describes the payments of a fixed-for-floating or "plain vanilla" swap.

A currency swap can be viewed the same way. If I lend you 1,000,000 euros at the euro rate of interest, and you lend me the equivalent amount of yen at today's exchange rate at the yen rate of interest, we have done a currency swap. We will "swap" back these same amounts of currency at the maturity date of the two loans. In the interim, I borrowed yen, so I make yen interest payments, and you borrowed euros and must make interest payments in euros.

For other types of swaps we just need to describe how the payments are calculated on the loans. For an equity swap, I could promise to make quarterly payments on your loan to me equal to the return on a stock index, and you could promise to make fixed-rate (or floating-rate) payments to me. If the stock index goes down, my payments to you are negative (i.e., you make a fixed-rate payment to me *and* a payment equal to the decline in the index over the quarter). If the index went up over the quarter, I would make a payment based on the percentage increase in the index. Again, the payments could be "netted" so that only the difference changes hands.

This intuitive explanation of swaps should make the following a bit easier to understand. Now let's dive into the mechanics and terminology of swaps. We have to specify exactly how the interest payments will be calculated, how often they are made, how much is to be loaned, and how long the loans are for. Swaps are custom instruments, and we can specify any terms both of us can agree on.

LOS 71.a: Describe the characteristics of swap contracts and explain how swaps are terminated.

Swaps are agreements to exchange a series of cash flows on periodic *settlement dates* over a certain time period (e.g., quarterly payments over two years). In the simplest type of swap, one party makes *fixed-rate* interest payments on the notional principal specified in the swap in return for *floating-rate* payments from the other party. At each settlement date, the two payments are *netted* so that only one (net) payment is made. The party with the greater liability makes a payment to the other party. The length of the swap is termed the *tenor* of the swap and the contract ends on the termination date. A swap can be decomposed into a series of forward contracts (FRAs) that expire on the settlement dates.

In many respects, swaps are similar to forwards:

- Swaps typically require no payment by either party at initiation.
- Swaps are custom instruments.
- Swaps are not traded in any organized secondary market.
- Swaps are largely unregulated.
- Default risk is an important aspect of the contracts.
- Most participants in the swaps market are large institutions.
- Individuals are rarely swaps market participants.

There are swaps facilitators who bring together parties with needs for the opposite sides of swaps. There are also dealers, large banks and brokerage firms, who act as principals in trades just as they do in forward contracts. It is a large business; the total notional principal of swaps contracts is estimated at over $50 trillion.

How Swaps are Terminated

There are **four ways to terminate a swap** prior to its original termination date.

1. *Mutual termination.* A cash payment can be made by one party that is acceptable to the other party. Like forwards, swaps can accumulate value as market prices or interest rates change. If the party that has been disadvantaged by the market movements is willing to make a payment of the swap's value to the counterparty, and the counterparty is willing to accept it, they can mutually terminate the swap.

2. *Offsetting contract.* Just as with forwards, if the terms of the original counterparty offers for early termination are unacceptable, the alternative is to enter an offsetting swap. If our 5-year quarterly-pay floating swap has two years to go, we can seek a current price on a pay-fixed (receive floating) swap that will provide our floating payments and leave us with a fixed-rate liability.

   Just as with forwards, exiting a swap may involve taking a loss. Consider the case where we receive 3% fixed on our original 5-year pay floating swap, but must pay 4% fixed on the offsetting swap. We have "locked in" a loss because we must pay 1%

©2009 Kaplan, Inc.

higher rates on the offsetting swap than we receive on the swap we are offsetting. We must make quarterly payments for the next two years, and receive nothing in return. Exiting a swap through an offsetting swap with other than the original counterparty will also expose the investor to default risk, just as with forwards.

3. *Resale*. It is possible to sell the swap to another party, with the permission of the counterparty to the swap. This would be unusual, however, as there is not a functioning secondary market.

4. *Swaption*. A **swaption** is an option to enter into a swap. The option to enter into an offsetting swap provides an option to terminate an existing swap. Consider that, in the case of the previous 5-year pay floating swap, we purchased a 3-year call option on a 2-year pay fixed swap at 3%. Exercising this swap would give us the offsetting swap to exit our original swap. The cost for such protection is the swaption premium.

LOS 71.b: Define, calculate, and interpret the payment of currency swaps, plain vanilla interest rate swaps, and equity swaps.

In a **currency swap**, one party makes payments denominated in one currency, while the payments from the other party are made in a second currency. Typically, the notional amounts of the contract, expressed in both currencies at the current exchange rate, are exchanged at contract initiation and returned at the contract termination date in the same amounts.

An example of a currency swap is as follows: Party 1 pays Party 2 $10 million at contract initiation in return for €9.8 million. On each of the settlement dates, Party 1, having received euros, makes payments at a 6% annualized rate in euros on the €9.8 million to Party 2. Party 2 makes payments at an annualized rate of 5% on the $10 million to Party 1. These settlement payments are both made. They are not netted as they are in a single currency interest rate swap.

As an example of what motivates a currency swap, consider that a U.S. firm, Party A, wishes to establish operations in Australia and wants to finance the costs in Australian dollars (AUD). The firm finds, however, that issuing debt in AUD is relatively more expensive than issuing USD-denominated debt, because they are relatively unknown in Australian financial markets. An alternative to issuing AUD-denominated debt is to issue USD debt and enter into a USD/AUD currency swap. Through a swaps facilitator, the U.S. firm finds an Australian firm, Party B, that faces the same situation in reverse. They wish to issue AUD debt and swap into a USD exposure.

There are **four possible types of currency swaps** available.

1. Party A pays a fixed rate on AUD received, and Party B pays a fixed rate on USD received.

2. Party A pays a floating rate on AUD received, and Party B pays a fixed rate on USD received.

3. Party A pays a fixed rate on AUD received, and Party B pays a floating rate on USD received.

4. Party A pays a floating rate on AUD received, and Party B pays a floating rate on USD received.

Here are the steps in a fixed-for-fixed currency swap:

The notional principal actually changes hands at the beginning of the swap. Party A gives USD to Party B and gets AUD back. Why? Because the motivation of Party A was to get AUD and the motivation of Party B was to get USD. *Notional principal is swapped at initiation.*

Interest payments are made without netting. Party A, who got AUD, pays the Australian interest rate on the notional amount of AUD to Party B. Party B, who got USD, pays the U.S. interest rate on the notional amount of USD received to Party A. Since the payments are made in different currencies, netting is not a typical practice. *Full interest payments are exchanged at each settlement date, each in a different currency.*

At the termination of the swap agreement (maturity), the counterparties give each other back the exchanged notional amounts. *Notional principal is swapped again at the termination of the agreement.* The cash flows associated with this currency swap are illustrated in Figure 1.

Figure 1: Fixed-for-Fixed Currency Swap

SWAP INITIATION

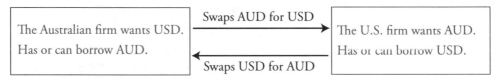

SWAP INTEREST PAYMENTS

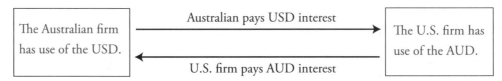

SWAP TERMINATION

©2009 Kaplan, Inc.

Calculating the Payments on a Currency Swap

Example: Fixed-for-fixed currency swap

BB can borrow in the U.S. for 9%, while AA has to pay 10% to borrow in the U.S. AA can borrow in Australia for 7%, while BB has to pay 8% to borrow in Australia. BB will be doing business in Australia and needs AUD, while AA will be doing business in the United States and needs USD. The exchange rate is 2AUD/USD. AA needs USD1.0 million and BB needs AUD2.0 million. They decide to borrow the funds locally and swap the borrowed funds, charging each other the rate the other party would have paid had they borrowed in the foreign market. The swap period is for five years. Calculate the cash flows for this swap.

Answer:

AA and BB each go to their own domestic bank:

- AA borrows AUD2.0 million, agreeing to pay the bank 7%, or AUD140,000 annually.
- BB borrows USD1.0 million, agreeing to pay the bank 9%, or USD90,000 annually.

AA and BB swap currencies:

- AA gets USD1.0 million, agreeing to pay BB 10% interest in USD annually.
- BB gets AUD2.0 million, agreeing to pay AA 8% interest in AUD annually.

They pay each other the annual interest:

- AA owes BB USD100,000 in interest to be paid on each settlement date.
- BB owes AA AUD160,000 in interest to be paid on each settlement date.

They each owe their own bank the annual interest payment:

- AA pays the Australian bank AUD140,000 (but gets AUD160,000 from BB, an AUD20,000 gain).
- BB pays the U.S. bank USD90,000 (but gets USD100,000 from AA, a USD10,000 gain).
- They both gain by swapping (AA is ahead AUD20,000 and BB is ahead USD 10,000).

In five years, they reverse the swap. They return the notional principal.

- AA gets AUD2.0 million from BB and then pays back the Australian bank.
- BB gets USD1.0 million from AA and then pays back the U.S. bank.

Interest Rate Swaps

The **plain vanilla interest rate swap** involves trading fixed interest rate payments for floating-rate payments. (A **basis swap** involves trading one set of floating rate payments for another.)

The party who wants floating-rate interest payments agrees to pay fixed-rate interest and has the *pay-fixed* side of the swap. The counterparty, who receives the fixed payments and agrees to pay variable-rate interest, has the *pay-floating* side of the swap and is called the *floating-rate payer.*

The floating rate quoted is generally the **London Interbank Offered Rate** (LIBOR), flat or plus a spread.

Let's look at the cash flows that occur in a *plain vanilla interest rate swap.*

- Since the notional principal swapped is the same for both counterparties and is in the same currency units, there is no need to actually exchange the cash. *Notional principal is generally not swapped* in single currency swaps.
- The determination of the variable rate is at the beginning of the settlement period, and the cash interest payment is made at the end of the settlement period. Since the interest payments are in the same currency, there is no need for both counterparties to actually transfer the cash. The difference between the fixed-rate payment and the variable-rate payment is calculated and paid to the appropriate counterparty. *Net interest is paid by the one who owes it.*
- At the conclusion of the swap, since the notional principal was not swapped, there is no transfer of funds.

You should note that swaps are a zero-sum game. What one party gains, the other party loses.

The net formula for the *fixed-rate payer,* based on a 360-day year and a floating rate of LIBOR is:

$$(\text{net fixed-rate payment})_t = (\text{swap fixed rate} - \text{LIBOR}_{t-1})\left(\frac{\text{number of days}}{360}\right)(\text{notional principal})$$

If this number is positive, the fixed-rate payer *owes* a net payment to the floating-rate party. If this number is negative, then the fixed-rate payer *receives* a net flow from the floating-rate payer.

 Professor's Note: For the exam, remember that with plain vanilla swaps, one party pays fixed and the other pays a floating rate. Sometimes swap payments are based on a 365-day year. For example, the swap will specify whether 90/360 or 90/365 should be used to calculate a quarterly swap payment. Remember, these are custom instruments.

Example: Interest rate risk

Consider a bank. Its deposits represent liabilities and are most likely short term in nature. In other words, deposits represent floating-rate liabilities. The bank assets are primarily loans. Most loans carry fixed rates of interest. The bank assets are fixed-rate and bank liabilities are floating. Explain the nature of the interest rate risk that the bank faces, and describe how an interest rate swap may be used to hedge this risk.

©2009 Kaplan, Inc.

Answer:

The risk the bank faces is that short-term interest rates will rise, causing cash payment on deposits to increase. This would not be a major problem if cash inflows also increase as interest rates rise, but with a fixed-rate loan portfolio they will not. If the bank remains unhedged as interest rates rise, cash outflows rise and bank profits fall.

The bank can hedge this risk by entering into a fixed-for-floating swap as the fixed-rate payer. The floating-rate payments received would offset any increase in the floating-rate payments on deposits. Note that if rates fall, the bank's costs do not. They still pay fixed for the term of the swap and receive (lower) floating-rate payments that correspond to their lower costs on deposits.

Calculating the Payments on an Interest Rate Swap

Example: Calculating the payments on an interest rate swap

Bank A enters into a $1,000,000 quarterly-pay plain vanilla interest rate swap as the fixed-rate payer at a fixed rate of 6% based on a 360-day year. The floating-rate payer agrees to pay 90-day LIBOR plus a 1% margin; 90-day LIBOR is currently 4%.

90-day LIBOR rates are:	4.5%	90 days from now
	5.0%	180 days from now
	5.5%	270 days from now
	6.0%	360 days from now

Calculate the amounts Bank A pays or receives 90, 270, and 360 days from now.

Answer:

The payment 90 days from now depends on current LIBOR and the fixed rate (don't forget the 1% margin).

Fixed-rate payer pays:

$$\left[0.06 \left(\frac{90}{360} \right) - (0.04 + 0.01) \left(\frac{90}{360} \right) \right] \times 1{,}000{,}000 = \$2{,}500$$

270 days from now the payment is based on LIBOR 180 days from now, which is 5%. Adding the 1% margin makes the floating-rate 6%, which is equal to the fixed rate, so there is no net third quarterly payment.

The Bank's "payment" 360 days from now is:

$$\left[0.06\left(\frac{90}{360}\right)-(0.055+0.01)\left(\frac{90}{360}\right)\right]\times 1,000,000 = -\$1,250$$

Since the floating-rate payment exceeds the fixed-rate payment, Bank A will *receive* $1,250 at the fourth payment date.

Equity Swaps

In an **equity swap**, the return on a stock, a portfolio, or a stock index is paid each period by one party in return for a fixed-rate or floating-rate payment. The return can be the capital appreciation or the total return including dividends on the stock, portfolio, or index.

In order to reduce equity risk, a portfolio manager might enter into a 1-year quarterly-pay S&P 500 index swap and agree to receive a fixed rate. The percentage increase in the index each quarter is netted against the fixed rate to determine the payment to be made. If the index return is negative, the fixed-rate payer must also pay the percentage decline in the index to the portfolio manager. Uniquely among swaps, equity swap payments can be floating on both sides and the payments are not known until the end of the quarter. With interest rate swaps, both the fixed and floating payments are known at the beginning of period for which they will be paid.

A swap on a single stock can be motivated by a desire to protect the value of a position over the period of the swap. To protect a large capital gain in a single stock, and to avoid a sale for tax or control reasons, an investor could enter into an equity swap as the equity-returns payer and receive a fixed rate in return. Any decline in the stock price would be paid to the investor at the settlement dates, plus the fixed-rate payment. If the stock appreciates, the investor must pay the appreciation less the fixed payment.

©2009 Kaplan, Inc.

Calculating the Payments on an Equity Swap

Example: Equity swap payments

Ms. Smith enters into a 2-year $10 million quarterly swap as the fixed payer and will receive the index return on the S&P 500. The fixed rate is 8%, and the index is currently at 986. At the end of the next three quarters, the index level is: 1030, 968, and 989.

Calculate the net payment for each of the next three quarters and identify the direction of the payment.

Answer:

The percentage change in the index each quarter, Q, is: Q1 = 4.46%, Q2 = –6.02%, and Q3 = 2.17%. The index return payer (IR) will receive 0.08 / 4 = 2% each quarter and pay the index return, therefore:

Q1: IR payer pays 4.46% – 2.00% = 2.46% or $246,000.
Q2: IR payer receives 6.02% + 2.00% = 8.02% or $802,000.
Q3: IR payer pays 2.17% – 2.00% = 0.17% or $17,000.

KEY CONCEPTS

LOS 71.a

Swaps are based on a notional amount of principal. Each party is obligated to pay a percentage return on the notional amount at periodic settlement dates over the life (tenor) of the swap. Percentage payments are based on a floating rate, fixed rate, or the return on an equity index or portfolio.

Except in the case of a currency swap, no money changes hands at the inception of the swap and periodic payments are netted (the party that owes the larger amount pays the difference to the other).

Swaps are custom instruments, are largely unregulated, do not trade in secondary markets, and are subject to counterparty (default) risk.

Swaps can be terminated prior to their stated termination dates by:
- Entering into an offsetting swap, sometimes by exercising a swaption (most common).
- Agreeing with the counterparty to terminate (likely involves making or receiving compensation).
- Selling the swap to a third party with the consent of the original counterparty (uncommon).

LOS 71.b

In a plain vanilla (fixed-for-floating) interest-rate swap, one party agrees to pay a floating rate of interest on the notional amount and the counterparty agrees to pay a fixed rate of interest.

The formula for the net payment by the fixed-rate payer, based on a 360-day year and the number of days in the settlement period is:

$$\left(\text{net fixed rate payment}\right)_t$$
$$= \left(\text{swap fixed rate} - \text{LIBOR}_{t-1}\right)\left(\frac{\text{number of days}}{360}\right)\left(\text{notional principal}\right)$$

In an equity swap, the returns payer makes payments based on the return on a stock, portfolio, or index, in exchange for fixed- or floating-rate payments. If the stock, portfolio, or index, declines in value over the period, the returns payer receives the interest payment and a payment based on the percentage decline in value.

In a currency swap, the notional principal (in two different currencies) is exchanged at the inception of the swap, periodic interest payments in two different currencies are exchanged on settlement dates, and the same notional amounts are exchanged (repaid) on the termination date of the swap.

©2009 Kaplan, Inc.

CONCEPT CHECKERS

1. Which of the following statements about swaps is *least likely* correct?
    A. In an interest rate swap, the notional principal is swapped.
    B. The default problem is the most important limitation to the swap market.
    C. In a plain vanilla interest rate swap, fixed rates are traded for variable rates.

2. Which of the following statements about swaps is *least likely* correct?
    A. The time frame of a swap is called its tenor.
    B. In a currency swap, only net interest payments are made.
    C. In a currency swap, the notional principal is actually swapped twice, once at the beginning of the swap and again at the termination of the swap.

3. Which of the following statements is *least likely* an advantage of swaps? Swaps:
    A. have little or no regulation.
    B. minimize default risk.
    C. have customized contracts.

4. In an equity swap:
    A. settlement is made only at swap termination.
    B. shares are exchanged for the notional principal.
    C. returns on an index can be swapped for fixed-rate payments.

5. In a plain vanilla interest rate swap:
    A. the notional principal is swapped.
    B. only the net interest payments are made.
    C. the notional principal is returned at the end of the swap.

6. Which of the following statements about swap markets is *least likely* correct?
    A. In an interest rate swap only the net interest is exchanged.
    B. The notional principal is swapped at inception and at termination of a currency swap.
    C. Only the net difference between the dollar interest and the foreign interest is exchanged in a currency swap.

Use the following data to answer Questions 7 through 10.

Consider a 3-year annual currency swap that takes place between a foreign firm (FF) with FC currency units and a U.S. firm (USF) with $ currency units. USF is the fixed-rate payer and FF is the floating-rate payer. The fixed interest rate at the initiation of the swap is 7%, and 8% at the end of the swap. The variable rate is 5% currently; 6% at the end of year 1; 8% at the end of year 2; and 7% at the end of year 3. At the beginning of the swap, $1.0 million is exchanged at an exchange rate of FC2.0 = $1.0. At the end of the swap period the exchange rate is FC 1.5 = $1.0.

Note: With this currency swap, end-of-period payments are based on beginning-of-period interest rates.

7.   At the initiation of the swap, which of the following statements is *most likely* correct?
       A. FF gives USF $1.0 million.
       B. USF gives FF $1.0 million.
       C. USF gives FF FC2.0 million.

8.   At the end of year 2:
       A. USF pays FC140,000; FF pays $60,000.
       B. USF pays FC60,000; FF pays $70,000.
       C. USF pays USD70,000; FF pays FC60,000.

9.   At the termination of the swap, FF gives USF which of the following notional amounts?
       A. $1 million.
       B. FC2,000,000.
       C. FC1,500,000.

10.   At the end of year 3, FF will pay which of the following total amounts?
       A. $1,080,000.
       B. $1,070,000.
       C. FC2,160,000

©2009 Kaplan, Inc.

Use the following information to answer Questions 11 through 13.

Lambda Corp. has a floating-rate liability and wants a fixed-rate exposure. They enter into a 2-year quarterly-pay $4,000,000 fixed-for-floating swap as the fixed-rate payer. The counterparty is Gamma Corp. The fixed rate is 6% and the floating rate is 90-day LIBOR + 1%, with both calculated based on a 360-day year. Realizations of LIBOR are:

Annualized LIBOR
Current   5.0%
In 1 quarter   5.5%
In 2 quarters 5.4%
In 3 quarters 5.8%
In 4 quarters 6.0%

11.   The first swap payment is:
      A. from Gamma to Lambda.
      B. known at the initiation of the swap.
      C. $5,000.

12.   The second net swap payment is:
      A. $5,000 from Lambda to Gamma.
      B. $4,000 from Gamma to Lambda.
      C. $5,000 from Gamma to Lambda.

13.   The fifth net quarterly payment on the swap is:
      A. 0.
      B. $10,000.
      C. $40,000.

ANSWERS – CONCEPT CHECKERS

1. **A**   In an interest rate swap, the notional principal is only used to calculate the interest payments and does not change hands. The notional principal is only exchanged in a currency swap.

2. **B**   In a currency swap, payments are not netted because they are made in different currencies. Full interest payments are made, and the notional principal is also exchanged.

3. **B**   Swaps do not minimize default risk. Swaps are agreements between two or more parties, and there are no guarantees that one of the parties will not default. Note that swaps do give traders privacy and, being private transactions, have little to no regulation and offer the ability to customize contracts to specific needs.

4. **C**   Equity swaps involve one party paying the return or total return on a stock or index periodically in exchange for a fixed return.

5. **B**   In a plain vanilla interest rate swap, interest payments are netted. Note that notional principal is not exchanged and is only used as a basis for calculating interest payments.

6. **C**   In a currency swap, full interest payments are made, and the notional principal is exchanged.

7. **B**   Because this is a currency swap, we know that the notional principal is exchanged. Because USF holds dollars, it will be handing over dollars to FF.

8. **A**   Remember, the currency swap is pay floating on dollars and pay fixed on foreign. Floating at the end of year 1 is 6% of $1.0 million. Since payments are made in arrears, FF pays $60,000 and USF pays FC140,000 at the end of year 2.

9. **A**   The notional principal is exchanged at termination. FF gives back what it borrowed, $1.0 million, and the terminal exchange rate is not used.

10. **A**   FF is the floating-rate dollar payer. FF will pay the return of $1.0 million in principal at the termination of the swap, plus the floating rate payment (in arrears) of 8% × $1.0 million = $80,000. The total payment will be $1,080,000.

11. **B**   The first payment is based on the fixed rate and current LIBOR + 1%, which are both 6%. There is no net payment made at the first quarterly payment date and this is known at the initiation of the swap.

12. **C**   The second quarter payment is based on the realization of LIBOR at the end of the first quarter, 5.5%. The floating rate is: $(5.5\% + 1\%)\left(\dfrac{90}{360}\right)4,000,000 = \$65,000$. The fixed rate payment is $60,000, making the net payment $5,000 from Gamma to Lambda.

13. **B**   The fifth quarterly floating-rate payment is based on the realization of LIBOR at the end of the fourth quarter, which is 6%. With the 1% margin, the floating rate is 7% compared to 6% fixed, so the net payment is $10,000.

©2009 Kaplan, Inc.

The following is a review of the Derivative Investments principles designed to address the learning outcome statements set forth by CFA Institute®. This topic is also covered in:

RISK MANAGEMENT APPLICATIONS OF OPTION STRATEGIES

Study Session 17

EXAM FOCUS

The most important aspect of this topic review is the interpretation of option profit diagrams. Payoff diagrams for single put or single call positions were covered in our options review. In this review, we introduce profit diagrams and two option strategies that combine stock with options. In a protective put position, we combine a share of stock and a put. With this strategy, we essentially purchase downside protection for the stock (like insurance). A covered call position consists of buying a share of stock and selling a call on it. This strategy equates to selling the upside potential on the stock in return for the added income from the sale of the call. On the Level 1 CFA® Exam, you will not be expected to draw payoff diagrams, but you will be expected to interpret them and find the breakeven price, maximum gains and losses, and the gains and losses for any stock price at option expiration.

LOS 72.a: Determine the value at expiration, profit, maximum profit, maximum loss, breakeven underlying price at expiration, and general shape of the graph of the strategies of buying and selling calls and puts, and indicate the market outlook of investors using these strategies.

Call Option Profits and Losses

Consider a call option with a premium of $5 and a strike price of $50. This means the buyer pays $5 to the writer. At expiration, if the price of the stock is less than or equal to the $50 strike price (the option has zero value), the buyer of the option is out $5, and the writer of the option is ahead $5. As the stock's price exceeds $50, the buyer of the option starts to gain (breakeven will come at $55, when the value of the stock equals the strike price and the option premium). However, as the price of the stock moves upward, the seller of the option starts to lose (negative figures will start at $55, when the value of the stock equals the strike price and the option premium).

The profit/loss diagram for the buyer (long) and writer (short) of the call option we have been discussing at expiration is presented in Figure 1. This profit/loss diagram illustrates the following:

- The maximum loss for the buyer of a call is the loss of the $5 premium (at any S ≤ $50).
- The breakeven point for the buyer and seller is the strike price plus the premium (at S = $55).
- The profit potential to the buyer of the option is unlimited, and, conversely, the potential loss to the writer of the call option is unlimited.

- The call holder will exercise the option whenever the stock's price exceeds the strike price at the expiration date.
- The greatest profit the writer can make is the $5 premium (at any $S \le \$50$).
- The sum of the profits between the buyer and seller of the call option is always zero; thus, options trading is a *zero-sum game*. There are no net profits or losses in the market. The long profits equal the short losses.

> *Professor's Note: Please notice that option profit diagrams show the gain or loss to the long and/or short option positions. They differ from the payoff diagrams that we used in our options review in that profit diagrams reflect the cost of the option (i.e., the option premium).*

Figure 1: Profit/Loss Diagram for a Call Option

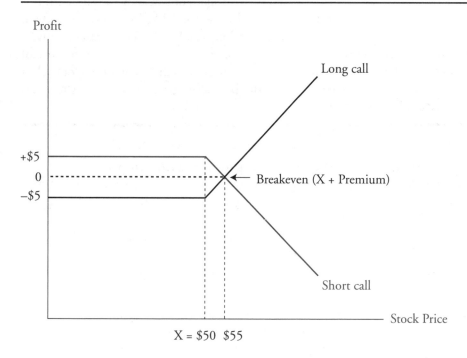

Put Option Profits and Losses

To examine the profits/losses associated with trading put options, consider a put option with a $5 premium. The buyer pays $5 to the writer. When the price of the stock at expiration is greater than or equal to the $50 strike price, the put has zero value. The buyer of the option has a loss of $5, and the writer of the option has a gain of $5. As the stock's price falls below $50, the buyer of the put option starts to gain (breakeven will come at $45, when the value of the stock equals the strike price less the option premium). However, as the price of the stock moves downward, the seller of the option starts to lose (negative profits will start at $45, when the value of the stock equals the strike price less the option premium).

©2009 Kaplan, Inc.

Figure 2 shows the profit/loss diagram for the buyer (long) and seller (short) of the put option that we have been discussing. This profit/loss diagram illustrates that:

- The maximum loss for the buyer of a put is the loss of the $5 premium (at any $S \geq \$50$).
- The maximum gain to the buyer of a put is limited to the strike price less the premium ($50 – $5 = $45). The potential loss to the writer of the put is the same amount.
- The breakeven price of a put buyer (seller) is at the strike price minus the option premium ($50 – $5 = $45).
- The greatest profit the writer of a put can make is the $5 premium ($S \geq \$50$).
- The sum of the profits between the buyer and seller of the put option is always zero. Trading put options is a *zero-sum game*. In other words, the buyer's profits equal the writer's losses.

Figure 2: Profit/Loss Diagram for a Put Option

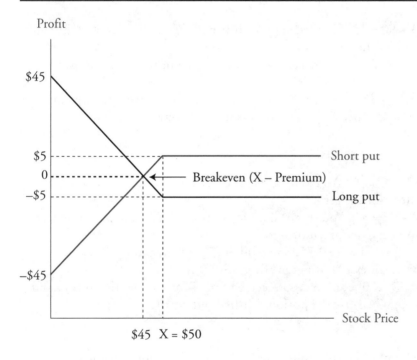

Example: Option profit calculations

Suppose that both a call option and a put option have been written on a stock with an exercise price of $40. The current stock price is $42, and the call and put premiums are $3 and $0.75, respectively.

Calculate the profit to the long and short positions for both the put and the call with an expiration day stock price of $35 and with a price at expiration of $43.

Answer:

Profit will be computed as ending option valuation – initial option cost.

Stock at $35:

- Long call: $0 – $3 = –$3. The option finished out-of-the-money, so the premium is lost.
- Short call: $3 – $0 = $3. Since the option finished out-of-the-money, the call writer's gain equals the premium.
- Long put: $5 – $0.75 = $4.25. You paid $0.75 for an option that is now worth $5.
- Short put: $0.75 – $5 = –$4.25. You received $0.75 for writing the option but you face a $5 loss because the option is in-the-money.

Stock at $43:

- Long call: –$3 + $3 = $0. You paid $3 for the option, and it is now worth $3. Hence, your net profit is zero.
- Short call: $3 – $3 = $0. You received $3 for writing the option and now face a –$3 valuation for a net profit of zero.
- Long put: –$0.75 – $0 = –$0.75. You paid $0.75 for the put option and the option is now worthless. Your net profit is –$0.75.
- Short put: $0.75 – $0 = $0.75. You received $0.75 for writing the option and keep the premium because the option finished out-of-the-money.

A buyer of puts or a seller of calls will profit when the price of the underlying asset decreases. A buyer of calls or a seller of puts will profit when the price of the underlying asset increases. In general, a put buyer believes the underlying asset is overvalued and will decline in price, while a call buyer anticipates an increase in the underlying asset's price.

©2009 Kaplan, Inc.

LOS 72.b: Determine the value at expiration, profit, maximum profit, maximum loss, breakeven underlying price at expiration, and general shape of the graph of a covered call strategy and a protective put strategy, and explain the risk management application of each strategy.

Professor's Note: Whenever we combine options with assets or other options, the net cost of the combined position is simply the sum of the prices paid for the long options/assets minus the proceeds from the option/asset sales (short positions). The profits and losses on a position are simply the value of all the assets/options in the positions at expiration minus the net cost.

In writing **covered calls,** the term *covered* means that owning the stock covers the obligation to deliver stock assumed in writing the call. Why would you write a covered call? You feel the stock's price will not go up any time soon, and you want to increase your income by collecting the call option premium. To add some insurance that the stock won't get called away, the call writer can write out-of-the-money calls. You should know that this strategy for enhancing one's income is not without risk. *The call writer is trading the stock's upside potential for the call premium.*

Figure 3 illustrates the profit/loss of a covered call position at option expiration date. When the call was written, the stock's price was $50. The call's strike price was $55, and the call premium was $4. The call is out-of-the-money. From Figure 3, we can observe that at expiration:

- If the stock closes below $50, the option will expire worthless, and the option writer's loss is offset by the premium income of $4.
- Breakeven *for the position* is at $46 = $50 – $4. Breakeven price = S_0 – call premium.
- If the stock closes between $50 and $55, the option will expire worthless. Since this option was an out-of-the-money call, the option writer will get any stock appreciation above the original stock price and below the strike price. So the gain (premium plus stock appreciation) will be between $4 and $9.
- If stock closes above $55, the strike price, the writer will get nothing more. The maximum gain is $9 on the covered out-of-the-money call.
- The maximum loss occurs if the stock price goes to zero; the net cost of the position ($46 = $50 stock loss offset by $4 premium income) is the maximum loss.

Figure 3: Covered Call Profit and Loss for S = 50, C = 4, X = 55

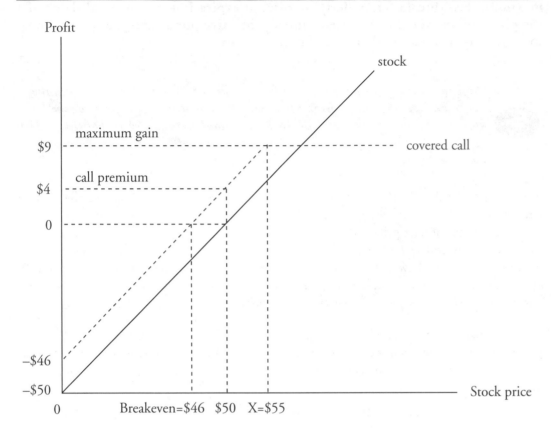

The desirability of writing a covered call to enhance income depends upon the chance that the stock price will exceed the exercise price at which the trader writes the call. In this example, the writer of the call thinks the stock's upside potential is less than the buyer expects. The buyer of the call is paying $4 to get any gain above $55, while the seller has traded the upside potential above $55 for a payment of $4.

A **protective put** is an investment management technique designed to protect a stock from a decline in value. It is constructed by buying a stock and put option on that stock.

Look at the profit/loss diagrams in Figure 4. The diagram on the left is the profit from holding the stock. If the stock's value is up, your profit is positive and if the stock's value is down, your profit is negative. Profit equals the end price, S_T, less the initial price S_t. That is, profit = $S_T - S_t$. The diagram on the right side of Figure 4 is the profit graph from holding a long put. If the market is up, you lose your premium payment, and if the market is down, you have a profit.

The value of the put at termination will be max[0, $X - S_T$]. Your profit will be max[0, $X - S_T$] less the price of the put.

                    ©2009 Kaplan, Inc.

Figure 4: Protective Put Components

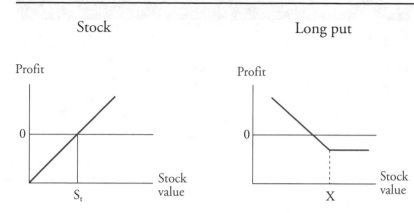

Figure 5 shows the profits from the combination of a long put and a long stock (i.e., a protective put). Here it is assumed that the stock is purchased at $100 and that a put with a strike price of $100 is purchased for $4. Note that the put described in Figure 5 is at the money.

Figure 5: Protective Put

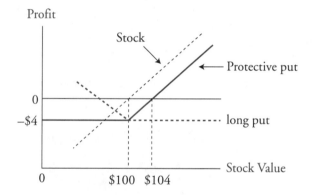

What we should observe in Figure 5 is that:

- A protective put cuts your downside losses (maximum loss = $4) but leaves the upside potential alone (unlimited upside gains).
- Your maximum loss occurs at any price below $100.
- Losses between $0 and $4 occur for stock prices between $100 and $104.
- You will not make a profit until the stock price exceeds $104 (breakeven).
- Breakeven price = S_0 + premium.

Note that *a protective put (stock plus a put) has the same shape profit diagram as a long call.* It could be replicated with a bond that pays (X – premium) at expiration and a call at X.

 Professor's Note: Recall that this relation was the basis for our derivation of put-call parity. The payoffs at expiration are identical for a protective put (S + P) and a fiduciary call $\left[\dfrac{X}{\left(1 + R_f\right)^{T-t}} + C \right]$, *a call with an exercise price equal to X and a pure discount bond that pays X at expiration.*

KEY CONCEPTS

LOS 72.a

Call option value at expiration is Max $(0, S - X)$ and profit (loss) is
Max $(0, S - X)$ – option cost.

	Call Option	
	Maximum Loss	Maximum Gain
Buyer (long)	Option Cost	Unlimited
Seller (short)	Unlimited	Option Cost
Breakeven	X + Option Cost	

Put value at expiration is Max $(0, X - S)$ and profit (loss) is
Max $(0, X - S)$ – option cost.

	Put Option	
	Maximum Loss	Maximum Gain
Buyer (long)	Option Cost	X – Option Cost
Seller (short)	X – Option Cost	Option Cost
Breakeven	X – Option Cost	

A call buyer (call seller) anticipates an increase (decrease) in the value of the underlying asset.

A put buyer (put seller) anticipates a decrease (increase) in the value of the underlying asset.

LOS 72.b

A covered call position is a share of stock and a short (written) call. Profits and losses are measured relative to the net cost of this combination $(S_0 - \text{premium})$.
- The purpose of selling a covered call is to enhance income by trading the stock's upside potential for the call premium.
- The upside potential on a covered call is limited to $(X - S_0)$ + call premium received. The maximum loss is the net cost $(S_0 - \text{premium})$.

A protective put consists of buying a share of stock and buying a put. Profits and losses are measured relative to the net cost $(S_0 + \text{premium})$.
- A protective put is a strategy to protect against a decline in the value of the stock.
- Maximum gains on a protective put are unlimited, but reduced by the put premium paid. Maximum losses are limited to $(S_0 - X)$ + put premium paid.

©2009 Kaplan, Inc.

CONCEPT CHECKERS

1. A call option sells for $4 on a $25 stock with a strike price of $30. Which of the following statements is *least accurate*?
    A. At expiration, the buyer of the call will not make a profit unless the stock's price exceeds $30.
    B. At expiration, the writer of the call will only experience a net loss if the price of the stock exceeds $34.
    C. A covered call position at these prices has a maximum gain of $9 and the maximum loss of the stock price less the premium.

2. An investor buys a put on a stock selling for $60, with a strike price of $55 for a $5 premium. The maximum gain is:
    A. $50.
    B. $55.
    C. $60.

3. Which of the following is the riskiest single-option transaction?
    A. Writing a call.
    B. Buying a put.
    C. Writing a put.

4. An investor will *likely* exercise a put option when the price of the stock is:
    A. above the strike price.
    B. below the strike price plus the premium.
    C. below the strike price.

5. A put with a strike price of $75 sells for $10. Which of the following statements is *least accurate*? The greatest:
    A. profit the writer of the put option can make is $10.
    B. profit the buyer of a put option can make is $65.
    C. loss the writer of a put option can have is $75.

6. At expiration, the value of a call option must equal:
    A. the larger of the strike price less the stock price or zero.
    B. the stock price minus the strike price, or arbitrage will occur.
    C. the larger of zero, or the stock's price less the strike price.

7. An investor writes a covered call on a $40 stock with an exercise price of $50 for a premium of $2. The investor's maximum:
    A. gain will be $12.
    B. loss will be $40.
    C. loss will be unlimited.

8. Which of the following combinations of options and underlying investments have similarly shaped profit/loss diagrams? A:
    A. covered call, and a short stock combined with a long call.
    B. short put option combined with a long call option, and a protective put.
    C. long call option combined with a short put option, and a long stock position.

ANSWERS – CONCEPT CHECKERS

1. **A** The buyer will not have a net profit unless the stock price exceeds $34 (strike price plus the premium). The other statements are true. At $30 the option will be exercised, but the writer will only lose money in a net sense when the stock's price exceeds X + C = $30 + $4. The covered call's maximum gain is $4 premium plus $5 appreciation.

2. **A** This assumes the price of the stock falls to zero and you get to sell for $55. Your profit would be $55 – 5 = $50.

3. **A** When buying either a call or a put, the loss is limited to the amount of the premium. When writing a put, the loss is limited to the strike price if the stock falls to zero (however, the writer keeps the premium). When writing an uncovered call, the stock could go up infinitely, and the writer would be forced to buy the stock in the open market and deliver at the strike price—potential losses are unlimited.

4. **C** The owner of a put profits when the stock falls. The put would be exercised when the price of the stock is *below* the strike price. The amount of the premium is used to determine net profits to each party.

5. **C** The greatest loss the put writer can have is the strike price minus the premium received equals $65. The other statements are true. The greatest profit the put writer can make is the amount of the premium. The greatest profit for a put buyer occurs if the stock falls to zero and the buyer makes the strike price minus the premium. Since options are a zero-sum game, the maximum profit to the writer of the put must equal the maximum loss to the buyer of the put.

6. **C** At expiration, the value of a call must be equal to its intrinsic value, which is Max[0, S – X]. If the value of the stock is less than the strike price, the intrinsic value is zero. If the value of the stock is greater than the strike price, the call is in-the-money and the value of the call is the stock price minus the strike price, or S – X.

7. **A** As soon as the stock rises to the exercise price, the covered call writer will cease to realize a profit because the short call moves into-the-money. Each dollar gain on the stock is then offset with a dollar loss on the short call. Since the option is $10 out-of-the-money, the covered call writer can gain this amount plus the $2 call premium. Thus, the maximum gain is $2 + $10 = $12. However, because the investor owns the stock, he or she could lose $40 if the stock goes to zero, but gain $2 from the call premium. Maximum loss is $38.

8. **C** A combined long call and a short put, with exercise prices equal to the current stock price, will have profits/losses at expiration nearly identical to those of a long stock position.

 Professor's Note: The easiest way to see this is to draw the payoff diagram for the combined option positions.

©2009 Kaplan, Inc.

The following is a review of the Alternative Investments principles designed to address the learning outcome statements set forth by CFA Institute®. This topic is also covered in:

ALTERNATIVE INVESTMENTS

EXAM FOCUS

"Alternative investments" collectively refers to the many asset classes that fall outside of the traditional definitions of stocks and bonds. This category includes mutual funds, exchange-traded funds, real estate, venture capital, hedge funds, closely held companies, distressed securities, and commodities. Each of these alternative investments has unique characteristics that require a different approach by the analyst. You should be aware of the different risk-return profiles, tax issues, legal issues, and other advantages and disadvantages associated with each of the alternative investments discussed in this topic review.

LOS 73.a: Differentiate between an open-end and a closed-end fund, and explain how net asset value of a fund is calculated and the nature of fees charged by investment companies.

Managed investment companies (mutual funds) are formed to collectively manage assets for a group of investors. Investment companies can be classified into one of two categories, depending upon the liquidity they provide or do not provide to their investors.

An open-end investment company, or **open-end fund**, stands ready to redeem shares at the closing value on any trading day. Shares of a closed-end company, or **closed-end fund**, are traded (after issuance) in the secondary markets through organized exchanges (e.g., NYSE). Thus, the liquidity of an open-end fund is provided by the investment company that manages it, whereas the liquidity of a closed-end fund is determined in the open market.

The managers of an open-end fund may charge a fee, or "load," to the investors upon purchase (a front-end load) or at redemption (a back-end load). A fund that charges no fee at purchase or redemption is called a "no-load" fund. All funds, regardless of whether they are load or no-load funds, will charge ongoing fees on an annual basis, which may include management fees, administrative fees, and distribution (marketing) fees, which are referred to as 12b-1 fees in the United States.

The shares of a closed-end fund will be issued at a small premium to the value of the underlying assets, the premium serving as compensation for issuance costs. The investment company will also charge an ongoing management fee. Since a closed-end fund is traded in the secondary market subsequent to issuance, the redemption cost for the investor is simply the commission charged on the sale of shares and a portion of the bid/ask spread of the shares. The terms "load" and "no-load" are not applicable to closed-end funds.

The **net asset value** (NAV) of a mutual fund is the value of the investment company's assets minus its liabilities, stated on a per-share basis. The share price of an open-end fund will always equal the NAV since the investment company is obligated to redeem shares at any time at current market value. The share price of a closed-end fund may or may not equal the NAV since the share price is determined in the secondary market. The shares may trade at a premium (share price greater than NAV) or at a discount (share price less than NAV) to the actual NAV of the fund's assets.

Investment Company Fees

Fees charged by investment companies can generally be classified as one-time fees or ongoing annual fees. Closed-end funds initially issue shares at a premium to the value of the fund's underlying assets, which essentially is a fee paid by the investors as compensation for issuance costs. Some open-end funds will charge a load (or sales commission) upon purchase, at redemption, or both. Sometimes the back-end load amount will decrease over time ("contingent deferred sales charges") in order to encourage longer investment holding periods for shareholders. Premiums, loads, and redemption fees are, in essence, compensation for the sales and marketing efforts, but they are not performance incentives for the portfolio managers.

Other fees or expenses are charged to shareholders on an annual basis. The annual fee may cover several components: management fees, which go to the portfolio manager and are typically the largest component; administrative expenses; and distribution fees which are part of overall marketing expenses (called 12b-1 fees in the United States). A fund's expense ratio is the ratio of operating expenses to average assets. Several investment industry groups examine expense ratios among funds in order to compare their relative operating efficiency. The expenses and fees charged by the investment companies decrease an investor's return and can have a significant effect on performance. Often, funds will have a different fee structure for different classes of shares. Different classes of shares are sold through different distribution channels. With differences in up-front, back-end, and ongoing distribution fees among the classes, an investor's anticipated holding period (time horizon) will be an important determinant of which class of shares and associated fee structure will be most advantageous.

©2009 Kaplan, Inc.

Example: Fee structures and the investment horizon

Consider the various fee and expense structures in the figure below.

Expenses for Fiduciary Fund Shares

	Class A Shares	Class B Shares	Class C Shares
Front-end load (charged at time of sale)	4% of investment	none	none
Back-end load (redemption fees)	none	initially 5% of sale proceeds—declines by 1% each year	2% during the first year
Annual fees (calculated on year-end values)			
Distribution fees	none	0.5%	1.0%
Fund management fees	0.8%	0.8%	0.8%
Other fund expenses	0.2%	0.2%	0.2%
Total annual fees	1.0%	1.5%	2.0%

Assume that the gross return on an investment in the Fiduciary Fund will be constant at 9% per year. Which class of shares would you recommend to an investor with an investment horizon of:

- two years?
- five years?
- ten years?

Answer:

Assuming a 2-year holding period, the total redemption value for an assumed $10,000 initial investment in:

Class A shares would be: $10,000 (1 - 0.04) (1.09)^2 (1 - 0.01)^2 = \$11,178.79$.

Class B shares would be: $10,000 (1.09)^2 (1 - 0.015)^2 (1 - 0.03) = \$11,181.43$.

Class C shares would be: $10,000 (1.09)^2 (1 - 0.02)^2 = \$11,410.51$.

Class C shares would provide the greatest net return.

Assuming a 5-year holding period, the total redemption value for an assumed $10,000 initial investment in:

Class A shares would be: $10,000 (1 - 0.04)(1.09)^5 (1 - 0.01)^5 = \$14,046.87$.

Class B shares would be: $10,000 (1.09)^5 (1 - 0.015)^5 = \$14,266.38$.

Class C shares would be: $10,000 (1.09)^5 (1 - 0.02)^5 = \$13,907.94$.

Class B shares would provide the greatest net return.

Assuming a 10-year holding period, the total redemption value for an assumed $10,000 initial investment in:

Class A shares would be: $10,000 \, (1 - 0.04)(1.09)^{10} \, (1 - 0.01)^{10} =$ $20,553.61.

Class B shares would be: $10,000 \, (1.09)^{10} \, (1 - 0.015)^{10} = \$20,352.95$.

Class C shares would be: $10,000 \, (1.09)^{10} \, (1 - 0.02)^{10} = \$19,343.08$.

Class A shares would provide the greatest net return.

Remember, closed-end funds are traded like shares of stock. There is an annual (or quarterly) fund management fee that is paid to the manager of the fund. Investors pay a stock commission when buying and when selling shares. There will also be a bid/ask spread as with any stock. This spread is typically larger for funds that are less actively traded and for funds with relatively high price volatility, just as we would expect for any publicly-traded stock.

LOS 73.b: Distinguish among style, sector, index, global, and stable value strategies in equity investment and among exchange traded funds (ETFs), traditional mutual funds, and closed-end funds.

An investment company will define which investment strategy it aims to pursue for each equity mutual fund. There are many broadly defined strategies in equity investment:

- The **style** of an equity fund describes the basic characteristics of the underlying assets, such as growth versus value or large cap versus small cap.
- A **sector strategy** would have the investment fund concentrate its assets in a specific industry (e.g., the automobile industry).
- An **index fund** strives to match returns to those of a particular stock index, such as the S&P 500.
- A **global fund strategy** will invest in securities from all over the world, including those from the investment company's home country.
- A **stable value fund** invests in short-term government securities or other investments that can provide timely principal payments and a set interest rate.

An **exchange traded fund** (ETF) is a special type of fund that invests in a portfolio of stocks or bonds and is designed to mimic the performance of a specified index. Shares are traded in the secondary market like the shares of a closed-end fund, with the investor having the ability to trade at any time during market hours, sell short, or margin the shares. Although they trade like shares of a closed-end fund, the legal structure of most ETFs in the United States is that of a traditional (open-end) mutual fund. The creation and redemption of shares is somewhat different, however, as is detailed later.

A feature unique to ETFs is their use of "in-kind" creation and redemption of shares. Exchange specialists, called authorized participants, are established by the fund to ensure an efficient, orderly market in the shares. Authorized participants can create new shares in the ETF by depositing with a trustee a portfolio of stocks that track the index. The authorized participant then receives from the trustee new ETF shares to be sold in the open market. Conversely, the authorized participant can redeem shares to the trustee in exchange for the underlying stocks.

The "in-kind" process used by ETFs has two primary advantages. First, the in-kind creation and redemption feature keeps market prices of ETF shares close to NAV and avoids the premiums and discounts typical for closed-end funds. It provides a mechanism for arbitrage by exchange participants between the shares of stock that make up the fund and shares of the fund. Second, there is a tax advantage to in-kind redemption. If the fund distributes shares as a redemption method, any capital gains on the shares are realized at their sale. It is not a capital gain to the fund, so existing fund shareholders do not incur a tax liability as they would when a traditional mutual fund redeems fund shares and must sell portfolio securities to meet the cash demand. While fund shareholders do have the right to cash redemption, it is discouraged by redemption fees and the fact that NAV for the redemption is calculated some days after the redemption request.

LOS 73.c: Explain the advantages and risks of ETFs.

Advantages of ETFs. The broad spectrum of ETFs may have some of the following advantages relative to other equity investments:

- ETFs provide an efficient method of diversification—one transaction yields exposure to a broad index or sector.
- ETFs trade in a similar fashion to traditional equity investments—through an exchange—and can be shorted or margined. ETFs can be traded throughout the day with continuously updated prices, unlike traditional open-end funds that trade once a day at prices determined at the close of market.
- Some ETFs are patterned after indexes that have active futures and option markets, allowing for better risk management.
- ETF investors know the exact composition of the fund at all times through a daily, published list of underlying assets.
- Because they are passively managed, ETFs typically have very efficient operating expense ratios, as well as no loads to purchase or redeem shares (just a normal commission) and a bid-ask spread.
- The use of "in-kind" creation and redemption of shares eliminates any trading at a discount or premium to NAV. Authorized participants can create or redeem shares to capture any arbitrage opportunities.
- Decreased capital gains tax liability for ETF shareholders compared to traditional open-end fund investors.
- For some ETFs, dividends received may be reinvested immediately, as opposed to index funds whose timing may be delayed.

Disadvantages of ETFs. The disadvantages with investing in ETFs are as follows:

- In some countries outside of the United States, there are fewer indices for ETFs to track, resulting in mid- or low-cap stocks not being well represented in the portfolio.
- The ability to trade ETFs intraday may not be significant to those investors with longer time horizons.
- Investors may encounter inefficient markets (large bid-ask spreads) in those ETFs with low trading volume.

- Larger investors may choose to directly invest in an index portfolio, resulting in lower expenses and lower tax consequences.

Risks of ETFs. The major risks associated with ETFs are somewhat applicable to all equity investments and may not apply to the same extent to all ETFs:

- Shareholders of ETFs are exposed to the market risk of the index tracked by the fund.
- An ETF may invest in only a particular portion of the market, thus subjecting investors to asset class or sector risk.
- Trading prices of ETFs can differ from NAV, depending upon depth and liquidity of the market.
- Like traditional index funds, ETFs may experience tracking error risk, where the portfolio is not identical to the benchmark index and thus does not perform identically to the index.
- Some ETFs that are able to purchase derivatives, such as futures contracts on the underlying index, are exposed to additional risk from the increased leverage as well as credit risk on the derivatives.
- Currency and country risk may be present in ETFs that are based on international indexes.

LOS 73.d: Describe the forms of real estate investment and explain their characteristics as an investable asset class.

Types of real estate investments. For investors, real estate is one of the most common tangible assets they can readily invest in. Other types of investments, such as stocks and bonds, are claims to intangible assets (i.e., future cash flows), represented by some form of documentation. Real estate as an asset class is broadly defined as land plus any permanently attached fixture. Each real estate property is unique, causing difficulty in accurately determining current market value. Real estate as an investment is fairly illiquid, resulting in higher transaction costs than other types of investments. Real estate investments can be categorized into one of four major groups:

1. **Outright ownership** (sometimes called "fee simple" or "free and clear equity"). This is the most straightforward form of ownership, which entitles the holder to full ownership rights for an indefinite time period.

2. **Leveraged equity position.** Investors have the same entitlements as those having outright ownership but with the addition of some type of loan with terms that must be met in order to maintain ownership.

3. **Mortgages.** The investor is the holder of a mortgage loan and receives the monthly principal and interest payments paid by a borrower. This is considered to be a form of real estate investment because the underlying real estate may revert to the mortgage investor if the borrower defaults on the mortgage. Investors may choose to diversify their real estate exposure by investing in a group or pool of mortgage loans.

4. **Aggregation vehicles.** These allow investors to increase diversification in direct real estate holdings by investing in groups of real estate projects. Common forms include real estate limited partnerships, commingled funds, and real estate investment trusts (REITs).

©2009 Kaplan, Inc.

There are several **characteristics unique to real estate** that differ from other asset classes. A real estate investment is immobile, not divisible, and unique from all other real estate properties. Since each property is unique, it is impossible to directly compare to other properties, making it difficult to determine true market value. For these reasons, real estate as an asset class is somewhat illiquid. Real estate investments tend to have high transactions costs and management fees.

When considering real estate in a portfolio context as an asset that can provide diversification benefits, there are some important issues to consider. A primary issue is the characteristics of the data used and their effect on real estate's expected return, standard deviation of returns, and the correlation with the returns of other investable asset classes.

Some indexes based on real estate performance are based on appraised values for the real estate. Frank Russell Company (FRC) and the National Council of Real Estate Investment Fiduciaries (NCREIF) both produce indexes of regional real estate performance that are based on appraised values. The use of appraised values tends to smooth the returns of appraisal-based indexes relative to market prices. In portfolio optimization models, appraisal-based indexes will tend to have very large weights because of their low volatility and low correlation with important asset-class proxies such as the S&P 500 stock index. Many analysts consider this a very serious drawback of appraisal-based indexes and consider their use in portfolio mean-variance optimization models to be inappropriate.

Other real estate indexes are based on the performance of the shares of Real Estate Investment Trusts (REITs). The National Association of Real Estate Investment Trusts (NAREIT) index is one example. REIT indexes tend to have returns volatilities very close to those of broad stock market indexes, such as the S&P 500 stock index. Correlations of REIT index returns with stock index returns are very close to one as well. The implication of these results is that portfolio diversification benefits of REITs as an asset class are likely quite small. Another thing to consider is that REIT index returns reflect the leverage used in the REITs that comprise the index, so the actual returns behavior of the underlying real estate is not what is being measured.

In a portfolio context, the ability of real estate investments to provide a hedge against inflation may be a primary concern. In this case, the type of real estate may be the most important consideration, since some types of income producing real estate have much greater ability to pass through price inflation over the short term than others.

LOS 73.e: Describe the various approaches to the valuation of real estate.

Investors may use one or more of the four common **methods to value real estate:**

1. With the **cost method**, value is determined by the replacement cost of improvements plus an estimate for the value of the land. The replacement cost is relatively easy to determine using current construction costs, but the valuation of the land may not be easily determined. Also, the market value of an existing property may differ significantly from its replacement cost, depending upon the current condition of the improvements.

2. The **sales comparison method** uses the price of a similar property or properties from recent transactions. Prices from other properties must be adjusted for changes in market conditions and for characteristics unique to each property. This approach cannot be used in an illiquid market without recent comparable sales. A more detailed method of the sales comparison approach is hedonic price estimation, where specific characteristics of a property are quantified and then the sales prices for all recent transactions are put into a regression model that determines a benchmark value of each of the characteristics.

3. The **income method** uses a discounted cash flow model to estimate the present value of the future income produced by the property. The **net operating income** (NOI) is a simplified estimate based on annual gross rental revenues minus operating expenses. The NOI is then divided by an estimated market required rate of return, resulting in an appraisal price. This approach ignores changes in NOI that may occur over time and also does not take into account investors' income tax implications.

4. The **discounted after-tax cash flow model** links the value of a property to an investor's specific marginal tax rate. The net present value of an investment equals the present value of after-tax cash flows, discounted at the investor's required rate of return, minus the equity portion of the investment. Only those projects with a positive expected net present value would make financial sense.

 Professor's Note: When we are calculating after-tax cash flow, after-tax refers to the investor's marginal tax rate.

LOS 73.f: Calculate the net operating income (NOI) from a real estate investment, the value of a property using the sales comparison and income approaches, and the after-tax cash flows, net present value, and yield of a real estate investment.

NOI is defined as the gross operating income less estimated vacancy, collections, and other operating expenses.

Example: Real estate NOI

An investor is considering the purchase of a small office building and, as part of his analysis, must calculate the NOI. The information on the building is as follows:

Gross potential rental income:	$250,000
Estimated vacancy and collection loss rate:	5%
Insurance:	$10,000
Taxes:	$8,000
Utilities and Maintenance:	$22,000

Answer:

NOI = $250,000 – ($250,000 × 0.05) – $10,000 – $8,000 – $22,000 = $197,500

©2009 Kaplan, Inc.

Professor's Note: Be aware that depreciation and financing costs are not factors in the calculation of NOI. It is assumed that maintenance will keep the property in good condition, and the value of the property is independent of any financing arrangements. Also note that the taxes that are relevant to the calculation of NOI for real estate are property taxes.

The Sales Comparison and Income Approaches

The **sales comparison approach** is based on sales prices of comparable properties. Valuation can then be done relative to a specific similar property or relative to a benchmark such as the mean or median home price in the area. Then additions (e.g., for more square feet) and subtractions (e.g., for poor locations) are made to estimate the value of the subject property.

Another approach under the general heading of sales comparison methods is "hedonic price estimation." This involves creating a statistical model of the sales prices of properties, showing how the prices are related to certain key characteristics that influence the value of a property. The model produces an estimate of how much each of these factors contributes to the value of a property on average. For example, "distance from nearest public transportation in miles" might have an estimated effect of –$5,000. This means that, other things equal, sales prices for properties five miles from public transportation have been $25,000 less than sales prices for properties adjacent to public transportation.

The **income approach** is based on taking the present value of the stream of annual NOI, assuming it is an infinite stream, using the required rate of return or "cap rate" estimated for the property. These approaches are illustrated in the following two examples.

Example: Real estate valuation

Continuing the previous example, the investor has obtained additional information regarding other recent sales of comparable office buildings in the vicinity. The investor can use the comparable sales information in a hedonic price model to estimate a current appraised value of the property. Assuming a current market cap rate of 10%, compute the value of the property using (1) the sales comparison approach and (2) the income approach.

Characteristics	Units	Estimated Effect on Property Value in $ per Unit
Proximity to downtown	In miles	–50,000
Vacancy rate	Percent	–35,000
Building size	Square feet	40

The potential investment is half a mile from downtown, has an estimated vacancy rate of 4%, and is 50,000 square feet.

Answer 1: Sales comparison approach

Using the price model, the estimated appraised value would be:

$$\text{value} = (-50{,}000 \times 0.5) + (-35{,}000 \times 4) + (40 \times 50{,}000) = \$1{,}835{,}000$$

Answer 2: Income approach

Using the income approach, the appraised value of the property equals the NOI divided by the market cap rate and can be calculated as:

$$\text{appraisal price} = \frac{\text{NOI}}{\text{market cap rate}} = \frac{\$197{,}500}{0.10} = \$1{,}975{,}000$$

Example: Computing after-tax cash flows, NPV, and yield for real estate

Continuing the previous example, assume the investor purchases the building for $1,850,000, putting down 20% cash and financing the remainder with a long-term mortgage at a rate of 10%. The annual payments on the mortgage are $156,997, and the interest portion is fully deductible for income tax purposes. The investor's marginal income tax rate is 28%. Depreciation per year, using the straight-line method, is estimated to be $45,000 per year. Calculate the after-tax cash flows, net present value, and the yield of the investment.

Answer:

After-tax cash flow: The first year's interest payment of $148,000 is calculated as the amount borrowed ($1,480,000) times the interest rate of the loan. After-tax net income (NOI less depreciation, less interest, net of taxes) is ($197,500 − 45,000 − 148,000) × (1 − 0.28) = $3,240. After-tax cash flow can be determined by adding depreciation back to and subtracting the principal component of the mortgage payment from the after-tax net income number. For this investment, the year 1 after-tax cash flow is $3,240 + $45,000 − $8,997 = $39,243.

Net present value: Three years forward, the investor plans to sell the building for $1,950,000. The remaining mortgage balance at payoff is $1,450,000. Assume that the cost of equity is 10% and the net cash flows for the investment are as follows:

Year 1: $39,243
Year 2: $38,991
Year 3: $538,721 (year of sale, net of mortgage payoff, no capital gains tax)

Study Session 18

The present value of the cash flows is:

$$\frac{\$39,243}{1.10} + \frac{\$38,991}{1.10^2} + \frac{\$538,721}{1.10^3} = \$472,649$$

The NPV is the present value of the cash flows minus the initial investment:

$$\$472,649 - \$370,000 = \$102,649$$

Yield: In summary, the cash flows of the investment are:

Year 0	−$370,000	=	CF_0
Year 1	$39,243	=	CF_{01}
Year 2	$38,991	=	CF_{02}
Year 3	$538,721	=	CF_{03}
CPT →	IRR	=	20.18%

LOS 73.g: Explain the stages in venture capital investing, venture capital investment characteristics and challenges to venture capital valuation and performance measurement.

Venture capital investments are private, non-exchange-traded equity investments in a business venture. Investments are usually made through limited partnerships, with investors anticipating relatively high returns in exchange for the illiquidity and high-risk profile of a venture capital investment. Investments may be made at any point of the business cycle of the company, from the initial planning stages of a new venture to an established firm ready to go public.

The **stages of venture capital investing**, which overlap somewhat, are as follows:

- *Seed stage*. Investors are providing capital in the earliest stage of the business and may help fund research and development of product ideas.
- *Early stage*. Early stage financing includes:
  - *Start-up financing*, which typically refers to capital used to complete product development and fund initial marketing efforts.
  - *First stage financing*, which refers to the funding of the transition to commercial production and sales of the product.
- *Formative stage*. Broad category that encompasses the seed stage and early stage.
- *Later stage*. Marketable goods are in production and sales efforts are underway, but the company is still privately held. Within the later stage period, *second-stage investing* describes investments in a company that is producing and selling a product but is not yet generating income. *Third-stage financing* would fund a major expansion of the company. *Mezzanine or bridge financing* would enable a company to take the steps necessary to go public.

Broad terms, such as "expansion stage financing," are used to describe the second and third stage, while the term "balanced stage" covers all stages, from seed through later stage.

Venture capital investment characteristics (may have some or all of the following):

- *Illiquidity.* Investors' ability to cash out is dependent upon a successful IPO, which probably will not occur in the short term, if ever.
- *Long-term investment horizon.* Market conditions must be conducive for a public offering, and the company most likely must be at a profitable point in order for investors to recognize returns on their investment.
- *Difficulty in valuation.* Because of the uniqueness of each investment, there are few comparable assets with meaningful trading volume available for market value comparisons.
- *Limited data.* There is not much comparable historical risk and return data, nor is there much information on which to base future cash flows and earnings estimates. There also is insufficient information on what competing ideas or products other entrepreneurs may be developing.
- *Entrepreneurial/management mismatches.* Entrepreneurs with good ideas don't always necessarily evolve into good managers as their company grows.
- *Fund manager incentive mistakes.* The primary incentive for fund managers must be performance, not size or some other criteria.
- *Timing in the business cycle.* Market conditions are a primary determinant of the timing of market entrance and exit strategies.
- *Requirement for extensive operations analysis.* A successful venture capital manager must act as both a financial and operations advisor to the venture.

Valuing and measuring the performance of a venture capital investment is tricky at best, due to the large probability of failure plus the overall uncertainty as to amount and timing of cash flows. The three most important factors that must be assessed are the expected payoff at exit, timing of exit, and the probability of failure. Prior to exit (or failure), evaluation of the venture's performance must be made, although precise measurement is challenging. Difficulties include deriving accurate valuations, establishing benchmarks, and lacking reliable performance measures.

LOS 73.h: Calculate the net present value (NPV) of a venture capital project, given the project's possible payoff and conditional failure probabilities.

Example: Computing NPV for a venture capital opportunity

A venture capital fund manager is considering investing $2,500,000 in a new project that he believes will pay $12,000,000 at the end of five years. The cost of equity for the investor is 15%, and the estimated probability of failure is presented in the figure below. These are conditional probabilities since they represent the probability of failure in year N, given that the firm has survived to year N.

Estimated Probability of Failure

Year	1	2	3	4	5
Failure probability	0.20	0.20	0.17	0.15	0.15

Calculate the NPV of the potential investment.

Answer:

The probability that the venture survives for five years is calculated as:

$(1 - 0.20)(1 - 0.20)(1 - 0.17)(1 - 0.15)(1 - 0.15) = 0.3838 = 38.38\%$

Under the original assumptions that the investment pays $12,000,000 at the end of year 5, the NPV of a successful project is $-\$2,500,000 + (\$12,000,000 / 1.15^5) = \$3,466,121$. The NPV of the project if it fails is $-\$2,500,000$. The expected NPV of the project is a probability-weighted average of the two possible outcomes:

$(0.3838 \times \$3,466,121) + (0.6162 \times -\$2,500,000) = -\$210,203$

The fund manager would not invest in the new project due to the negative expected NPV.

LOS 73.i: Define hedge fund in terms of objectives, legal structure, and fee structure, and describe the various classifications of hedge funds.

Hedge funds today utilize a wide variety of strategies, which may or may not utilize hedging techniques to reduce or eliminate risk. The term "hedge fund" does not begin to describe this broad asset class that has evolved over the past two decades. The common objective of hedge funds is that they strive for absolute returns. That is to say that hedge funds are not constrained by the fact that they must perform relative to some specific benchmark or index and simply seek to maximize returns in all market scenarios.

Most hedge funds are in the form of either a limited partnership, a limited liability corporation, or an offshore corporation. In the U.S., limited partnerships that abide by certain guidelines (regarding the maximum allowable number of investors, the "qualifications" of the investors, and the prohibition of advertising) are exempt from most SEC regulations. Because the number of investors is limited, the amount of their individual investments is relatively large, usually $200,000 or more.

The manager of the fund receives compensation that is comprised of two components. The base fee is typically around 1% of assets, and the manager receives this fee regardless of performance of the hedge fund. The second component, the incentive fee, is paid based on the actual returns of the fund. Some structures allow the manager to participate in all returns, while other structures pay the manager only if performance exceeds a target return, such as the risk-free rate.

Sometimes an additional provision allows incentive fees to be paid only after the fund has produced returns in excess of any negative returns from the previous year. A "high watermark provision" is sometimes included, which stipulates that incentive fees are only based on returns above the highest value achieved over the life of the fund. Provisions such as these may encourage the fund manager to take additional risk after periods of negative returns because of the option-like characteristics of the manager's incentive payment.

Classifications of Hedge Funds

Hedge funds can usually be classified by investment strategy; however, there is a great deal of overlap among categories. Some **hedge fund classifications** are:

- *Long/short funds* make up the largest category of hedge funds in terms of asset size. These funds take long and short common stock positions, use leverage, and are invested in markets worldwide. By definition they are not market-neutral but seek to profit from greater returns on the long positions than on the short positions.
- *Market-neutral funds* are a type of long/short fund that strive to hedge against general market moves. Managers may try to achieve this through any of several strategies, some involving derivatives. The fund may still have long and short positions, but the positions will offset each other so that the effect is a net zero exposure to the market.
- *Global macro funds* make bets on the direction of a market, currency, interest rate, or some other factor. Global macro funds are typically highly leveraged and rely heavily upon derivatives.
- *Event-driven funds* strive to capitalize on some unique opportunity in the market. This may involve investing in a distressed company or in a potential merger and acquisition situation.

LOS 73.j: Explain the benefits and drawbacks to fund of funds investing.

Fund of funds investing involves creating a fund open to both individuals and institutional investors, which in turn invests in hedge funds.

Benefits. Funds of funds enable investors with limited capital to invest in a portfolio of hedge funds. Likewise, investors with more capital can diversify their holdings by investing in several hedge funds via a fund of funds for roughly the same amount required for directly investing in a single hedge fund. Fund of funds investing may grant new investors access to hedge funds that might otherwise be closed to them due to limitations on the number of investors. A fund of funds manager will have the expertise necessary to choose high-quality hedge funds and will also perform the due diligence required by investing in hedge funds.

Drawbacks. Fund of funds managers charge a management fee in addition to those fees already charged by the hedge fund manager. Diversification among hedge funds will decrease the investor's risk but most likely his return as well, from which additional fees must be subtracted. Fund of funds managers may or may not deliver returns superior to what an investor might achieve by selecting her own hedge funds.

LOS 73.k: Discuss the leverage and unique risks of hedge funds.

The majority of hedge fund managers utilize some form of leverage in order to enhance returns. Some arbitrage opportunities may have such a small return that leverage is necessary to make the strategy meaningful. However, leveraged positions can sometimes backfire and cause losses to be magnified. Hedge funds typically limit the amount of leverage that can be used, and fund managers are legally required to operate within the limit. One way a hedge fund can increase its leverage is by borrowing through a margin

Study Session 18

account. Also, a hedge fund manager could borrow external funds to either buy more assets or sell short more than the equity in the fund. A third way is for hedge fund managers to utilize those securities that only require posting margin versus trading in cash securities requiring full payment.

Risks associated with hedge funds include:

- *Illiquidity.* Investing in those markets with little liquidity, such as derivatives, decreases a hedge fund's trading flexibility.
- *Potential for mispricing.* Investments in esoteric securities that trade infrequently may lead to difficulty in determining true current market value. Broker-dealers who are financing such securities tend to be conservative in their valuations, thereby increasing the amount of cash that is required to be posted by the hedge fund.
- *Counterparty credit risk.* A broker-dealer is involved in almost every transaction a hedge fund enters into, thereby creating significant counterparty risk to the hedge fund.
- *Settlement errors.* Hedge funds bear the risk that the counterparty will fail to deliver a security as agreed on settlement day.
- *Short covering.* Short selling is a component of many common hedge fund strategies. Hedge fund managers run the risk that they will have to cover their shorts and repurchase securities at a price higher than where they originally sold.
- *Margin calls.* Margin calls on an already highly leveraged position can result in forced selling of assets, possibly at a loss.

LOS 73.l: Discuss the performance of hedge funds, the biases present in hedge fund performance measurement, and explain the effect of survivorship bias on the reported return and risk measures for a hedge fund database.

There are numerous hedge fund indices designed to measure historical performance; however, they may not provide much meaningful information on hedge funds as an asset class because each hedge fund's structure is so unique. Since hedge funds are not legally required to publicly disclose performance, only those hedge funds that elect to disclose performance information are included in the indices. Some general conclusions regarding hedge funds can be derived.

- Hedge funds have demonstrated a lower risk profile than traditional equity investments as measured by standard deviation.
- In recent years, the Sharpe ratio, which is a reward-to-risk ratio, has been consistently higher for hedge funds than for most equity investments and has been comparable to that of fixed-income investments.
- There is a low correlation between the performance of hedge funds and conventional investments. This correlation tends to be lower in down equity markets and higher when equities perform well.

As with the evaluation of historical data for any investment instrument, certain **biases may exist** that should be considered. It is common investment knowledge that past performance is not a reliable indicator of future performance. Some significant biases are:

- *Self-selection bias.* The only information available to be included in the indices is what the fund managers submit. Managers may be unwilling to disclose poor performance and choose to offer information only on those funds with successful track records. The index may overestimate returns for the hedge fund industry as a whole.
- *Backfilling bias.* Again, because disclosure is voluntary, only fund managers with a respectable track record would be willing to be included in an index. Past performance of the industry is inflated by an index because funds with poor past performance are not included.
- *Survivorship bias.* As with any industry, only the best-performing hedge funds survive. By design, an index only includes ongoing funds and excludes those that have failed. The index in effect is biased toward only the "success stories" of the industry.
- *Smoothed pricing of infrequently traded assets.* Because many of the assets held in hedge funds are not actively traded, managers rely upon broker-dealers to mark their positions and estimate "market" value. Because they are estimates and not based upon actual transactions, values tend to be more stable over time, thereby reducing reported volatility.
- *Option-like strategies.* Some investment strategies used by hedge funds may have a limited upside potential but unlimited downside potential. Traditional risk measures, such as standard deviation or value at risk, do not fully account for this asymmetric return profile.
- *Fee structures and gaming.* A typical hedge fund fee structure pays the manager a small fixed fee and then a substantial percentage of gains. This structure may cause fund managers to take big risks, especially if past performance is bad and they have "nothing to lose."

Effect of Survivorship Bias

The **effect of survivorship bias** is greater for a hedge fund database than for other asset classes because of the lack of required reporting standards in the industry. Hedge funds are normally exempt from SEC regulations regarding reporting and only publicly disclose performance information on a voluntary basis. Fund managers tend to "cherry pick" the information they choose to release, reporting on their more successful funds while not providing information on poorly performing or defunct funds. Reported returns for a hedge fund database are therefore overstating performance because of survivorship bias.

Survivorship bias has the opposite effect on the risk measures of a hedge fund database. Hedge funds with highly volatile returns tend to fail more frequently, and defunct funds are not generally included in the database. Because the database would only include the more stable funds that have survived, the risk measure of hedge funds as an asset class would be understated.

LOS 73.m: Explain how the legal environment affects the valuation of closely held companies.

The equity shares of **closely held companies** are not publicly traded and are not subject to the same SEC regulations as public companies regarding reporting and disclosure. As the name implies, closely held companies are held by a relatively small group of owners. The companies may be in the form of any number of legal entities: corporations, partnerships, or sole proprietorships. Some corporations' legal structures are designed to take advantage of current tax codes, such as subchapter S corporations. Other corporations may elect to operate as general or limited partnerships, which dictate the extent of a partner's liability for the corporation. The choice of structure affects the investors' rights and responsibilities and, ultimately, the value of their investments.

When litigation situations arise, there can be questions as to the "value" of the corporation. The legal definitions of intrinsic value, fundamental value, and fair value can differ among jurisdictions. There are not frequent transactions in the open market upon which to estimate value. Valuation, therefore, is based upon either a forecast of future cash flows, actual past cash flows, or a combination of both. Both the purpose of the valuation and the legal jurisdiction affect the factors on which value is based and how it is calculated.

LOS 73.n: Describe alternative valuation methods for closely held companies and distinguish among the bases for the discounts and premiums for these companies.

There are three different valuation methods for closely held companies:

1. The **cost approach**. What is the cost today to replace the company's assets in their present state?

2. The **comparables approach**. What is the value relative to an appropriate benchmark value? The benchmark would be based upon market prices of similar companies, adjusted for such factors as transaction date and any unique characteristics of the company. The benchmark may be difficult to establish if no comparable companies have been sold recently.

3. The **income approach**. What is the net present value of the company based upon discounted future cash flows?

When valuing closely held companies, lack of liquidity and lack of marketability can both be important factors. Value can be determined by analyzing operationally similar publicly traded companies to establish a base value, to which the liquidity and marketability discounts can be applied. Another factor to be considered is whether the block of shares being valued represents a controlling interest in the company. A discount for minority interest may be necessary for valuing a position that lacks the ability to influence corporate decision making if the benchmark value is for a controlling interest in a private company. Likewise, a premium would be appropriate for the valuation of a controlling ownership position if the benchmark value is for publicly traded shares, which represent a minority interest.

The application of premiums and discounts depends on the characteristics of the subject securities relative to the characteristics of the securities used in estimating the base value. If the base value used is the market price of publicly traded shares, the valuation of a majority interest in a closely held company may require the application of discounts for lack of liquidity and marketability and of a premium for control, for example.

LOS 73.o: Discuss distressed securities investing and compare venture capital investing with distressed securities investing.

When companies are on the brink of bankruptcy or have already filed for bankruptcy protection, their securities are considered "distressed." Also included in the group of **distressed securities** are those companies attempting to avoid bankruptcy by pursuing an out-of-court debt restructuring. In a typical bankruptcy scenario, the original holders of the company's debt negotiate for an equity position in the new, restructured corporation. The original equity shareholders then receive a somewhat diluted equity position in the reorganized company. A typical distressed security investment strategy would be to purchase the debt of the struggling company, pre-reorganization, in the hopes of ultimately owning an equity position in a new, revitalized operation. Pursuing a distressed security strategy is somewhat similar to venture capital investing. Both asset classes are illiquid, have a long expected investment horizon, and require heavy involvement by investors in order to be successful. Both situations mandate extensive analytical work in order to avoid pricing or valuation mistakes.

LOS 73.p: Discuss the role of commodities as a vehicle for investing in production and consumption.

Investing in commodities gives an investor exposure to an economy's production and consumption growth. When the economy experiences growth, the demand for commodities increases, and price increases are likely. When housing starts to increase, the demand for lumber will increase; when automobile sales are high, the demand for steel is likely high as well. During recessions, commodity prices are likely to fall with decreased demand. Overall, swings in commodity prices are likely to be larger than changes in finished goods prices.

LOS 73.q: Explain the motivation for investing in commodities, commodities derivatives, and commodity-linked securities.

The motivation for investing in commodities may be as an inflation hedge for hedging purposes or for speculation on the direction of commodity prices over the near term. Most investors do not invest directly in commodities that need to be transported and stored. *Passive investors* who hold commodities as an asset class for diversification or those who hold commodities as a long-term inflation hedge are more likely to invest in a collateralized futures position. A collateralized futures position or collateralized futures fund is a combination of an investment in commodity futures and an investment in Treasury securities equal in value to the value of the futures position. *Active investors* may invest in commodity futures in an attempt to profit from economic growth that is associated with higher commodity prices.

©2009 Kaplan, Inc.

Commodity-linked equity investments also provide exposure to commodity price changes. Shares of commodity-producing companies are likely to experience returns that are strongly tied to the prices of the commodities produced. This may be especially true for the shares of smaller, less diversified commodity producing firms.

Commodity-linked bonds provide income as well as exposure to commodity price changes since the overall return is based on the price of a single commodity such as gold or oil. Other commodity-linked bonds are linked to inflation through payments based on inflation or a commodity price index. These bonds may be attractive to a fixed-income portfolio manager who wants exposure to commodity price changes but cannot invest either directly in commodities or in derivative securities.

LOS 73.r: Discuss the sources of return on a collateralized commodity futures position.

Establishing a **collateralized commodities futures position** requires simultaneously purchasing (going long) a specific futures contract and purchasing government securities, such as T-bills, with a *market* value equal to the *contract value* of the futures contract. Any gains from the futures position are used to buy T-bills, and any margin calls are covered by selling T-bills. The total return on this strategy will equal the percentage change in price of the futures contract plus the percentage interest earned on the government securities.

Example: Commodity futures returns

A passive manager purchases a position worth $50 million in underlying value of a futures contract. The manager also buys $50 million worth of 10-year U.S. Treasury notes at par that pay an interest rate of 5%. Compute the gain in the value of the position if, at the end of one year, the futures contract position is worth $51 million and the price of the 10-year notes is unchanged. Ignore any interest gained or lost on variation margin over the life of the contract.

Answer:

gain on the futures position = $1,000,000

interest earned on the notes = $50,000,000 × 0.05 = $2.5 million

total gain = $1,000,000 + $2,500,000 = $3,500,000

Note that the total return, $\dfrac{3,500,000}{50,000,000} = 7\%$, is equal to the interest on the notes of

5% plus the gain, $\dfrac{1,000,000}{50,000,000} = 2\%$, on the futures contract.

KEY CONCEPTS

LOS 73.a

An open-end fund will create new shares upon purchase or redeem existing shares for cash.

A closed-end fund has a fixed number of shares that trade like shares of stock.

The net asset value of investment company (mutual fund) shares is the value, at a point in time, of fund assets minus fund liabilities divided by the number of shares outstanding.

Mutual funds have ongoing management fees, administrative fees, and possibly marketing fees, all of which can significantly affect fund performance.

LOS 73.b

Strategies of investment company portfolios can be categorized as:
- Style (e.g., growth).
- Sector (e.g., biotech).
- Index (e.g., S&P 500 Index).
- Global (all countries of the world).
- Stable value (e.g., short-term high quality debt securities).

An exchange traded fund (ETF) holds a portfolio that matches a specific published index. ETF shares are traded like closed-end fund shares.

LOS 73.c

Advantages of ETFs:
- Efficient method of diversification.
- Shares can be traded intraday, shorted, and margined.
- Underlying assets are published daily.
- Low expenses.
- In-kind creation and redemption of shares keeps premiums and discounts to NAV at a minimum.
- Less capital gains liability compared to open-end funds.

Risks of ETFs:
- Exposure to market risk of the index tracked.
- Class or sector risk for ETFs that invest in specific portions of the market.
- Prices can differ from NAV.
- Tracking error risk.
- Leverage and credit risk for ETFs that use derivatives.
- Currency and country risk for ETFs based on international indexes.

©2009 Kaplan, Inc.

LOS 73.d

Forms of real estate investment are:

- Outright ownership.
- Leveraged equity positions.
- Mortgages.
- Aggregation vehicles such as limited partnerships and REITs.

Real estate is immobile, indivisible, and somewhat illiquid, and each property is unique, making valuation difficult.

LOS 73.e

Approaches to real estate valuation are:

- Cost approach.
- Sales comparison approach.
- Income approach.
- Discounted after-tax cash flow approach.

LOS 73.f

Net Operating Income for a real estate investment is calculated as:

NOI = gross potential income – vacancy and collection loss estimate – insurance – real estate taxes – utility expense – estimated maintenance expense

The sales comparison approach of real estate valuation begins with recent sales prices for comparable properties and makes adjustments for differences.

The income approach begins with a calculation of NOI and divides by the required rate of return (the cap rate).

With the discounted after-tax cash flow model, annual NOI is adjusted for specific financing cash flows and computed on an after-tax basis using the investor's marginal tax rate.

- The net present value of the investment is the present value of these after-tax cash flows based on the required rate of return.
- The yield of the investment is the IRR of the after-tax cash flows based on the purchase price of the property.

LOS 73.g

The stages of venture capital investing are:

- Seed stage.
- Early stage.
- Formative stage.
- Later stages (after the company is making and selling a product). These later stages are alternatively called second stage, third stage (to fund a major expansion), or mezzanine/bridge financing (in preparation for an IPO).

Venture capital investments are illiquid, have long horizons, have limited comparable historical data, and require substantial input from the investor.

Valuation and performance measurement are difficult for venture capital investments due to problems in estimating the probability of failure, the payoff at exit (sale or IPO of the firm), and the timing of the exit.

LOS 73.h

The NPV of a venture capital investment can be estimated as the difference between the original investment amount and the present value of the estimated payment at exit multiplied by 1 minus the probability of failure for each year of the assumed holding period.

LOS 73.i

Hedge funds are typically structured as partnerships, are exempt from SEC regulation, have an absolute return objective, and charge a performance-based management fee. Many hedge funds have no hedging objective or strategy.

Some major hedge fund categories are:
- Long/short (to benefit from overpriced securities).
- Market neutral (to hedge market risk).
- Global macro (to profit from trending factors).
- Event-driven (to exploit unique opportunities).

LOS 73.j

Fund of funds investing allows an investor to gain diversification across funds and styles and provides professional fund selection but is also more costly in terms of overall management fees.

LOS 73.k

Many hedge funds use leverage to magnify the gains (and losses) from their strategies.

Hedge fund investments have additional risks from illiquidity, counterparty risk, pricing/valuation problems, settlement errors, and possible margin calls.

LOS 73.l

Hedge funds have historically exhibited lower standard deviations and higher Sharpe ratios than traditional equity investments, as well as low correlations of returns with those of conventional asset classes.

Hedge fund performance figures may be biased upward because of self-selection bias, backfilling bias, survivorship bias, smoothed pricing of assets that trade infrequently, option-like investment strategies, and gaming based on fee structures.

Databases of hedge fund performance that contain only surviving hedge funds will provide performance statistics that are biased upward (poor performing funds tend to cease to exist) and risk measures that are biased downward (funds that employ riskier strategies are more likely to cease to exist).

©2009 Kaplan, Inc.

LOS 73.m

The legal structure of a closely held investment (e.g., S corporation or partnership), the absence of SEC reporting requirements, the purpose of the analysis, and the valuation methods accepted in its specific legal jurisdiction can all affect the valuation of closely held companies.

LOS 73.n

Valuation of closely held companies can be done by:
- Cost method.
- Comparables method.
- Income approach.

Discounts for lack of liquidity, for lack of marketability, or for a minority position, and a premium for controlling interest are applied when the characteristics of the subject security differ in these dimensions from the characteristics of the securities used to establish a base value.

LOS 73.o

Investing in distressed securities is like venture capital investing in that the investments are often illiquid, have a long time horizon, require extensive valuation analysis, and can require active participation in dealing with management or with a court-appointed trustee in the case of a firm in bankruptcy reorganization.

LOS 73.p

Indirect investment in commodities can be achieved through futures, commodity-linked bonds, and the shares of commodity-producing firms in order to gain exposure to commodity price gains associated with higher economic growth.

LOS 73.q

While a passive investor may invest in commodities for diversification benefits through a collateralized futures fund, an active investor seeks to profit from anticipating moves in commodity prices and is more likely to use futures.

Commodity-linked securities are used by investors who want exposure to commodity price moves for either hedging or speculation.

LOS 73.r

A collateralized commodity futures position involves investing in futures along with an investment in Treasury securities equal to the value of the futures contract and will have returns from futures price changes and from the interest income of the Treasury position.

CONCEPT CHECKERS

1. What is the NAV for the ABC fund, given the following information?
   - Assets $250,000,000
   - Liabilities $25,000,000
   - Shares outstanding   10,500,000
   - Base management fee   0.75%
   A. $21.43.
   B. $23.81.
   C. $225,000,000.

2. An investor is considering purchasing shares of the ABC fund that has an NAV equal to $21.25. Given that the current market price is $22.50, which of the following statements is *most accurate*?
   A. ABC is an open-end fund.
   B. ABC charges a front-end load.
   C. The investor can purchase shares of the ABC fund at a premium to NAV.

3. An investment company that invests primarily in stocks with high price-to-earnings ratios is pursuing a:
   A. style strategy.
   B. sector strategy.
   C. global strategy.

4. An important benefit of an exchange-traded fund's creation and redemption process is that it:
   A. provides diversification to shareholders.
   B. increases liquidity for investment company managers.
   C. provides capital gains tax relief to existing shareholders.

5. The real estate valuation method which assigns quantitative rankings to a property's characteristics for use in a regression model is the:
   A. cost approach.
   B. income approach.
   C. hedonic price estimation approach.

6. What is the NOI for an office building, calculated with the following information:
   - Gross rental income $250,000
   - Estimated vacancy and losses   7%
   - Taxes and insurance $18,000
   - Utilities and maintenance $21,000
   - Depreciation $20,000
   A. $173,500.
   B. $193,500.
   C. $211,000.

©2009 Kaplan, Inc.

7.   An investor is considering investing $2,000,000 in a venture capital project that promises to pay $12,000,000 at the end of four years. The investor realizes there is some risk that the project will fail prior to the end of four years, in which case the investor will lose the entire investment. Using the following information, determine the probability that the project survives until the end of the fourth year.

Year	1	2	3	4
Failure probability	0.22	0.20	0.18	0.15

A. 18.8%.
B. 43.5%.
C. 56.5%.

8.   A portfolio manager has been researching a potential venture capital investment. The venture, ABC, Inc. has recently received patent approval for a new widget but has yet to begin production and marketing of the new product. Which of the following *best* describes this stage of venture capital investing?
A. First stage.
B. Seed stage.
C. Second stage.

9.   The one characteristic that hedge funds as an asset class have in common is that they typically:
A. are highly leveraged.
B. seek absolute returns.
C. utilize some type of hedging strategy.

10.   The biggest advantage for a U.S. hedge fund to be structured as a limited partnership organized under Section 3(c)(1) of the Investment Company Act is:
A. to gain exemption from most SEC regulations.
B. to lower the minimum initial required investment.
C. to be able to freely advertise to prospective investors.

11.   An investor makes a $1 million investment in a venture capital project that has an expected payoff of $5,000,000 at the end of four years. The cost of capital is 10%. If the conditional annual failure probabilities over the first four years are 10%, 15%, 20%, and 15%, the expected NPV of the project is *closest* to:
A. $366,067.
B. $775,834.
C. $698,057.

12.   A hedge fund that seeks to invest in the equity and debt of companies emerging from bankruptcy reorganization can *best* be described as a(n):
A. event-driven fund.
B. global macro fund.
C. risk arbitrage fund.

13.   A fund of funds (FOF) is *least likely* to provide its investors with which of the following advantages?
A. Performance of due diligence.
B. Diversification across several markets.
C. Lower fees through economies of scale.

14. Historical data regarding hedge fund returns has limitations because hedge fund managers tend to submit data on only those hedge funds with impressive track records, while omitting data on those with poor past performance. This bias in performance data can *best* be described as:
    A. gaming.
    B. self-selection.
    C. smoothed pricing.

15. Investments in closely held companies require extensive analysis, beyond what is required by traditional investments. This is due to questions regarding:
    A. valuation.
    B. management accountability.
    C. disclosure of financial information.

16. A portfolio manager is considering taking a 5% position in a closely held company. Currently, the company's founder/CEO holds over 60% of the company's equity. The portfolio manager is valuing his potential investment based upon a the market value of a comparable company whose stock is actively traded. In this case, the value of the comparable company will be adjusted by a:
    A. control discount.
    B. control premium.
    C. liquidity discount.

17. The main motivation for a passive investor to participate in the commodities market is that it provides:
    A. for speculative profits.
    B. a hedge against inflation risk.
    C. participation in the real economy.

18. A major benefit of investing in commodity-linked securities rather than holding commodities is that:
    A. commodity-linked securities may provide current income.
    B. counterparty risk is lower with commodity-linked securities.
    C. there is higher liquidity in the commodity-linked securities market.

©2009 Kaplan, Inc.

COMPREHENSIVE PROBLEMS

1. Assume an expected annual gross return of 8% and the various fee and expense structures in the table below.

	Class A Shares	Class B Shares	Class C Shares
Front-end load (charged at time of sale)	4% of investment	none	none
Back-end load (redemption fees)	none	initially 5% of sale proceeds—declines by 1% each year	2% during the first year
Annual Fees (calculated on year-end values)			
Distribution fees	none	0.5%	1.0%
Fund management fees	0.8%	0.8%	0.8%
Other fund expenses	0.2%	0.2%	0.2%
Total annual fees	1.0%	1.5%	2.0%

A. What are the holding period returns for each class of fund shares over a 4-year period?

B. Which class of shares would produce the highest average annual compound rate of return for an investor over a 4-year period?

C. Which class of shares would be the best choice for a short holding period of one or two years? Answer without calculations and explain your reasoning.

2. A model derived from a large sample of house prices (U.S. dollars) based on three important characteristics yielded the following results.

Average value, net of model characteristics   134,534
Estimated effects on price:
    Square feet   7.54
    Number of bathrooms   14,345
    Miles from subway station   −13,980

An appraiser is using this model to value a house with two bathrooms and 1,300 square feet of living space that is 4.3 miles from the closest subway station. What will the estimated value be?

3.   A real estate investor is considering the purchase of a building for $7 million, putting 30% down and financing the rest of the purchase price with a 30-year mortgage loan (fully amortizing with 30 equal annual payments) at an interest rate of 9%. The net operating income on the building is estimated to be $675,000 the first year and to grow at the expected inflation rate of 3%. At the end of the third year, the investor expects to sell the building for $7.4 million. The investor is in the 28% marginal tax bracket and interest is tax deductible. He will use straight-line depreciation for the building only (not the land) which is $200,000 per year. Assume for this problem that the tax rate on any gain on the sale of the property is 15%.

A. What are the after-tax cash flows the investor expects in years 1, 2, and 3?

B. What are the net (after-tax) proceeds of the sale at the end of year 3?

C. If the investor requires an after-tax rate of return of 15% on such investments, should he purchase the building?

4.   The trustee of a retirement fund has been told by a consultant that for diversification purposes his fund should invest approximately 35% of assets in real estate in the major cities of the North Atlantic region in the U.S. When asked about the source of his data on real estate returns, the consultant informs the trustee that returns based on the NCREIF index for the North Atlantic region were used. What would your advice to the trustee be?

5.   Consider the following four hedge fund fee structures.

   I.   1% per year plus 20% of gross returns in excess of the risk-free rate.

   II. 20% of gross returns in excess of the absolute value of any negative returns from the previous year.

   III. 1% per year plus 20% of any returns in excess of the total returns on the S&P 500 index.

   IV. 1% per year plus 20% of any returns for the fund above its previous highest value (high watermark provision).

Assume that for the current year the risk-free return was 4.5%, the S&P 500 Index had a total return of 9.5%, and the gross return on the fund was 17%. Further, assume that the fund gross returns last year were +2% and that it has never had negative gross returns in any year.

A. Calculate the returns (net of fees) that an investor would earn under each of the above fee structures.

B. If all remains the same, except that the previous year's gross return had been –10%, calculate the returns an investor would earn under each of the above fee structures.

C. If all remains the same (as in part A), but the current year's return is –13% and the current year's total return on the S&P 500 Index is –20%, which fund structure will give an investor the lowest return net of fees?

Study Session 18

6.   A trustee for a large tax-deferred institutional portfolio has hired a consultant to advise her on the possible advantages of investing a portion of the portfolio's assets in hedge funds as an asset class to potentially increase returns, decrease portfolio risk, or both. Based on a database of 5-year performance for all the currently investable hedge funds that have both been in existence and reported returns for the entire 5-year period, the consultant states: "The average annual fund gross return has been 17.8% with a standard deviation of returns of 15%. The standard deviation of returns on the S&P 500 Index over the same period was 10%. The Sharpe ratio for the hedge funds as an asset class has been 0.80 while the Sharpe ratio for an investment in the S&P 500 Index has been 0.70 for the same 5-year period. Based on the correlation of hedge-fund returns with the returns on the assets currently in the institutional portfolio and the average returns on the hedge funds, I recommend a 30% allocation of existing portfolio assets to hedge funds."

   A. What was the average risk-free rate over the period?
   B. What was the average annual return for the S&P 500 Index over the 5-year period?
   C. How would you respond to the consultant's recommendation of a 30% allocation to hedge funds? Refer to as many characteristics of the hedge fund data used as you can.

7.   Gold has a negative beta.

   A. Based on the CAPM, how will the expected return on an investment in gold compare to the risk-free rate?
   B. How can you use what you know about modern portfolio theory to explain why investors would choose to hold gold, based on your answer to A above.

ANSWERS – CONCEPT CHECKERS

1. **A** The net asset value is the investment company's assets minus its liabilities, stated on a per-share basis.

$$NAV = \frac{\$250,000,000 - \$25,000,000}{10,500,000 \text{ shares}} = \$21.43 \text{ per share}$$

2. **C** The market price of $22.50 is at a premium to NAV at $21.25. The fund is not an open-end fund because shares of an open-end fund always trade at NAV. The fund does not charge a load because it is a closed-end fund.

3. **A** A style strategy concentrates on equities that share similar underlying characteristics. Sector strategies focus on a specific industry. Global strategies invest in securities from around the world.

4. **C** The in-kind process allows for the creation and redemption of shares through market makers, which operate outside the legal structure of the fund. In a traditional open-end fund, when shares are redeemed, the manager must sell fund assets to pay off the redemption, thus possibly creating capital gains issues for the remaining fund shareholders.

5. **C** Hedonic price estimation is a variation of the sales comparison approach that uses recent transactions as a benchmark to estimate market value. The cost approach only considers what it would cost today to rebuild improvements on a property. The income approach values a property based on an estimate of future income.

6. **B** NOI is gross income less vacancy and collection costs, taxes and insurance, and utilities and maintenance. Depreciation is not a factor because it is assumed that proper maintenance will keep the property in its current condition. The calculation is: $250,000 – ($250,000 × 7%) – $18,000 – $21,000 = $193,500.

7. **B** The probability that the venture will survive to the end of the fourth year is calculated as follows:

$$(1 - 0.22)(1 - 0.20)(1 - 0.18)(1 - 0.15) = 0.435, \text{ or } 43.5\%$$

8. **A** First-stage financing refers to capital provided to begin manufacturing and sales. Seed-stage is prior to first-stage financing and involves providing capital for developing a business idea. Second-stage financing is used for expansion of a company already producing and selling a product.

9. **B** Hedge funds as an asset class follow a vast array of strategies as far as leverage and hedging strategies. The only common characteristic is their search for absolute returns.

10. **A** Forming as a limited partnership frees the hedge fund from most SEC regulations. The structure does, however, place strict limitations on the number of "qualified" investors, which in turn effectively raises the minimum initial investment. Also, under this structure, advertising is prohibited.

©2009 Kaplan, Inc.

11. **B** The probability of surviving four years is $(0.9)(0.85)(0.8)(0.85) = 0.52$. The expected value of the payoff in four years is $0.52(\$5 \text{ million}) = \$2.6 \text{ million}$.

$$NPV = \frac{\$2.6 \text{ million}}{(1.10)^4} - \$1 \text{ million} = \$775,835.$$

12. **A** An event-driven fund makes bets on some event specific to a company or security, such as the successful emergence from bankruptcy. A global macro fund bets on the direction of some macroeconomic variable, such as interest rates or currencies. A risk arbitrage fund focuses on arbitrage opportunities arising from mergers and acquisitions.

13. **C** The FOF manager will charge a management fee in addition to those fees charged by the underlying hedge funds.

14. **B** Self-selection bias occurs because unsuccessful managers and their funds tend not to disclose their performance, leaving only successful managers with impressive track records in the performance database. Gaming refers to managers either taking big risks to make up for past poor performance or refraining from taking more risk to avoid damage to a good track record. Smoothed pricing refers to the use of estimated values for assets that trade infrequently.

15. **A** Questions regarding valuation arise from differences in legal structures among closely held companies, each of which have unique ownership differences and tax implications for the investor. Disclosure of financial information and management accountability are not typical causes for additional analysis.

16. **C** From the portfolio manager's viewpoint, the value of the position should be discounted by some amount for the lack of liquidity in the equity of a closely held company.

17. **B** A passive investor is seeking diversification benefits because commodities tend to have a positive correlation with inflation. An active investor is seeking speculative profits in periods of economic growth. Some investors may regard gold as a good store of value, but not all commodities hold their value over time. Participation in the real economy is an unlikely motivation for investing in commodities.

18. **A** Commodity-linked securities can provide current income, while pure commodities afford returns through price increases. There is no evidence that the commodity-linked securities market is more liquid or provides less counterparty risk.

ANSWERS – COMPREHENSIVE PROBLEMS

1. A. Assuming a 4-year holding period, the holding period returns for:
        Class A shares would be: $(1 - 0.04)(1.08)^4(1 - 0.01)^4 - 1 = 25.46\%$.
        Class B shares would be: $(1.08)^4(1 - 0.015)^4(1 - 0.01) - 1 = 26.79\%$. (Back-end load is 1% after 4 years)
        Class C shares would be: $(1.08)^4(1 - 0.02)^4 - 1 = 25.49\%$.

    B. Class B shares would provide the greatest holding period return and therefore the greatest average annual compound rate of return.

    C. Over short holding periods such as one or two years, Class C would be the best choice. Although Class C shares have higher annual expenses, the relatively high front-end charges for Class A shares and redemption charges for Class B shares in the early years will outweigh the savings from lower total annual fees.

2. $134,534 + 7.54(1,300) + 14,345(2) - 13,980(4.3) = \$112,912$

3. A. The amount borrowed is $4.9 million ($0.7 \times 7$ million). At 9% and with 30 level payments, the payments will be $476,948.

        Year 1 (rounding to whole dollars):
        Interest will be 0.09×4.9 million = $441,000
        Principal repayment will be $476,948 - 441,000 = \$35,948$

        After-tax cash flow for year 1 will be:
        (NOI – interest – depreciation)(1 – tax rate) – principal repayment + depreciation
        $(675,000 - 441,000 - 200,000)(1 - 0.28) - 35,948 + 200,000 = \mathbf{\$188,532}$

        At the end of year 1, the remaining principal on the mortgage loan is $4,900,000 - 35,948 = \$4,864,052$
        Year 2 interest will be $4,864,052 \times 0.09 = \$437,765$
        Year 2 principal payment will be $476,948 - 437,765 = \$39,183$

        After-tax cash flow for year 2 will be:
        (NOI – interest – depreciation)(1 – tax rate) – principal repayment + depreciation
        $[675,000(1.03) - 437,765 - 200,000](1 - 0.28) - 39,183 + 200,000 = \mathbf{\$202,206}$

        At the end of year 2, the remaining principal on the mortgage loan is $4,864,052 - 39,183 = \$4,824,869$
        Year 3 interest will be $4,824,869 \times 0.09 = \$434,238$
        Year 3 principal payment will be $476,948 - 434,238 = \$42,710$

        After-tax cash flow for year 3 will be:
        (NOI – interest – depreciation)(1 – tax rate) – principal repayment + depreciation
        $[675,000(1.03)^2 - 434,238 - 200,000](1 - 0.28) - 42,710 + 200,000 = \mathbf{\$216,236}$

Study Session 18

©2009 Kaplan, Inc.

B. At the time of sale, the remaining mortgage balance is $4,824,869 - 42,710 = 4,782,159$

The depreciated book value is: $7,000,000 - (3 \times 200,000) = 6,400,000$

Cash from sale is: $7,400,000 - 4,782,159 = \$2,617,841$

Capital gains tax is: 7.4 million – 6.4 million = 1 million $(0.15) = 150,000$

After-tax proceeds from sale are: $2,617,841 - 150,000 = \$2,467,841$

Total after-tax cash flow at the end of year 3 is: $2,467,841 + 216,236 = \mathbf{\$2,684,077}$

C. With a down payment of $2.1 million, and the three cash flows calculated above (in bold), we can calculate the IRR on the investment, which is 14.64%. Since this is an after-tax return, we can compare it to the required rate of 15% and conclude that the investment will have a negative NPV and should not be undertaken.

4. The NCREIF index is based on appraised values and likely underestimates the true volatility of prices and the correlation of real estate returns with U.S. stock market returns. Both sources of bias will lead to overestimates of the optimal allocation to real estate in efficient portfolios based on portfolio optimization models.

5. A. I. $17 - 1 - 0.2 (17 - 4.5) = 13.5\%$

II. $17 - 0.2 (17) = 13.6\%$

III. $17 - 1 - 0.2 (17 - 9.5) = 14.5\%$

IV. The fund has never had negative gross returns so its beginning value this year was its previous highest value.

$17 - 1 - 0.2 (17) = 12.6\%$

B. I.   Same as part A, 13.5%

II. $17 - 0.2 (17 - 10) = 15.6\%$

III. Same as part A, 14.5%

IV. As an example, assume the fund's value was $1,000 at the beginning of last year and it fell 10% to 900. The 17% gross return this year brings the fund's ending value to $900(1.17) = \$1,053$. The returns on the fund above its highest value ($1,000) are therefore 5.3%. Investor returns net of fees are: $17 - 0.2 (5.3) - 1 = 14.94\%$.

If your approach to this part of the problem gave you a slightly different answer, don't be disheartened. The important part here is to understand the implications of a high watermark provision compared to an incentive structure without such a provision.

C. Because the fund's returns were less than the risk-free rate, under structure (I) there would be no incentive fee, only the fixed 1% fee. Since the fund did not have a positive return, structure (II) would result in no fee and structure (IV) would result in only the 1% fee. Since the fund did outperform the S&P 500 index, structure (III) would result in an incentive fee of 20% of the fund return in excess of the index return, $0.2 [-13 - (-20)] = 1.4\%$. Therefore, structure (III) would result in the lowest return net of fees: $-13 - 1 - 1.4 = -15.4\%$.

6. A. Sharpe ratio = $\dfrac{R_p - R_f}{\sigma_p}$. Therefore, $R_f = R_p - \text{Sharpe ratio} \times \sigma_p$.

Using the hedge fund asset class data: $R_f = 17.8 - 0.8(15.0) = 5.8\%$.

B. $R_p = R_f + \text{Sharpe ratio} \times \sigma_{index}$

Using the S&P 500 Index data: $R_{index} = 5.8 + 0.7(10.0) = 12.8\%$

C. By including only funds that have been in existence for five years and reported results for the entire period, the consultant's data are subject to significant biases. The data do not include funds whose managers choose not to report results, which are likely to be the poorer performers. Likewise, the managers who do report results can engage in "cherry picking," reporting results only for their more successful funds. These characteristics will lead to an overestimate of average fund returns.

The data would be influenced by survivorship bias as they do not include funds that ceased to exist during the 5-year period. Funds that ceased to exist would tend to be those with poor returns (biasing average fund returns upwards) and those that took on more risk (biasing fund standard deviation downward). All of these biases would pull the average return for funds in the database above the true average return for hedge funds as an asset class.

Hedge funds often deal in infrequently traded assets for which market values must be estimated using a pricing model. This tends to smooth the assets' reported values and make the funds' volatility appear lower than it really is. At the same time, such model pricing will likely lead to a downward bias in the correlation of fund returns with the returns of other asset classes.

Also, for funds that use strategies with asymmetrical returns (i.e., limited upside potential but unlimited downside potential), standard deviation may not adequately capture the true risk taken.

The 30% recommended allocation is very likely too high for all of these reasons. The artificially high expected returns and artificially low standard deviation and correlation will all tend to increase the estimate of the allocation to hedge funds in an optimal portfolio.

7. A. The CAPM relation is $E(R_i) = RFR + \beta_i [E(R_{mkt}) - RFR]$. A negative beta means the expected return on gold is less than the risk free rate (assuming a positive market risk premium).

B. The question here is why investors would choose to hold a risky asset that has an expected return less than the risk-free rate. The negative systematic risk (beta) of gold gives it attractive hedging properties. When market returns are negative, returns on gold will be less so or even positive. The benefits in terms of risk reduction more than compensate for the decrease in portfolio expected returns from including gold in the portfolio.

©2009 Kaplan, Inc.

INVESTING IN COMMODITIES

Study Session 18

EXAM FOCUS

This topic appears in both the Level 1 and Level 2 curricula. The part you are responsible for at Level 1 includes only three LOS. The concepts of backwardation and contango are based on the relation between current (spot) prices and futures prices and are important for understanding the component of returns called the roll yield, which stems from the necessity to re-establish long commodity positions as they reach their settlement (delivery) dates. The fact that positions must be periodically closed out and re-established makes even a commodity indexing strategy "active" compared to a long equity or bond indexing strategy.

LOS 74.a: Explain the relationship between spot prices and expected future prices in terms of contango and backwardation.

Contango refers to a situation in commodities futures contracts where the futures price is above the spot price, the price for current purchase and delivery of the physical commodity. This is the current situation (as of the time of writing) in the oil futures market. One way to view the explanation for this is based on the needs of either long or short hedgers. With oil prices rising sharply over the last year, users of oil and oil-related commodities are concerned with the risk they face from rising oil prices. Airlines, for example, sell tickets at prices based on expected fuel prices and are exposed to the financial consequences of increases in fuel prices above those expected to prevail in the future.

When an end user of a commodity buys futures contracts to protect against unexpected future price increases, we refer to that futures buyer as a *long hedger*, as they are hedging commodity price risk with long positions. If the predominant reason for futures positions in a commodity is to hedge the risk of price increases, long hedgers will be paying for the protection of long futures positions, which will produce gains as the futures price increases. In a situation of contango, long hedgers are bidding up the price of commodity futures and, in effect, paying a premium for the hedging benefit they get from taking long futures positions.

Backwardation refers to a situation in commodities futures contracts where the futures price is below the spot price. If the dominant traders in a commodity future are producers of the commodity hedging their exposure to financial losses arising from unexpected price declines in the future, the result will be backwardation. In this situation, producers are paying for protection against price declines and that is reflected in futures prices which are lower than current market prices (spot prices). Historically, producers hedging the price risk of future production have been dominant in futures markets, so that backwardation was the typical situation and sometimes referred to as **normal backwardation**.

LOS 74.b: Describe the sources of return and risk for a commodity investment and the effect on a portfolio of adding an allocation to commodities.

An investor who desires long exposure to a commodity price will typically achieve this exposure through a derivative investment in forwards or futures. Some physical commodities cannot be effectively purchased and stored long term, and for others, such as precious metals, derivative positions may be a more efficient means of gaining long exposure than purchasing the commodities outright and storing them long term.

To take a position in forwards or futures, a speculator or hedger must post collateral. If U.S. Treasury bills are deposited as collateral, the **collateral yield** is simply the yield on the T-bills. Active management of the collateral, within the bounds of what is acceptable collateral, can increase the collateral yield above the 90-day T-bill rate.

The **price return** on a long-only investment in commodities derivatives can be positive or negative depending on the direction of change in the spot price for the commodity over the life of the derivatives contract employed.

Since commodity derivative contracts expire, a speculator or hedger who wants to maintain a position over time must close out the expiring derivative position and re-establish a new position with a settlement date further in the future. This process is referred to as "rolling over" the position and leads to gains or losses which are termed the **roll yield**. The roll yield can be positive or negative depending on whether the derivative contract used to establish the long exposure is in backwardation or contango. You can view this roll yield as the gains or losses that would be realized on the position if the spot price remained unchanged over the life of the contract.

The futures price at expiration must equal the spot price at that time. For a future or forward in backwardation (i.e., the futures/forward price is less than the current spot price) the roll yield is positive, since an unchanged spot price at contract settlement would mean the futures/forward price increased over the life of the contract, and the investor would have gains at settlement. For a future or forward in contango, the roll yield is negative. Since contango means the forward/futures price is greater than the spot price, an unchanged spot price over the life of the contract means the futures price will have fallen and losses will result when the position is closed out.

When commodity derivative markets were dominated by short hedgers (commodity producers) and markets were typically in backwardation, the roll yield was positive. In current market conditions, with futures and forwards typically in contango, the roll yield is negative. It may be the case that structural changes in the markets for commodities derivatives mean that a zero or negative roll yield has become the new norm for these markets.

Adding a long commodities index position to a portfolio can provide several benefits, particularly for pension fund portfolios. Commodities provide diversification benefits because their prices tend to be uncorrelated with securities prices, and they can serve as a hedge against inflation.

LOS 74.c: Explain why a commodity index strategy is generally considered an active investment.

An index strategy in equities is considered a passive strategy. While changes may be necessary if one of the component stocks of the index is changed, in the absence of any change in the component stocks, no active management of an index portfolio is required. Because of the necessity of closing out and re-establishing long derivative positions to maintain long exposure to changes in commodity prices, a commodity index strategy is considered an active strategy. Managers can add value to the long-only commodity index strategy by choosing the maturities of the derivative contracts they buy and by their decisions about when to roll over their positions. To the extent that many long-only commodity derivative managers attempt to roll their positions over at the same time, they pay a premium in transactions costs, which reduces both the roll yield and overall yield of their commodity index strategy.

There are two other aspects of commodity index investing that require active management. The weightings of various commodities and commodity blocks (such as metals or energy) in indexes do not necessarily change with the values of the derivative positions in the portfolio. Since commodities index weightings, whether based on commodity production or consumption, change over time, a manager who seeks to match an index must actively manage the size of the exposure to various commodity markets as positions are rolled over. Additionally, as mentioned earlier, the short-term debt used to collateralize derivative positions must be managed as well. The collateral debt securities mature and new ones must be purchased, and the collateral yield can be enhanced by taking advantage of market conditions as maturing collateral debt securities are replaced.

KEY CONCEPTS

LOS 74.a

A commodity futures market is in contango if futures prices are greater than the spot price. The market is in backwardation if futures prices are less than the spot price.

Futures markets that are dominated by long hedgers (users of the commodity who buy futures to protect against price increases) tend to be in contango. Futures markets that are dominated by short hedgers (producers of the commodity who short futures to protect against price decreases) tend to be in backwardation.

LOS 74.b

The return on a commodity investment includes:

- Collateral yield: the return on the collateral posted to satisfy margin requirements.
- Price return: the gain or loss due to changes in the spot price.
- Roll yield: the gain or loss resulting from re-establishing positions as contracts expire.

Roll yield is positive if the futures market is in backwardation and negative if the market is in contango.

Commodities can provide diversification benefits to a portfolio of securities because commodity returns tend not to be highly positively correlated with securities returns.

LOS 74.c

A commodity index strategy is considered an active investment because the manager has to decide what maturities to use for the forward or futures contracts and determine when to roll them over into new contracts. Active management is also required to manage portfolio weights to match those of the benchmark index selected and to determine the best choice of securities to post as collateral and how these should be rolled over as they mature.

©2009 Kaplan, Inc.

CONCEPT CHECKERS

1. A commodities market tends to be in backwardation if:
    A. it is dominated by end users of the commodity.
    B. the spot price is greater than futures prices.
    C. futures prices are greater than the spot price.

2. The source of return on a long-only commodity investment that represents the change in the spot price over the life of the forward or futures contract used is the:
    A. roll yield.
    B. price return.
    C. spot yield.

3. For a commodity market that is in contango, an unchanged spot price over the life of a contract will result in a roll yield that is:
    A. zero.
    B. positive.
    C. negative.

4. A manager following a long-only commodity index strategy is *least likely* to adjust the portfolio:
    A. to reduce exposure to a declining commodity market.
    B. for changes in the composition of the commodity index.
    C. by closing out expiring contracts and re-establishing positions in new contracts.

ANSWERS – CONCEPT CHECKERS

1. **B** Backwardation refers to the situation in which futures prices are less than the spot price. Commodity markets tend to be in backwardation when they are dominated by producers of the commodity.

2. **B** The price return results from the change in the spot price. The roll yield is the gain or loss that results from closing a position in an expiring contract and re-establishing it in a new contract. The collateral yield is the return on the collateral deposited to establish the position.

3. **C** For a commodities market in contango, if the spot price remains unchanged, the futures price will decrease over its life and the investor will realize a loss at expiration. Thus, the roll yield is negative.

4. **A** A long-only commodity index strategy is always long the commodities in the index and the weights are not adjusted based on the performance of the positions. The manager must actively manage the roll out of expiring contracts, as well as matching any changes in the commodity index weightings.

©2009 Kaplan, Inc.

12 questions, 18 minutes

1. Which of the following is *least likely* a similarity between a forward rate agreement based on LIBOR + 1.5% and an interest rate option on LIBOR?
    A. A long position in either one will result in a positive payment if interest rates increase above the contract rate.
    B. The payments to either are based on the difference between a contract rate and a market (reference) rate.
    C. If both have the same contract rate, notional principal, expiration date, and reference rate, they will make equal payments to their (long) owners.

2. Adam Vernon took a long position in four 100-ounce July gold futures contracts at 685 when spot gold was 670. Initial margin is $4,000 per contract and maintenance margin is $3,200 per contract. If the account is marked to market when spot gold is 660 and the futures price is 672, the additional margin the investor must deposit to keep the position open is *closest* to:
    A. $2,000.
    B. $4,000.
    C. $5,000.

3. The value of a call option on a stock is *least likely* to increase as a result of:
    A. an increase in asset price volatility.
    B. a decrease in the risk-free rate of interest.
    C. a decrease in the strike price of the option.

4. Kurt Crawford purchased shares of Acme, Inc., for $38 and sold call options at $40, covering all his shares for $2 each. The sum of the maximum per-share gain and maximum per-share loss (as an absolute value) on the covered call position is:
    A. $36.
    B. $40.
    C. unlimited.

5. Craig Grant has entered into a $10 million quarterly-pay equity swap based on the NASDAQ stock index as the 8% fixed rate payer when the index is at 2,750. Which of the following is *most accurate*?
    A. He will make a payment of $200,000 on the second payment date if the index is 2,750.
    B. He will neither make nor receive a payment on the first settlement date if the index is 2,805.
    C. If the index at the first settlement date is 2,782, he must make a payment at the second settlement date.

6. It is *least likely* that a forward contract on a zero-coupon bond:
    A. has counterparty risk.
    B. can be settled in cash.
    C. requires a margin deposit.

7. Among a no-load mutual fund, a closed-end fund, and an exchange-traded fund (ETF), which *most likely* has the lowest transactions costs and which *most likely* will trade at a discount to NAV?

Low transactions costs	Trade at a discount
A. No-load fund	ETF
B. No-load fund	Closed-end fund
C. ETF	Closed-end fund

8. Jodi Monroe has purchased an office building for $10 million and financed the purchase with a 20-year $8 million loan at 9%, which requires equal end-of-year payments of $876,372. The building has 30,000 square feet and will lease at an annual rate of $40 per square foot with expected vacancy and bad debt expense of 6%. Maintenance cost is expected to be $150,000 per year. Depreciation on the building is $250,000 per year and Monroe is in the 38% marginal tax bracket. The first-year annual after-tax cash flow on this investment is *closest* to:
    A. −$100,000.
    B. $0.
    C. $100,000.

9. A consultant has made a presentation to a pension fund manager that shows that based on the last ten years of available hedge fund data, the mean return after fees was 14%, which exceeded the return on a popular broad-based large-cap index by more than 3%. The standard deviation of net returns was estimated to be 12%, which is less than that of the index. For the hedge fund returns, it is *least likely* that:
    A. standard deviation fails to describe risk well.
    B. the estimate of risk is too low due to survivorship bias.
    C. self-selection bias tends to smooth the reported returns of each included fund.

10. The probabilities that a venture capital investment will fail, given that it has survived all prior periods, are:

1st year	15%
2nd year	18%
3rd year	10%
4th year	8%

    An investment of €1.5 million is expected to return €9 million if the venture survives until the end of the fourth year. The expected annual compound rate of return on this investment is *closest* to:
    A. 36%.
    B. 33%.
    C. 31%.

©2009 Kaplan, Inc.

11. Jeff Stephenson runs a hedge fund that takes offsetting long and short positions so that the systematic risk of the portfolio is close to zero. Jane Carroll runs a hedge fund that primarily seeks to profit from large leveraged long or short positions in currencies and interest rate derivatives. These funds would *most appropriately* be classified as:

	Stephenson	Carroll
A.	Long/short fund	Event-driven fund
B.	Long/short fund	Global macro fund
C.	Market neutral fund	Global macro fund

12. Harriet Lansing has used the recent sales price of a private company to value the shares a client holds in a private company in a similar line of business. Given that the client's shares represent only 55% of the issued and outstanding shares, she should:
    A. apply a minority discount to the client's shares.
    B. adjust the price by adding a liquidity premium.
    C. make no adjustment for a minority interest or lack of liquidity.

SELF-TEST ANSWERS: DERIVATIVES AND ALTERNATIVE INVESTMENTS

1. **C** Since the FRA pays at the expiration of the forward contract, it pays the present value of the interest savings that would be realized at the end of the (hypothetical) loan term. The interest rate option will pay the interest savings on the (hypothetical) loan after expiration at the end of the loan term and its payment will be greater (since it's not discounted back to the expiration date).

2. **C** The initial margin is 4 × $4,000 = $16,000 and the maintenance margin is 4 × $3,200 = $12,800. The loss on the position is (672 − 685) × 4 × 100 = −$5,200, leaving a balance of $16,000 − $5,200 = $10,800. Since the account has fallen below the maintenance margin, a deposit of $5,200 is required to bring the balance back up to the initial margin.

3. **B** A decrease in the risk-free rate of interest will decrease call values. The other changes will tend to increase the value of a call option.

4. **B** The net cost of the covered call position is 38 − 2 = 36, so the maximum loss (if the stock price goes to zero) is $36. The maximum gain (if the stock price goes to 40 or more) is $4. The sum is 36 + 4 = 40.

5. **B** If the index has risen to 2,805 (+2%), the index payer's liability (2% × $10 million) just offsets the fixed rate payer's liability (8% / 4 × $10 million). The payment at the second settlement date cannot be determined without knowing the change in the index level between the first and second settlement dates. The index level at the first settlement date does not determine the payment at the second settlement date.

6. **C** Forward contracts typically do not require a margin deposit. They are custom instruments that may require settlement in cash or delivery of the underlying asset, and they have counterparty risk.

7. **B** The no-load fund has transactions costs that are essentially zero while an ETF buyer must pay a stock commission and is subject to the effects of the bid-ask spread. Closed-end fund shares often trade at significant premiums or discounts to NAV while ETF shares trade close to their NAVs because of their in-kind redemption and creation feature.

8. **C** after-tax cash flow = (net operating income − depreciation − interest expense)(1 − tax rate) + depreciation − principal portion of the annual loan payment

   net operating income = gross potential rent × (1 − % vacancy and collection losses) − maintenance expense

   = [30,000 × $40 × (1 − 0.06)] − $150,000

   = $978,000

   interest expense = 0.09($8,000,000) = $720,000

   principal reduction = $876,372 − $720,000 = $156,372

©2009 Kaplan, Inc.

after-tax cash flow = ($978,000 − $250,000 − $720,000)(1 − 0.38) + $250,000 − $156,372

= $4,960 + $250,000 − $156,372

= $98,588

9. **C** Self-selection bias refers to the practice of reporting returns only for funds that do relatively well and tends to bias reported returns upward. The fact that many hedge funds contain infrequently traded assets that must be valued with pricing models is what tends to smooth reported returns for each fund. Hedge fund returns are often asymmetric, and standard deviation as a risk measure does not account for the fact that many hedge fund strategies have limited upside potential (with relatively high probability) and almost unlimited downside risk (with low probability). Survivorship bias tends to inflate return estimates and leads to an underestimate of risk.

10. **A** The probability that the venture survives four years is:
(1 − 15%)(1 − 18%)(1 − 10%)(1 − 8%) = 57.7%.

The expected payoff is 0.577(9 million) = €5,194,044.

The expected return is $(5{,}194{,}044 / 1{,}500{,}000)^{1/4}$ = 36.4%.

Note that with a required return of 36.4% the NPV of this investment is zero, so at any discount rate less than 36.4%, the NPV is positive and the venture investment should be undertaken based on the NPV decision method.

11. **C** A long/short fund takes both long and short positions but does not necessarily take equal size positions to minimize market risk as a market neutral fund does. Global macro funds make bets on the direction of currencies, interest rates, and other factors.

12. **C** Since the 55% represents a controlling interest in the subject firm and neither firm's shares are traded in a liquid market, no adjustment is required for either characteristic.

FORMULAS

full price = clean price + accrued interest

$$\text{duration} = -\frac{\text{percentage change in bond price}}{\text{yield change in percent}}$$

value of a callable bond = value of an option-free bond − value of the call

$$\text{TIPS coupon payment} = \text{inflation-adjusted par value} \times \frac{\text{stated coupon rate}}{2}$$

absolute yield spread = yield on the higher-yield bond − yield on the lower-yield bond

$$\text{relative yield spread} = \frac{\text{absolute yield spread}}{\text{yield on the benchmark bond}}$$

$$\text{yield ratio} = \frac{\text{subject bond yield}}{\text{benchmark bond yield}}$$

after-tax yield = taxable yield × (1 − marginal tax rate)

$$\text{taxable-equivalent yield} = \frac{\text{tax-free yield}}{(1 - \text{marginal tax rate})}$$

$$\text{zero-coupon bond value} = \frac{\text{maturity value}}{(1+i)^{\text{number of years}\times 2}}$$

$$\text{current yield} = \frac{\text{annual cash coupon payment}}{\text{bond price}}$$

$$\text{bond equivalent yield} = \left[\left(1 + \text{monthly CFY}\right)^6 - 1\right] \times 2$$
$$= \left[\sqrt{1 + \text{annual-pay YTM}} - 1\right] \times 2$$

$$\text{effective annual yield} = \left(\frac{1 + \text{semiannual-pay YTM}}{2}\right)^2 - 1$$

spot rate from forward rates:

$$S_3 = [(1 + {}_1f_0)(1 + {}_1f_1)(1 + {}_1f_2)]^{1/3} - 1$$

forward rate from spot rates:

$$_1f_2 = \frac{\left(1 + S_3\right)^3}{\left(1 + S_2\right)^2} - 1$$

©2009 Kaplan, Inc.

$$\text{effective duration} = \frac{(\text{bond price when yields fall} - \text{bond price when yields rise})}{2 \times (\text{initial price}) \times (\text{change in yield in decimal form})} = \frac{V_- - V_+}{2V_0(\Delta y)}$$

percentage change in bond price = −effective duration × change in yield in percent

portfolio duration = $w_1 D_1 + w_2 D_2 + \ldots + W_N D_N$

percentage change in price = duration effect + convexity effect

$$= \{[-\text{duration} \times (\Delta y)] + [\text{convexity} \times (\Delta y)^2]\} \times 100$$

price value of a basis point = duration × 0.0001 × bond value

value of a long FRA at settlement: $(\text{notional principal})\dfrac{(\text{floating} - \text{forward})\left(\dfrac{\text{days}}{360}\right)}{1 + (\text{floating})\left(\dfrac{\text{days}}{360}\right)}$

intrinsic value of a call: $C = \text{Max}[0, S - X]$

intrinsic value of a put: $P = \text{Max}[0, X - S]$

option value = intrinsic value + time value

lower and upper bounds for options:

Option	Minimum Value	Maximum Value
European call	$c_t \geq \text{Max}[0, S_t - X / (1 + RFR)^{T-t}]$	S_t
American call	$C_T \geq \text{Max}[0, S_t - X / (1 + RFR)^{T-t}]]$	S_t
European put	$p_t \geq \text{Max}[0, X / (1 + RFR)^{T-t} - S_t]$	$X / (1 + RFR)^{T-t}$
American put	$P_t \geq \text{Max}[0, X - S_t]$	X

put-call parity: $c + X / (1 + RFR)^T = S + p$

put-call parity with asset cash flows: $C + X / (1 + RFR)^T = (S_0 - PV_{CF}) + P$

plain-vanilla interest rate swap:

$$(\text{net fixed-rate payment})_t = (\text{swap fixed rate} - LIBOR_{t-1})\left(\frac{\text{number of days}}{360}\right)$$
$$\times (\text{notional principal})$$

income method for real estate:

$$\text{appraisal price} = \frac{\text{net operating income}}{\text{market cap rate}}$$

net operating income = gross potential income − collections and
vacancy losses − total operating expenses

INDEX

©2009 Kaplan, Inc.

©2009 Kaplan, Inc.

©2009 Kaplan, Inc.

Notes

Notes

Notes

Notes

Notes

Notes

Notes

Notes

Notes

Required Disclaimers:

CFA Institute does not endorse, promote, or warrant the accuracy or quality of the products or services offered by Kaplan Schweser. CFA Institute, CFA®, and Chartered Financial Analyst® are trademarks owned by CFA Institute.

Certified Financial Planner Board of Standards Inc. owns the certification marks CFP®, CERTIFIED FINANCIAL PLANNER™, and federally registered CFP (with flame design) in the U.S., which it awards to individuals who successfully complete initial and ongoing certification requirements.
Kaplan University does not certify individuals to use the CFP®, CERTIFIED FINANCIAL PLANNER™, and CFP (with flame design) certification marks.
CFP® certification is granted only by Certified Financial Planner Board of Standards Inc. to those persons who, in addition to completing an educational requirement such as this CFP® Board-Registered Program, have met its ethics, experience, and examination requirements.

Kaplan Schweser and Kaplan University are review course providers for the CFP® Certification Examination administered by Certified Financial Planner Board of Standards Inc. CFP Board does not endorse any review course or receive financial remuneration from review course providers.

GARP® does not endorse, promote, review, or warrant the accuracy of the products or services offered by Kaplan Schweser of FRM® related information, nor does it endorse any pass rates claimed by the provider. Further, GARP® is not responsible for any fees or costs paid by the user to Kaplan Schweser, nor is GARP® responsible for any fees or costs of any person or entity providing any services to Kaplan Schweser. FRM®, GARP®, and Global Association of Risk Professionals™ are trademarks owned by the Global Association of Risk Professionals, Inc.

CAIAA does not endorse, promote, review or warrant the accuracy of the products or services offered by Kaplan Schweser nor does it endorse any pass rates claimed by the provider. CAIAA is not responsible for any fees or costs paid by the user to Kaplan Schweser nor is CAIAA responsible for any fees or costs of any person or entity providing any services to Kaplan Schweser. CAIA®, CAIA Association®, Chartered Alternative Investment Analyst℠, and Chartered Alternative Investment Analyst Association®, are service marks and trademarks owned by CHARTERED ALTERNATIVE INVESTMENT ANALYST ASSOCIATION, INC., a Massachusetts non-profit corporation with its principal place of business at Amherst, Massachusetts, and are used by permission.

CPCU® is a registered mark owned by the American Institute for CPCU and the Insurance Institute of America.

ChFC®, Chartered Financial Consultant®, CLU®, Chartered Life Underwriter®, and CASL®, Chartered Advisor for Senior Living® are registered marks owned by The American College. Kaplan Schweser is not affiliated or associated in any way with The American College. The American College does not endorse, promote, review, or warrant the accuracy of any courses, exam preparation materials, or other products or services offered by Kaplan Schweser and does not verify or endorse any claims made by Kaplan Schweser regarding such products or services, including any claimed pass rates.